The
RESTAURANT

For Emily and Walter

The RESTAURANT

A HISTORY of EATING OUT

WILLIAM SITWELL

SIMON & SCHUSTER

London · New York · Sydney · Toronto · New Delhi

A CBS COMPANY

MMXX

First published in Great Britain by Simon & Schuster UK Ltd, 2020
A CBS COMPANY

1 3 5 7 9 10 8 6 4 2

Simon & Schuster UK Ltd
1st Floor
222 Gray's Inn Road
London WC1X 8HB

www.simonandschuster.co.uk
www.simonandschuster.com.au
www.simonandschuster.co.in

Simon & Schuster Australia, Sydney
Simon & Schuster India, New Delhi

A CIP catalogue record for this book is available from the British Library.

Publishing Director: Iain MacGregor
Senior Editor: Melissa Bond
Design: Keith Williams, sprout.uk.com

Hardback ISBN: 978-1-4711-7961-7
eBook ISBN: 978-1-4711-7963-1

Printed in China

Contents

Introduction 6

1 The Romans 10

2 The Ottoman Empire 22

3 The Legacy of Ibn Battuta 34

4 Medieval England 46

5 The Coffee House Revolution 58

6 The French Revolution 72

7 The British Industrial Revolution 84

8 Carême and the *New Paris Guide* 98

9 The Victorian Era 110

10 Britannia & Co. Opens in Bombay 124

11 The Invention of the Taco Machine 134

12 Postwar Britain 146

13 The Invention of the Sushi Conveyor Belt 162

14 Le Gavroche Opens in London 176

15 Chez Panisse Opens in the US 192

16 Bibendum Opens in London 206

17 The Death of Bernard Loiseau 220

18 The Future of Eating Out 234

Acknowledgements 249

About the Author 250

Select Bibliography 251

Picture Credits 257

Index 258

Introduction

The tentacles of inspiration wrap around the world; they cross continents, they infiltrate cultures and they instil themselves in people's minds. They also curl themselves along the course of history. Sometimes the tentacles pause; sometimes they seem to stop altogether, before springing up centuries later and in a very different place.

Those tentacles – those roots of the restaurant story – I will endeavour to describe in this book.

From the ancient to the futuristic, there are few things quite as multifarious as a restaurant. It is a business, a hobby, a passion and a calamity. Between a restaurateur and a chef, or the two combined, it takes ingenuity, business acumen, creativity, technical expertise, design or artistic sensibility, accounting sense, literacy, people skills, public relations proficiency, marketing know-how, negotiating talent – and it helps if you can cook.

Restaurants can be dreamt up in a passion and gobbled up in a frenzy. They can be wild successes or horrendous failures. As many fortunes have been made, many people have been ruined.

The history of eating out is a story of politics, of terror, of courage, of madness, of luck, of innovation, of art, of love and of quiet, earnest endeavour.

It is a story that could be explained by simply studying individuals with unique attributes, whose passions and foresight saw them open extraordinary places, implement novel kitchens, or settle on a manner of service or a style of food that changed the way many of us ate.

And, across the pages of this book, you will find such people. There is the amazing fourteenth-century Ibn Battuta, who journeyed and ate out in forty countries over thirty years, bringing home ideas and writing about his culinary adventures for people to learn from. And the nineteenth-century Frenchman, Marie-Antoine Carême, who created serious distinction between the food of the professional kitchen and that of the home.

You'll meet Juvencio Maldonado, a Mexican-born immigrant in New York City, whose patented taco machine from 1951 unleashed a fast-food craze. And Yoshiaki Shiraishi, whose 1958 sushi conveyor belt revolutionised the eating of fish.

There are the Roux bothers, Albert and Michel, who transformed the bleak dining scene of postwar Britain as they opened Le Gavroche in London in 1967, training and inspiring generations of chefs. And Alice Waters, who, with her US counterculture restaurant Chez Panisse in California, attempted to beat down the beasts of fast food with her love of the farmer and the seasons.

These men and women have influenced others in countries thousands of miles from their own. Millions have tasted their personal philosophies, wittingly or unwittingly, for good or ill.

But, if this book rests on the great man/woman theory, it also firmly posits the theory of unintended consequences. The French revolutionary Maximilien Robespierre did not foresee that his politics – or bloody methods of implementing them – would usher in an era of fine dining. Nor did Richard and Maurice McDonald predict that their business's spiral into a global monster would inspire people like Alice Waters to create a completely opposite type of restaurant.

Intended or not, restaurants have been instruments and symbols of transformation. They can signpost both the decline and success of a nation – or, indeed, an empire. The extraordinary sophistication of the dining scene of ancient Pompeii was indicative of the Roman Empire's vision, breadth, sophistication and prosperity. The bleak restaurant scene of the United Kingdom after the Second World War showed quite how the horrors and disruption of conflict had damaged both the country's food culture and palate. Fast-forward to 2018, London's status as a global player was exemplified by its dining scene – this time in a positive light. In the words of the restaurateur and designer Sir Terence Conran, the UK capital went from a 'culinary joke to being the absolute envy of the world'.

Yet Conran's view reflects another theme in the story of restaurants: the constant fantasy of the glory of the present. Writers frequently assert that there is no better time to dine out than now, but, some twenty years before Conran's remarks, in 1997, *The Good Food Guide* pronounced that 'there has never been a more exciting time to eat out'.

And what of the much-maligned restaurant scene in the decades of postwar Britain? The film director and *Sunday Times* newspaper critic Michael Winner once referred to it as: 'The golden period of the 1950s, when food tasted like it was meant to be.'

In 1791, Samuel Johnson wrote that 'there is nothing which has yet been contrived by man, by which so much happiness is produced, as by a good tavern or inn'. So the food can't have been too awful then. And how about in 1170, when William Fitzstephen's 'Description of London' talked of a public eating house, open day and night, 'where every thing desirable is instantly procured'?

If it were true that eating out only became worth thinking about relatively recently, the story would be a rather narrow one. But I don't believe that – and, if you travel back a few thousand years with me, I might be able to convince you, too. While some of the tales might be considered more eating 'away' than 'out', I still think they are relevant, as the graduation from 'away' to 'out' influenced the restaurants of the future.

Of course, the modern world, with its possibilities of communication and travel, means that millions are now lucky to have developed much broader and experienced palates. And that heightens the symbolism of the restaurant, for many of us can now judge a nation by its food. Indeed, a restaurant alone can provide people with a reason to travel. Restaurants have become as vital to culture as museums, art, nightclubs or beaches, and are now just as crucial as the landscape, the people or climate of a country.

But, while restaurants are a reason to travel, they are also a reason not to. If you live in a city with brilliant vendors of the cuisine of India, China, Japan, Peru, France or Italy, then why bother getting on a plane? In the words of the British writer Nicholas Lander: 'Menus represent the least expensive form of travel.'

And, just as restaurants can be symbolic of a country, so, too, can they be a status symbol for the diner. How complex the idea of dining out becomes when the reason someone picks a restaurant is because of the reflected glory they believe they revel in by simply being there.

'Tell me where you eat and I will tell you what you are,' wrote historian John Burnett (deftly editing the words of his predecessor Jean Anthelme Brillat-Savarin). That conversation about your favourite restaurants might be more nuanced than you think, as you demonstrate your credentials based on the type of establishment you enthuse about. Perhaps you need to add some vegan cafés in among the smart/casual fashionable eateries you keep talking about.

Restaurants have also become forms of entertainment, if not an intrinsic part of the entertainment industry. One wonders if some of them are merely an adjunct to a chef's TV show or book-publishing career. It can be hard to see which is the product and which is the marketing tool. Some chefs open restaurants after winning televised cooking competitions, and some win such competitions after having run restaurants, going on to cook only for television.

Yet, as restaurants have become part of the leisure business, so their raison d'être has become less defined. If you need to take exercise, walk or run to make space for dinner, should you even go out to eat? What mad kind of world do we live in where people go to restaurants when they're not hungry? But, of course, food is not the only reason we eat out. As the British restaurant critic A. A. Gill once put it: 'You go to a restaurant because you have an appetite, and appetite is not the same as hunger.'

Whatever the shape or form of a place where we eat out, its inspirations are varied and multifaceted. And they are often the joyous result of immigration, whereby food has been introduced by a community to satisfy its own people – the Japanese communities of North America in the 1960s or the Bangladeshi immigrants in the East End of London in the 1940s, for example – but then the host nation has got a taste of it, and, while its citizens may have disparaged the original immigration that brought it about, they enjoy the cuisine so much that they embrace it, before assuming it as a key part of their own culture (as in the case of Britain with Indian food).

However, before you tackle this complex and wonderful story, I feel I should add an apology. This is my history of eating out, written within 272 pages, so there are many people, restaurants and stories not mentioned herein. There are whole countries and cuisines that have not made the final cut, but whose food and restaurants remain as delicious as they are influential. I apologise to them, and I apologise to you for not covering them.

But the storyteller's privilege is to tell his own tale. This is not a countdown of the best restaurants of all time or a list of the greatest chefs, finest ovens or most innovative kitchen tools ever. The stories I have chosen to tell will give you a delicious backstory. It's also a narrative that shapes the modern world we live in today.

William Sitwell
Weston, Northamptonshire

1

The Romans

An inn discovered in ancient Pompeii reveals a city with a very sophisticated array of hotels, bars and restaurants.

23 August AD79. A blazing hot day on which we can imagine a citizen of Pompeii stumbling out into the street from his favourite bar. It could have been the Inn of Primus, a very real watering hole situated on the north-east corner of Holconius's crossroads. From the main entrance, he steps out onto the Via dell'Abbondanza. This, the main street of the town, once dissected a metropolis of some 12,000 souls and stretches out for almost a kilometre.

Perhaps our friend, weary from drink – wine, possibly, which was watered down to suit a customer's taste – and wishing to avoid the crowds of this Pompeiian Oxford Street, a Fifth Avenue of the ancient world, turns right out of the bar and then takes a sharp right again down the narrower Via Stabiana. He passes the open window of Primus's, where a counter abuts the street, offering food to go. There's even a wide step up to it so that passers-by, our worse-for-wear Pompeiian included, don't bump into it as they make their way down the busy little street.

This Primus regular, irritable from the heady mix of alcohol and losing at dice, wishes merely to get home for a siesta. He looks ahead of him down Stabiana, the view into the distance dominated by the hulk of a mountain. This is Vesuvius. Having grown up with this large feature of the landscape, it is as familiar to him as his own hands. But today there is something unusual about it. From the summit of the mountain, a thin plume of smoke can be seen – what the younger poet Pliny described as looking 'like an umbrella pine'.

Opposite: The thoroughfare of Via dell'Abbondanza – a Fifth Avenue of the ancient world – was filled with popular eating and drinking establishments visited by rich and poor. Emperor Nero, even, was known to frequent such taverns.

There had also been a rumble that morning, an earth tremor that residents of the town had remarked upon. But they were not uncommon; this part of Campania often experienced such minor shakes – the gods grumbling, perhaps, like humans did when offered a bad hand at the gambling table. Certainly Vesuvius's smoke and a minor rattling of the ground would not have alarmed the residents of the town, nor would they have connected the two. Indeed, the idea that a volcano such as Vesuvius might erupt was ridiculous. While there had been a serious earthquake seven years previously, she hadn't actually erupted for 1,500 years.

And so we follow our man as he stumbles home, ducking and weaving along the vast cobblestones, attempting to avoid both pedestrian and stray dog. Once home, maybe he takes another few drinks, pushing him beyond sunset and into the night. And then, fully sated, he retires to bed, falling into a deep sleep. Perhaps the effects of the best part of a day at Primus's meant that one of the gods looked kindly upon him and never woke him up.

For 24 August arrives and visits upon the little city of Pompeii a tragedy. Within hours, Vesuvius does erupt, spewing lava, deadly fumes and dust across the region. A great number of Pompeii's residents die quickly, unable to escape from their houses. Those who do escape with their lives return in the weeks or months that follow to look for their possessions, their houses and the bodies of loved ones, but in vain.

An airtight blanket of ash and lava has coated the city. Rainfall has set the lava to pumice stone. Recovery of anything – human or inanimate – is impossible. So they give up. Pompeii disappears from the map. And, for eighteen centuries, it remains that way.

Excavations continue today after some 250 years, but what the visitor can see is, in the words of one historian, 'the Pompeiians, their joys, sorrows, their work and play, their virtues and vices'.

And nowhere is this more pertinent than in a scribbler's searches for concrete evidence of the dining scene of the Roman Empire over 2,000 years ago. For, as we all know, eating out is at the heart of things: be it fuelling happiness, appeasing grief, aiding and abetting both business and pleasure, or encouraging our best and our worst natures.

And, because Pompeii did not seek nor anticipate the oblivion that struck it, what we see is truth. It is a town that was in full swing at the very moment the Roman Empire was at its peak. Pompeii in AD 79 was a big deal. It was a shining example of the Roman dream, the magnificent vision that meant a citizen of

Rome could travel across the empire knowing that he was protected by a unified legal system and a single administrative language, and that, if he wished to buy drinks, snacks and meals, he needed only one currency. The empire's downfall was precipitated by Barbarian invasions at its furthest borders – some say the upshot of uncontrolled immigration. Arguably, the last Roman emperor was Romulus Augustulus, but, while he may have been the final emperor, thus technically the most disastrous, he wasn't so egregious as to offer the people a referendum...

So there was not a whiff of impending doom when Pompeii was trending in the AD 70s. All that was good in the empire was great in Pompeii – law, technology, culture, language, religion, architecture, food, drink... And the town was well situated, too. Geographically, it was by the sea, but also nestling between the warm waters of the Mediterranean and the slopes of Mount Vesuvius in the region of Campania, a fertile area whose land, soil and slopes were perfect for the growing of vines.

The wines of the region were famous and its makers enjoyed a healthy export business. Indeed, the most famous wine of ancient Greece, Falernian, from Aglianico grapes, was produced on nearby Mount Falernus. This prized white wine was often made from late-harvested grapes and left to mature in amphoras until it oxidised, taking on a rusty colour and packing a punch with a high alcohol content. A price list on the wall of a bar in Pompeii states: 'For one [coin] you can drink wine / For two you can drink the best / For four you can drink Falernian.'

Shaded by Mount Vesuvius and cooled by the sea, Pompeii had it all. A tourist destination, a fashionable seaport, a magnet for the smart set, an outward-looking internationalist stopping point for traders and businesspeople. That the amphitheatre could seat 20,000 spectators indicates that people would visit Pompeii from neighbouring towns, if not further afield. It was, in the words of Cambridge Classics professor Dame Mary Beard, 'a cross between Las Vegas and Brighton'.

It was to Pompeii that Romans came for partying – to gamble, to find girls, to eat and to drink. And both visitors and residents were well catered for. Hospitality was a cornerstone of the town, if not the wider empire.

The term originates from the word *hospes*, which describes a Roman who is connected to a fellow Roman by ties of hospitality. The word was both legal and sacred. It was stronger than blood. They even had a God who oversaw it. It fell under the remit of Jupiter (also known as Zeus in Greek mythology), when he wasn't dealing with sky and thunder, to watch over *ius hospitia*, the law of hospitality.

And so it applied to all, rich or poor, as a unifying concept. Regardless of your wealth, one was expected to embrace and offer hospitality. Perhaps it developed from more mercurial intentions. If Romans were hospitable wherever they went, it helped expand the empire both by enabling traders to do business more comfortably and by softening up those who were about to be conquered. And, if the latter didn't succumb, the Romans slaughtered them anyway.

So traders, merchants and sailors arrived in towns and cities across the empire seeking and expecting a warm welcome – comfort, food, company and a little entertainment. As the historian Livy wrote of Rome: 'Throughout the city, the front gates of the houses were thrown open and all sorts of things placed for general use in the open courts, all comers, whether acquaintances or strangers, being brought in to share the hospitality.'

It became traditional for courtyards of private houses to be adorned with items for passing travellers: a wonderful respite for the weary stranger. It helped to forge friendships and fuelled hope – an essential element if you're building an empire. When someone returned home with tales of adventure and warm receptions, it would encourage others to set forth.

So the tradition gradually became formalised and, eventually, the violation of it was perceived as a terrible crime. This Roman custom meant that, by the time we drop in on Pompeii in AD 79, commercial hospitality had become highly organised.

There were hotels, coaching inns, bars, restaurants and brothels. Because of the vast number of saucy images found on the walls of many of these establishments, some argue that virtually all of them doubled as brothels. Juvenal, a Roman poet of the late first and early second centuries AD, described the typical Roman bar as 'liberty hall', where your typical customer could be found 'lying next to a cut-throat, in the company of sailors, thieves and runaway slaves, beside hangmen and coffin makers, or beside a passed-out priest'.

But less excitable scholars, such as the rather more contemporary Mary Beard, believe that, while there were some brothels in the town (and one in particular, with its dingy little bedroom and stone bed, makes one pity the poor sex workers), the images are less indicative of brothels everywhere, more that the Romans just had a dirty sense of humour.

As with most Roman provincial towns, several inns and taverns can be found at the entrance to Pompeii, having provided handy shelter to visiting merchants. Then there are other establishments spread across the town. In total, archaeologists have identified some 160 properties that seem to have been bars and restaurants, in addition to a great many hotels. This relatively large number owed to the fact that many people would not have had access in their homes to the utilities required to prepare food – from ovens to sinks. It's not dissimilar to the circumstances that the dwellers of modern-day Manhattan find themselves in. Limitations on space and power provision mean that a great many New Yorkers have no kitchens and can't even boil a kettle. And such is the convenience, affordability and fashion for consuming everything out – from coffee to three-course meals – that, even if they can cook, they don't throw dinner parties.

Many of Pompeii's establishments are what we would today call a restaurant with rooms, which the Romans called a *hospitium*. In various shapes and sizes, there were modest establishments in poorer parts of town that probably had long-term residents who couldn't afford to rent a home, some of which appear to have had enough bedrooms for up to fifty people.

Then there were: coaching inns (*stabula*), which were simple bars, sometimes located just outside the metropolis; restaurants known as *popina*; and the inevitable *lupanar* (brothels).

Of those eating and drinking establishments, the Inn of Primus was doubtless very popular. Situated on the main drag of Via dell'Abbondanza, it would have attracted a wide clientele from the local businesses and residences that existed at the heart of Pompeii.

Along that street were found shops and workshops offering anything and everything one could imagine. There were builders' merchants, blacksmiths, iron and bronze dealers, arts and crafts stores, shops selling cloth, olive oil, hardware and tools. There was a wine store, a bakery, a barber shop, as well as a grocer, a fruit store, a bank, several brothels, a laundry and the local public baths. The latter advertised itself as 'elegant baths for the best people', and that perhaps included those who lived in the extremely smart and unbelievably lavish villas, houses and apartments along the road: noblemen, generals and prosperous professionals such as surgeons and physicians.

Indeed, adjacent to the Inn of Primus were two impressive residences belonging to Pompeiians Marco Epidio Rufo and L. Rapinasi Optati. Both are architecturally remarkable, with inner courtyards, columns and fountains that must have felt like cool, calm refuges from the steamy streets beyond the grand front doors.

Of course, we know the names, if not the lives, of those who inhabited these homes, because – as with so many shops, baths and blacksmiths' – their monikers and titles are written either on signs at the front or inside on the walls. And we know which buildings were bakeries, because the vicious discharge of Vesuvius covered, concealed and preserved not just the mills, ovens and loaves, but also the unground wheat kernels. In the olive oil shops, there are traces of oil in the jugs; amphoras are still stacked in the wine shops. In fact, archaeologists claim to have even found evidence of rosemary, garlic, olive oil, cheese and anchovies in the fossilised flatbreads in some of the bakeries. Not far from the forum is the sign of a shop belonging to local baker Podiscus Pricus, in whose building historians say was a wood-fired oven. There were likely other ovens across Pompeii, too, similar to a small one found in the Greco-Roman market area of Naples. Some 4ft in diameter, these ovens would not have been a good shape for bread, but you could bake smaller rounds: in other words, pizza – that classic Italian street food staple.

The spirit of some of the Pompeiians who chomped on these pizzas can be seen in the graffiti across town.

On the wall of a bar owned by one Athictus are the words: 'I screwed the barmaid.' A little more poetic and found at the bar of Astylus and Pardalus is: 'Lovers are like bees in that they live a honeyed life.' And at the bar of Innulus and Papilio – most likely also a brothel – an individual recorded the occasion of his coming out: 'Weep you girls. My penis has given you up. Now it penetrates men's behinds. Goodbye, wondrous femininity!'

And thus at the epicentre of this energy and industry was the Inn of Primus. It was excavated on two separate occasions, in 1853 and 1857.

Stepping into the inn – amid the throng of locals (Pompeiians rich and poor lived cheek by jowl, meaning they likely rubbed shoulders in bars) and visitors new to the town – was an L-shaped bar. It was noisy and maybe a little smoky. While drinks were served at the bar, the circular holes cut into the top of the adjacent side suggest it was used to house a small grill, and there was likely a metal tripod secured over coals to hold a pan for soups or to keep food warm. It's also probable that wine and other drinks were stored under the counters in terracotta or earthenware vessels.

To the right of the bar was a hearth, which may have doubled as a fireplace and second grill or oven. To the back on the left are steps that would have led to accommodation on a second storey, and to the right is a door that leads to a back room. The remnants of some ornate paintwork on the walls suggest that this room wasn't a back kitchen or store room, but rather a dining room. The existence of red paint with gold stripes denotes a smart interior room – red blocks lined with gold.

It was in here, perhaps, that our local Pompeiian had spent the afternoon, drinking and gambling, before calling it a day. The existence on the wall of an advert for an electoral campaign suggests that discussions in such a place included politics. Indeed, across town and at nearby Herculaneum, similarly destroyed and preserved intact, one can find several painted declarations for political candidates. Doubtless many inns became meeting places for these discussions. In fact, Roman leaders eyed them with suspicion, believing some taverns to be harbouring political hostility, and so began to inflict regulations.

Tiberius (Roman emperor AD 14–37) was so incensed that he imposed, according to the decree, 'restrictions on ... eating houses as not to allow even pastry to be exposed for sale'. Presumably the less food a place could offer, the less attractive it became for people to meet there.

The Mercury Street tavern would have resembled a modern-day, but traditional, Italian trattoria. Herbs, grapes, cheeses and cured meats would have hung from the ceilings, and wine would have arrived in animal skins, transported on carts and decanted into amphoras.

Clearly that didn't quite do the job, as Claudius (emperor AD41–54) went a bit further and actually abolished a number of establishments that caused him concern. In the words of the historian Dio Cassius, writing some 100 years later, Claudius 'abolished the taverns where they were wont to gather and drink and commanded that no boiled meat or hot water should be sold'. Then Nero – whose thirteen-year reign ended in AD68 – imposed his own culinary restrictions, with historian Suetonius (d. AD126) recording that, under the emperor, 'the sale of any kind of cooked viands in the taverns was forbidden, with the exception of pulse and vegetables, whereas before every sort of dainty was exposed for sale'.

But, having done this, Nero decided to embrace the issue of political hostility being stirred in inns by visiting them himself. Suetonius reported that, as soon as the sun set, Nero went off to make his rounds of the taverns. Dio Cassius went further, stating that Nero 'spent practically his whole existence amid the tavern life', but that he also 'forbade others to sell in taverns anything boiled, save vegetables and soup'.

However, it is likely that these restrictions, laboriously inflicted by each ruler, did not reach Pompeii, or, if such regulatory measures were applied, they were ignored in the town.

The evidence is in the number of inns in Pompeii. It was one of the most widespread businesses; its growth seemed to have no limitations. And it's another reason the town became so popular. A Roman citizen could visit Pompeii and fill his boots with wine, pastries, meat and other delicacies.

The atmosphere in those establishments can also be evoked by looking at surviving pictures and fragments painted on the walls. There is a painting in a tavern on Pompeii's Mercury Street, for example. Customers sit around a table on stools, and one of them wears a hooded cloak, indicating his status as a traveller. A young serving boy stands nearby and, on a wall behind them, various types of food hang on a rack.

The scene would be familiar to those who have visited a modern-day, but traditional, Italian trattoria, where one can find the likes of grapes, sausages, onions and cheeses, not to mention dried bunches of herbs – thyme, oregano and rosemary – hanging from the ceilings and wooden beams. Other paintings around the town show simple moments in hospitality, such as a customer asking a serving boy for wine and the method by which wine, mainly local, was transported around the town. It was driven about in carts, in large animal skins, and then poured into empty amphoras, ingeniously, using a spout made from one of the legs of the animal skin.

A drinking bowl fragment from 480 BC shows a man reclining on a couch, seemingly about to slap a server who has spilt some wine onto his waist – an early example of the plight of the waitress.

Wine was usually served diluted with water, and some tavern keepers had a reputation for mixing in a little more than the customer would have liked. This is recorded in some graffiti left by a tavern near one of the entrances to the town, the Stabian gate: 'Curses on you, *copo* [landlord], you sell water and drink unmixed wine yourself.'

Doubtless some places were more raucous than others, establishments where – particularly in an era of slavery – it might not have been wholly pleasant to have worked. A very early example of this, casting us back another 500 years or so, can be found among the ancient Greek artefacts at the Martin von Wagner Museum in the northern Bavarian German town of Würzburg. Item number L483, dated around 480 BC, is a fragment of a drinking bowl, with a gold design painted onto the sheer black piece of pottery. It is an image of universal suffering – that of the plight of the waitress.

A long-bearded man reclines on quite a high couch – his shoes are removed and placed on the floor. He is attended by a woman who, pouring wine from a small and decorative amphora, manages to spill some of it onto his waist. Neither the vessel nor history records whether this was done by mistake or on purpose. But what can be seen is that the man's hand is raised and, judging by the muscles drawn distinctly on his arm, she's due quite a hard slap for her misdemeanour.

If the abuse of staff is a symbol of inequality, Roman taverns, like taverns throughout history, can actually be social levellers, as we have seen with some notorious emperors who cruised bars after office hours. Furthermore, the eating

The inns of Pompeii were lavishly decorated. The circular holes cut into the bars may have contained coals, with small grills above either to cook food or warm pans of soup. Wine and other drinks were kept under the counters and in store rooms at the back.

habits of Pompeiians suggest that food was also a common bond generally among Romans. Evidence for this comes firstly from skeletons found in a cellar in a suburb of Pompeii called Oplontis. There lie the remains of several dozen people who had sought shelter from the erupting volcano. But, while their luck ran out, they offer us some fascinating insights. There are two groups of people. One group has money and jewels; the other has nothing. Slaves died alongside members of the upper classes, yet their skeletal remains show no distinct differences. There are no signs of malnutrition, nor is there evidence of those general assumptions about rich and poor in history: that the rich are big and strong, the poor weak and slight; the wealthy live lives of gluttony, the underprivileged go hungry.

Studies of teeth in the cellar show similar wear and tear, abrasions that would have been caused by the remnants of millstone grit left in the flour from milling. There were around thirty bakeries in Pompeii, and it seems they served both rich and poor. Studies of cesspits in Herculaneum draw similar conclusions.

About 15ft below the streets lies what some might call 2,000-year-old shit, but what Cambridge University historian Andrew Wallace-Hadrill described as 'gold'. 'Down here was the story of the Roman diet, waiting to be found,' he said. His analysis of 700 bags of human waste, albeit a rather more pleasant job now than 2,000 years ago, revealed a very varied diet of chicken, fish, nuts and eggs – locally sourced ingredients and imported food. Above the sewer were shops and modest apartments. These weren't the abodes of the rich or the poor, but rather the Roman middle class, and it's clear that they enjoyed a good diet.

What was a horror story is now fodder for holidaymakers, perusing Pompeii as a day-off from the beach, sun-tanning and water-skiing. Yet this trauma reveals itself as a frozen slice of history – the extraordinary evidence of the most ordinary lives. Rich and poor lived side by side – as they do today in so many cities across the world, from London to Bombay – and some even chose to gather in the same places. As the English country pub sees the squire landlord sipping alongside farmers and labourers, new and old money propping up the bar, so, too, did the Roman nobles mix with merchants in the establishments of Pompeii. Their diets were similar – their teeth and stomachs revealing amazing similarities – though the rich undoubtedly dined in splendour in private houses as well.

But our obsession here is the public sphere, the rough and tumble of the hospitality business. It's an exciting and vivid place to start a journey across 2,000 years of eating out. And, while we can only guess as to the fate of our imaginary friend who staggered along the streets of Pompeii that day in AD 79, we do know for sure that, if he did live, he never again propped up the bar at the Inn of Primus.

2

The Ottoman Empire

A study of the Ottoman Empire, disparaged by many historians as an ancient and backward civilisation, reveals a magnificent array of food that casts a bright light a very long way into the future.

It is derogatory, derisory, dismissive, not to mention disrespectful, that people talk of the 'collapse' of the Ottoman Empire. I mean, if you'd been going for 600 years, you might need a bit of a lie-down. But then, as you take your well-earned rest, look what happens. Before you can say 'baba ganoush', you're being slated, your reputation trashed. Centuries of tradition are labelled 'conservative', as in 'backward'. Those eyes that were all looking to the east suddenly swivel; now it's the west where it's at. When the Republic of Turkey was established in 1923, the buzzword was 'modernisation', and so Turkey – a somewhat smaller landmass than the Ottoman Empire, though still at the centre of it – shunned even the Ottoman food traditions. Instead, cooks looked to France. Even though the empire was created in 1299, those 600 years of humanity were dismissed as insular, irrelevant.

But, while political ideology has a way of gripping the psyche, food is different. If things taste good, if drinks do more than just quench thirst, then they find a way of reaching the surface, coming up for air, seeing the light.

And so it is with the food of the Ottoman Empire. Because now, as the west trundles along into the first quarter of the twenty-first century, it cannot avoid the influences of the east that began right at the end of the thirteenth century. For that tub of houmous you dip your carrots into in the park at lunchtime, or those falafels you pop into your mouth on the move, or the simple fact that you are dining in a fancy new restaurant where sharing is the norm, all owe their origins to this beast of an ancient culture. Your on-the-go snacks and your smart little restaurant plates are not the inventions of the latest trendy chefs. Instead, they are the creations of the likes of the Seljuks, the Mongols, the Ilkhanids and the Memluks.

As these tribes battled for supremacy, their territory expanded and contracted from Iran to Algeria, Greece to Yemen, in between mouthfuls of *imam bayildi*, *soslu patican* and *tavuk*. As the Abbasids and Safavids and Byzantines fought it out, and as the empire reached its peak in the mid-sixteenth century (when it included modern-day Egypt, Iraq and the Balkans), it had a food culture as complex as its landmass was vast.

The Ottomans were proud of their cuisine: it reflected the greatness of their empire and, as the empire grew in size and stature, so, too, its ingredients permeated and extended beyond its borders. By the seventeenth century, foods of the empire had reached the shores of England. In fact, so successful were Ottoman merchants in finding export hubs that local markets back home began to go short.

This came to a head in the 1670s when the export of figs and raisins to England had to be banned to preserve indigenous supplies. This greatly upset the fashionable English, who had developed a taste for these exotic dried fruit snacks. And no one was more upset than the incumbent sovereign, Charles II. This was a time when dining was a defining aspect of the king. At banquets, he would sit at a raised table so that everyone could see him. Dishes were elaborate, presented on glinting, sparkling platters. It is said that one of Charles's favourite fruits was pineapple. But we can be sure he also loved figs. Indeed, so upset was the royal household by the Ottoman ban on their export that representations were made and, in 1676, an exemption was announced. A shipload of figs would be exported from the Ottoman Empire to England twice a year, for exclusive use in the kitchens of that merry monarch.

And, in the same way that we can say the Roman Empire was at its pinnacle when its sauces – cooked in Rome by

Fifteenth-century Sultan Mehmed II had 160 staff working in his kitchens; his successor, Murad II, employed almost 1,500.

Apicius – were at their thickest, so, too, can the Ottoman Empire's peak be measured by the number of staff employed in the sultans' kitchens.

During the reign of Mehmed II (1451–81), there were 160 employees in the kitchen. At the start of Suleiman the Magnificent's reign in 1520, the number was 250; by 1566, when Selim II acceded to the throne, it was 600; and, in the final years of Murad II (1574–95), it was around 1,500. In the 1590s, there is a record of a contemporary writer complaining about the excessive number of kitchen personnel. The pantry alone employed 286 men.

By this time, the HQ of the sultan was firmly in Constantinople. It had, over the years, been in the cities of Bursa (north-west of what is now Turkey) and Edirne (in the far eastern corner of today's Marmara region). But, in 1453, following a seven-week siege, the incumbent Byzantines lost the city to an army commanded by a 22-year-old Ottoman sultan, Mehmed II. Constantinople became the new capital of the empire and, six years later, Mehmed II ordered the building of a palace. He summoned the finest builders and craftsmen from across the land and they built him private apartments, associated buildings for his entourage, pavilions, peaceful courtyards and, of course, kitchens – ten of them. This large complex – the Topkapi Palace – was then made even larger by Suleiman the Magnificent between 1520 and 1560.

The food that the palace cooked, the menus and the eating traditions, had all been developed and formalised by Mehmed's father, Murad II. That Ottoman cuisine was a combination, or fusion, of culinary culture from a very broad region: the Arabic world, north Africa, the Balkans, Anatolia, the Black Sea, the Aegean, the Caucasus and parts of Persia. (By the 1500s, the empire extended to what is today Hungary in the north and Yemen in the south, and from Algeria in the west to Iraq in the east.)

These influences, the recipes and the ingredients that reached the capital, were then shaped by the habits of the sultan and his subjects, the ancestors of today's Turks. From the Black Sea came grain, barley, salt, beef, lamb, chicken, eggs, apple and honey. Dates, prunes, rice, lentils, spice, sugar and pickled meats arrived from Egypt. From regions in modern-day Hungary and Romania (Moldavia and Transylvania) came honey and recipes for making sherbets and meat stews. Olive oil appeared from Greece. And, across the empire, there was rice – lots of it. A contemporary traveller recorded a visit to the town of Tabriz where he noted forty different variations of the rice dish *pilav* (pilau).

Of course, different periods saw different influences, but one can make three generalisations: the Ottomans shared dishes; the Ottomans drank milk (from

The food cooked at the Topkapi Palace was a fusion of the vast Ottoman Empire: meals from the palace kitchens were served to citizens, who waited outside.

horses, as well as from goats and cows); and the Ottomans consumed a lot of vegetables. A seventeenth-century visitor described Ottomans as 'milk-drinking barbarians'; a nineteenth-century observer wrote that it is 'in the preparation of vegetables [that] the Turkish cook expands all his art'; a French traveller considered 'the great plenty of fruits, salads, and among the rest of cucumbers half ripe, together with their stalks, a dyet very proper to break a French horse's belly'; and a sixteenth-century German talked of the vegetables he came across as 'all eaten raw like cattle do'.

At the palace, there were kitchens that prepared food for the sultan, kitchens for his queen, princes, eunuchs and royal household, and then kitchens that catered for the public. From across the empire came bakers, pastry chefs and specialists in the likes of yoghurt, pickles and confectionery. Alongside this was a complicated structure of kitchen brigades. There was the chief cook – the executive chef of today's grand hotels – who was head of the private kitchen of the sultan, but also had overarching responsibility for all the brigades, budgeting and tableware.

Under him were heads of sections, as well as clerks, butlers, page boys and many others. Indeed, the structures of today's grandest catering institutions, be they royal households or public restaurants, clearly have their origins in the Ottoman era.

Palace chefs were marked out from others by the white caps they wore. They began work at sunrise in order to create an immense amount of food. A mid-fifteenth-century visitor recorded the quantities of food ordered to the palace as '200 sheep, 100 kids, 10 calves, 50 geese, 200 hens, 100 chickens and 200 pigeons'. This fed the sultan and the eunuchs, servants, pages, army officers and government officials stationed at the palace. And the kitchens geared up further, of course, for feasts and celebrations. A mid-sixteenth-century writer recorded a list of ingredients for a feast that would celebrate the circumcision of a prince as '1,100 chickens, 900 lambs, 2,600 sheep, almost 8,000kg of honey and 18,000 eggs'.

It was not just elaborate food prepared daily for the sultan and his crew, however. Out of those kitchens was ferried simpler food for those who lived nearby, both wealthy locals and those with nothing.

So one of the ways to eat out in the days of the Ottoman Empire was to linger near the palace at meal times. Meals occurred twice a day: breakfast was mid-morning and dinner took place after mid-afternoon prayer. For the sultan, breakfast would normally start with a hearty soup, and, according to tradition, he would sit at a low round table, or a large round spread of leather material, with his knees crossed, and a napkin, made of silk or some other valuable material, across his front. A second towel was placed in his left hand to clean his mouth and fingers. When meat was served, it was brought in by his attending maids intact, but slow-cooked, so that the sultan could tear it into pieces himself. This he would do with his hands, never with a knife or fork, although spoons were provided so the sultan could eat porridge or syrupy, fruit-based desserts.

That meat could have been gently cooking for hours with tomato paste, onions and garlic. It might have been pigeon, goose, lamb, chicken, mutton or wild fowl. Apparently fish was only eaten when the sultan was by the sea, so that he could watch it being caught first. There could also be meatballs and kebabs, rice pilaus, and a vast array of hot and cold vegetables: little dishes of tomatoes, peppers, okra, squash, artichoke, leek and cabbage. There would be doughs, too, some shaped into fritters, stuffed with vegetables, cheese or spinach, and fried. Dozens of sweets were then offered, and meals often ended with sherbet, a sweet drink made with the likes of sugar and dates. As was the custom across the empire, food would be eaten in silence, without conversation – although the sultan, according to one visitor, would be entertained by 'mutes and buffoons', who fooled around in silence, playing tricks and making fun of each other.

While there were two main dining times, snacks were often served at the palace between meals. An ambassador to the Ottoman capital from Venice – Ottaviano Bon, who served from 1603 to 1609 – wrote a detailed account of the dining habits of the then sultan Ahmed I. His appetite saw him eat three or four meals a day, which began with one at ten in the morning and ended with dinner at six o'clock at night. Feeling peckish, he would first inform his chief white eunuch, who would then pass the message on to a junior eunuch, who would, in turn, inform an attendant, who would finally send a message to the kitchen. Individual dishes would then arrive, tried first by a taster.

While the sultan's private kitchen catered elaborate meals to please him and impress his visitors, the public kitchens offered more humble fare. However, though it may have been plain, it was also free. The role of sultan was all-powerful and absolute, answerable only to God. He was head of the military and entitled to all land and possessions. Ottoman sultans were, or so they felt, natural successors to the Roman Empire, but perhaps with more paternal notions. For, if they owned all land and property, they also had a duty to their people to sustain them. So – and this was key to the successful expansion of the empire – the sultan provided and regulated all food, and out of his palace's public kitchens came that humble fare, often broths and pilaus. The latter was, wrote a seventeenth-century visitor, often boiled stiff until 'it crumbleth'.

Like the sultan, the people ate sat upon the floor. A German botanist, Leonhard Rauwolf, travelled to the eastern region of the Mediterranean, the Levant, in the sixteenth century, publishing his account in 1582. He described how, 'in these eastern countries, they eat upon the plain ground, and, when it is dinner time, they spread a round piece of leather, and lay about it tapestry, and sometimes cushions, whereupon they sit cross-legged'. Grace was said first, he reported, 'then they eat and drink hastily ... and do not talk much'. The meal over, Rauwolf noted the skill with which the diners stood up: 'After they have done, they rise altogether with a jerk, swinging themselves about, which our countrymen cannot easily imitate, 'til after they have been there a while, for the limbs are numbed in sitting cross-legged, so that one hath a great deal to do to bring them to themselves again.' If Rauwolf managed to get up without feeling numb, enduring pins and needles or losing his balance, he then watched as the leather spread, with the day's bread still on it, was drawn together with string, like a purse, and then hung up in a corner.

While the sultan fed his people at the fringes of the palace, food was also served at imarets – places that we might now recognise as soup kitchens (many of which were part of a mosque complex). Again, the food here was free and, while imarets were frequented by the poor, they also provided food for the general populace, from government officials to local mosque workers, scholars, students and travellers. Wooden trays would bear dishes of broth or thicker porridge made with barley, in which pieces of meat would sit stewing.

An imaret in Jerusalem, recorded in 1552, was attached to a mosque and served two free meals a day – one in the morning that offered rice soup, and another in the evening with wheat soup. The morning offering came with chickpeas, parsley, courgettes or squash, with a little dish on the side of yoghurt and another of lemon juice. The evening soup was made with cracked wheat, onions and salt or cumin. There was bread as well, and, according to historical deeds, diners were fed in strict order of status. First would be the staff of the imaret, then local residents, then each of the two categories of the poor: those who were learned and those without education. The last to be served were women...

Another imaret, in Damascus, served the poor, but also provided fodder for horses. And one in Constantinople, located near the Grand Bazaar, offered soup, but also supplied condiments such as pickled grapes, aubergines and onions; it catered for staff and students at a nearby college, so only gave food to the poor if there were leftovers.

As to the quality of these meals, an Ottoman bureaucrat – one Mustafa Ali, working in the late 1500s – doubled as a critic when he pronounced on his visits to two imarets. Of one in the capital, he wrote that 'their bread has become black as the earth and looks like a lump of dry clay, their soup has turned into dishwater, their rice and puddings into vomited matter'. As for the meat, it was, he reckoned, processed after the animals had died of natural causes – 'emaciated sheep that were slaughtered after having died'. But the place had some use, he added: if you have a pet, 'they pour their soup to their dogs'.

Of another imaret in Rumeli, a town in what is now the Balkans, he was ecstatic: 'The food offered to the travellers is so delicious and soul-nourishing. Their stewed meat is well seasoned, their soup and hamburgers are plentiful, and

Opposite: The sultan ate his meals seated on the floor at a low, round table. Breakfast was often a hearty soup, and it was traditional for meat to be brought slow-cooked, but intact, so the sultan could tear off strips himself.

their noodles and noodle soup are of equal quality.' He also wrote of fresh fruits distributed after each meal, as well as little boxes of 'sweet confections', and, on special occasions, diners being offered 'baclava like the disk of the shining moon and sweeter than sugar and countless tasty delicacies of the sausage'.

Across the towns and cities of the Ottoman Empire, you would also find places not bestowed upon the people by their benevolent sultans. (One should note that, when not providing for his people, Mehmed II had a tidy line in killing all his male relatives, infants included, and sultans insisted that their burly gardeners, when not tending flowers, must double as executioners – the preferred method of executing officials being strangulation, so that blood would not be spilled.) Run by entrepreneurs, the cook shops and eating houses had different approaches to food. Eating houses tended to serve variations on three themes: lamb or goat cooked in a tandoor-style oven; stewed sheep's head or trotters; and tripe soup or a porridge made from wheat and mutton. As for the cook shops, they all tended to specialise in individual dishes. Some sold vegetables stuffed in cabbage or vine leaves (early dolma), others sold sausages, a few sold salads, many sold stews or soups, and then there were those that sold kebabs, which are, of course, still familiar today.

Early miniatures from the seventeenth century record the cooking of *döner kebaps* in, for example, the dainty setting of a picnic. While a small group of men sits around a cloth laden with fruit, reading books to one another, a cook – a suitable distance behind the men – carves pieces of meat from a long wedge, which is being turned on a spit over hot coals by another cook.

Meanwhile, other cook shops specialised in *sis kebaps*, with small-time cooks setting up 'shop' almost anywhere they could, digging holes in the ground and laying coals under a grill, upon which they would cook their skewers of meat. Other food vendors erected similar stands, often simply large trays with a grill in the middle and a pot in which to keep the food warm. They would create their pitch in public squares and then pack and carry their equipment away at the end of the day. But this street food was not just for the poor; it is said that Sultan Ahmed III, who ruled until 1736, sent his vizier – his highest-ranking adviser – out into the streets each day to fetch him his favourite pastry from a specialist vendor.

There were shops for sweeter pleasures, too. Some establishments sold clotted cream sprinkled with sugar, and others sold various types of milk puddings, although it seems many men who had sweet teeth were also partial to the fairer sex – so much so that, in 1573, women were banned from entering clotted cream shops in one district of Constantinople, because some were using the venues to solicit men.

As the food offerings grew throughout the empire, regulations began to be imposed. While the sultan gave food away, others prospered from selling it, and so price controls were brought in, as well as food hygiene standards. A law in 1502 decreed that: food be cooked in a clean manner and served in clean bowls; pots be washed properly; cloths that dry the cooking equipment be clean; and staff wear clean aprons. Furthermore, in the same way that French wine appellations today decree to the letter the percentages of varieties of grapes used in specific wines, so, too, did the Ottomans control the recipes for popular foods sold in eating houses in the sixteenth and seventeenth centuries. Thus, tripe soup had to be served with garlic, spices and vinegar; a roasted sheep's head or feet had be sprinkled with vinegar, melted butter and spices; a rice and chicken soup had to come flavoured with lemon juice. Very specific detail was reserved for a flaky filled pastry called *börek*. Good-quality flour had to be used, and the dough mixture had to be (an ancient measure that translates as) precisely 1.283kg of pure butter to 25kg of flour. The filling was specified at a ratio of 70 dirhems of meat to 10 dirhems of onion, and then seasoned with black pepper. The regulations created a culture of cleanliness that pervaded the ensuing centuries. A visitor to Constantinople in the 1850s, George Matthew Jones, was impressed by the cook shops, writing that they were 'kept really very clean and neat'.

As to drinking, given that Ottoman culture was predominantly Islamic, one might assume that it was booze-free. But that was not, in fact, the case. Many deviated from the official code and drank wine at parties and other gatherings. The wife of an English ambassador visiting Constantinople in 1718 is reported to have been shocked when one of her Ottoman hosts drank wine in her presence. He explained to her that the prohibition of wine was a very wise maxim, but that it was intended for the common people. Furthermore, he added, the prophet Muhammad never intended to forbid from drinking wine those who knew how to consume it in moderation.

However, there were periods when the public consumption of wine was more fiercely policed. Rauwolf wrote that, while the residents he came across in Aleppo (in what is now Syria) drank a non-alcoholic drink flavoured with berries, they preferred to drink wine. But, he wrote, 'anybody that did smell of wine was imprisoned immediately', as well as fined and 'punished severely with many blows under his soals'. Rauwolf also noted that one local commander, upon

By the mid-sixteenth century, there were coffee houses across the Ottoman Empire. Mehmet III employed a personal coffee maker with forty attendants.

seeing a member of his brigade drunk and staggering, 'drew his scimeter and cut off his head'. But apparently, during the reign of a previous sultan, drinking was permitted, and so, wrote the German, many men 'met together daily in drinking houses and drunk ... not only two or three glasses of strong wine not mixed with water, but four or five of such ... [and] so quickly, one after another, and with such eagerness that they would not allow themselves a morcel or two between it; and so, as you may easily guess, they become to be sordid presently'. They were 'hoggish', he said, adding that they were such big boozers that they could have represented their country at drinking. Or, as he put it, 'they excel all other nations in it'. The successor to that particular sultan took a dimmer view. But, noted Rauwolf, it didn't stop the people from drinking. In the summer months, he wrote that they would 'carry in privately (just like the ants) great quantities of wine', which they would open 'at night and drink together until they have their bellies full and so rest after it all night that they might not smell of wine the next day'.

If drinking wine was covert, the consumption of another liquid was not. 'They have a very good drink', noted Rauwolf, 'called *chaube* [coffee] that is almost black as ink.' It was, he'd been told, a drink that settled the stomach if one felt ill. He saw it drunk in the morning 'out of china cups, as hot as they can, they put it often to their lips, but drink little at a time'.

While coffee originated from Ethiopia or Yemen, it was, as Rauwolf attests, alive, well and thriving among the Ottomans by the middle of the sixteenth century. Such was its popularity that coffee houses sprang up across the empire and, as one historian noted, became entrenched 'as the very centre of male public life'. Conservative Muslim scholars disapproved of this stimulating drink, but they failed to stem its rise and rise. Elaborate ceremony was developed in its brewing, and the sultan Mehmed III was soon enjoying the drink himself – employing a coffee maker who, of course, came with forty assistants.

Coffee was often served with Turkish delight, sometimes flavoured with pistachio and always drunk hot. In 1615, a visiting physician wrote that 'one hardly sees a gathering where it is not drunk'. However, so prevalent were the gatherings at coffee houses that the upper political echelons became paranoid that the storytellers, poets and thinkers of the day were gathering to sip coffee and ridicule the corrupt elite. And so, just as Roman emperors had cracked down on inns as alleged centres of intrigue and conspiracy, between 1623 and 1640, during the reign of Murad IV, many coffee houses were forced to close. There are records, even, of coffee drinkers – and tobacco smokers – being executed. Ponder on that the next time you're in Starbucks having a gossip over some flaky pastry and a latte...

3

The Legacy of Ibn Battuta

When Ibn Battuta took a gap year in the early fourteenth century, it was a dangerous time to travel – but he was hungry for change, adventure and food. He ate out. A lot. And his gap year lasted for over thirty years.

The solid, imposing doors of windowless, sandstone buildings in the Moroccan city of Fez shield many of the residents from the hot, bustling, dusty and narrow streets of the capital. Behind one such door, its heavy wood studded with iron roundels and two large knockers, is a contrasting courtyard of idyllic peace. Over the refreshing sound of drips from the fountain at its centre, past the decorative columns and shadowed floor, the cool tiles of which are adorned with elaborate rugs and cushions, the murmur of conversation can be heard.

It is 1356. Reclining there in the shade, sipping occasionally from pretty little glass cups of tea, is a man in his fifties, dressed in the traditional robes and white headdress of a Muslim scholar. With him is a younger man, a literary scholar, sent to this house on a mission from Sultan Abu Inan, no less, ruler of Morocco.

As the older man speaks, the more youthful chap listens intently and writes with frantic eagerness. His name is Ibn Juzayy. He is there to record for posterity one of the most extraordinary tales of adventure in history. It is the story of the travels of Shams al-Din Abu'Abdallah Muhammad ibn'Abdallah ibn Muhammad ibn Ibrahim ibn Muhammad ibn Yusuf al-Lawati al-Tanji ibn Battuta, whom we shall simply call Ibn Battuta.

Opposite: Behind the heavy wooden door of a riad in Fez, in the shade of a quiet and cool courtyard, scholar Ibn Battuta dictated tales of his extraordinary thirty-year journey.

‘I braced my resolution to quit all my dear ones, female and male, and forsook my home as birds forsake their nests,’ he said, perhaps settling among the cushions and delving deep into his memory.

Aged twenty-two, he had set off from his family home in Tangier without companions and with very little luggage or money. His mission was a pilgrimage to Mecca, the tomb of the prophet Muhammad, in what is now Saudi Arabia. But, while such a journey is mandatory for all Muslims, Ibn Battuta’s mission was a little different. Leaving home, he had the idea that this journey could be a little longer. His appetite was more for an adventure than a trip. And an adventure it proved to be, for this gap year lasted for thirty-two years and took him from north Africa to Syria, across the Black Sea to central Asia, back through modern-day Turkey, east to Afghanistan and India, and then on to China. He visited forty countries in today’s geography, and covered a distance of some 75,000 miles.

And, where he stopped and rested, he dined – which makes Ibn Battuta’s journey not only a fascinating medieval tale, but also an extraordinary culinary adventure. He was a man who ate out for over three decades.

‘My parents being yet in the bonds of life, it weighed sorely upon me to part from them, and both they and I were afflicted with sorrow at this separation,’ Battuta spoke to the young Ibn Juzayy at the start of what must have been many sessions of intense reflection. Juzayy’s finished manuscript went on to be distributed and copied, but it would be 400 years until his words reached a European audience, with a French translation appearing in the 1850s. In the 150 years that followed that version, Battuta’s words were further translated into most continental languages. Indeed, it was as recently as 2001 that an index was produced for an English translation, the final volume of which was only completed in 1994. Those who have read *A Gift to Those Who Contemplate the Wonders of Cities and the Marvels of Travelling* (*Rihla* for short in Arabic – *Travels*) have compared Battuta to Marco Polo.

The western world thinks of Polo as the greatest ever traveller: a Venetian explorer who journeyed through Asia and became the first to chronicle life in China. Like Battuta, he travelled by whatever means possible, from boat to camel, facing life-threatening circumstances along the way, from storms to bandits. Like Battuta, he dictated his tales – albeit from a prison cell rather than a peaceful courtyard. (Polo returned home after his 24-year trip to find his town overrun by hostile Genoans.) And, like Battuta, scrupulous historians have questioned the veracity of some of his stories, with Polo being accused of both errors and plagiarism.

And yet the positive contributions of Marco Polo far outweigh any unhelpful elements. His travels took place between 1271 and 1295, and he died the year before Ibn Battuta left home (1324), so one could say that Polo (unknowingly) handed over the baton of epic travel to the hero of this chapter.

Battuta has suffered some intense criticism himself on the fronts of both accuracy and chronology. One historian analysing the original text has questioned, for example, how it was that Battuta might 'have crossed 800 miles of Anatolia in an afternoon'. However, other analysis, which cross-references with contemporary accounts, actually points to an extraordinary level of accuracy. Though Battuta dictated his story, there are some 1,500 mentions of names of specific individuals. And, as Tim Mackintosh-Smith, editor of a recent abridgement of Battuta's tales, says: 'How he remembered them – and, where they can be checked, with generally impressive accuracy – is one of the mysteries of the *Travels*.'

In fact, Battuta admits, for example, that he did, at one point, copy down the names of a number of learned men inscribed on a tomb in Bukhara (in modern-day Uzbekistan). But he then says that 'they were lost with all that I lost when the Indian infidels robbed me at sea'. This would cause panic in the minds of most writers (especially the author of this very tome, who can barely recall his dog's name unless he's written it down), but Battuta was raised in the tradition of learning and memorising text. His era was closer to the ancient days of aural tradition. The muscle in his brain that remembered people and places was fit and supple – unlike ours today, which has been rendered virtually extinct by technology and laziness.

Mackintosh-Smith didn't confine himself to the library when abridging the *Travels*, though; he physically followed some of Battuta's journey, which he found to, alongside other records, 'corroborate the traveller's accounts ... I have discovered sometimes startling evidence of his accuracy: to find, for instance, a certain piece of furniture seen by him in an obscure Anatolian mosque, still in the same spot 670 years on, is a spine-tingling experience.'

Battuta was born into a respected family of Muslim legal scholars in 1304 in Tangier. Like his father and grandfather, he became a *qadi*, a judge of Islamic law. Perhaps he felt that, being so qualified, he would find nothing in Tangier but a life of tortuous jurisprudence. Instead, if he travelled through the Islamic world, the theory of the philosophy of law he had in his head could prove more useful than any money he had in his purse.

He would go on his pilgrimage (or Hajj), but he would go further, to Delhi in India, where his qualifications could serve him well. And, indeed, when he arrived there and was able to impress the local sultan, he was installed as a judge and given a serious salary.

Battuta was obviously curious and brave, as well as brazen at times. In due course, he would collect slave girls and wives (and have children with both), and escape shipwrecks and deadly muggings. But he did set out as a pilgrim, a believer in mystical Islam. He was a scholar looking for like-minded intellectuals, and he saw himself as a citizen of Islamic civilisation, wherever that might reach.

As Battuta travelled, and, specifically, as he ate, he was guided by a morality and a constitution that chimed. He would have taken seriously the fundamental ethics of being a Muslim when it came to food. As Al-Ghazali, the prominent eleventh-century philosopher of Sunni Islam, once wrote: 'The greatest moral peril into which mankind may fall is the desire of the stomach.' Indeed, British professor of Islamic studies, and Battuta expert, David Waines suggests that 'even sexual desire ranked second to the stomach as a source of temptation and error'. A healthy body was needed to enable one to acquire the knowledge of God's guidance and, as Waines says, 'a healthy body was achieved only through food in necessary quantities over time'. But, in addition to Battuta's philosophically modest appetite, he also disparaged over-eating.

Travelling through western Persia (modern-day Iran), he was perturbed and a little embarrassed at having been provided with a meal and then presented with additional food, which he reckoned could have fed four more people. In Mogadishu, he was shocked by the locals, whom he called 'very corpulent; they are enormous eaters, one of them eating as much as a congregation ought to'. And in Ceylon (Sri Lanka), he described a distressing time when some citizens were so stricken with hunger that they killed and ate a small elephant. Battuta then added that, sated from their elephant dinner, the people lay down and went to sleep, but, as they snored, 'the elephants came in a body, and, smelling one of them, put him to death'.

In the course of his travels, as one would expect, Battuta experienced a huge variety of food, from meat and vegetables to pulses and fruit, but, whether he was in Cairo or Delhi, Morocco or China, there were three defining characteristics to his food consumption: he rarely ate alone; when he dined, dishes were shared; and there is no actual account of him ever having paid for anything.

Of the third point, it may be that moments when money changed hands for a coconut or a piece of bread were not considered worthy of description, so he decided not to record them. However, it is likely that he did manage to travel for a long time without having to call for a bill at the end of meals. As the sultans fed their people (Chapter 2) and the Romans opened their courtyards for passing travellers, so, too, did the kindness of strangers become something Ibn Battuta relied upon. This is one searing difference between the earliest records of hospitality and the present day.

In modern times, if you knock on someone's door asking for a bed and a bowl of soup, the person who answers is more likely to call the police than ask you in and give you a seat at their kitchen table. For all the joys of digital communication, we now tend to see the approach of strangers as the potential for a financial transaction.

Today, the word 'hospitality' has lost its original meaning (that legal and sacred term discussed in Chapter 1). Hospitality is now judged on its quality based on the knowledge that the person dispensing it will benefit financially. However, there are still some corners of the planet where strangers are ushered in for food – a few Greek islands, for example, where tourists are at first alarmed and then overwhelmed by such natural giving with no quid pro quo.

It's striking that the writer Patrick Leigh Fermor travelled from Rotterdam to Istanbul in the early 1930s and was largely able to live off the comfort provided by strangers. Unlike Battuta, he had some good contacts to look up along the way, but, like Battuta, he was also robbed of money and notebooks. However, they both were able to sing for their supper. Fermor had a talent for languages and was a gifted conversationalist. Battuta had a similarly great brain. One assumes that, as he travelled, his experiences made him a popular story-teller. His writings also indicate a good sense of humour. For example, visiting an orchard of pomegranates in Beirut, Battuta was given a tour by a man who worked there. As they walked about the shrubs, Battuta was handed several pomegranates to try, but, as the fruit was cut open, he found that all the seeds tasted sour.

'Have you been all this while in the orchard and do not yet know a sweet pomegranate from a sour one?' he said, castigating the worker.

The man replied curtly: 'I was hired to keep the orchard, not to eat the pomegranates.'

Battuta also revelled in the eccentricities he came across, especially in the courts of sultans and kings. There was the Persian king in whose presence one had to stand straight while holding one's earlobes, and the Anatolian king who gave his guest Battuta the greatest honour by offering him provisions and money – but not before being sick in front of him. In Sumatra, Battuta had an audience with the king in which a loyal subject bowed before him, made a long speech ('not a word of which I could understand') and then proceeded to cut his own head off with a knife. Battuta was alarmed by this, but managed to keep his composure ('I was wondering much at the circumstance,' he said – a considerable understatement). With his subject now dead on the floor in a pool of blood, the king looked at Battuta.

'Servants do this out of loyalty for us,' he said, ordering the body to be removed, taken away and burnt. 'Does anyone among you do such a thing as this?'

Battuta considered the situation before replying: 'I never saw one do so.'

Both Fermor and Battuta also attracted strong female interest; we know Fermor cut a dash as a handsome man in his late teens, and perhaps Battuta had similar attributes. He certainly didn't shy away from mentioning some of his exploits. In the Maldives, among lashings of coconut and fish, he recalled that the locals drank 'palm wine', as well as consuming large amounts of honey, sweetmeats and dried fruit, a combination of which, he said, was 'a strong incentive to venery', and, as a consequence, 'I had some slave girls and four wives during my residence there'. He also wrote of his frustration with tradition: 'In these islands, the women never eat with the men, but in their own society,' which, he said, was a shame because 'their conversation is very pleasing and they themselves are exceedingly beautiful'. Battuta even attempted to change the culture: 'I endeavoured to get my wives to eat with me, but I could never prevail.'

While Battuta appears to have sired children with a variety of women in various countries across the decades, there is no evidence that his English counterpart Fermor, operating a few centuries later, made any of his hosts pregnant. But both men enjoyed the concept of hospitality in its truest forms, though it seems that world war and massive cultural change have rendered modern society considerably less generous.

When today's cooks talk of the concept of sharing plates, they see it as a trend and a way to get people into their restaurants. For Battuta, communal dining was the norm, eating alone only in extremis – snatching food while on the run from bandits, for example. In China, he was captured by forty men on horseback, stripped and bound by thieves, but he managed to escape: 'I hid myself in a forest thickly interwoven with trees and thorns ... my food was the fruit and leaves

Battuta lived on the kindness of strangers. An Egyptian holy man gave him a bed and, on departure, a package of small cakes and silver coins.

of the mountain trees.' In India, attacked this time by 'infidels', he escaped and hid in a bamboo forest. Desperate with hunger, he found berries on a bush, which he plucked 'until the thorns pricked my forearms, some traces of which still remain'. At this point, Battuta may have paused in the courtyard to roll up his sleeves and show the scars on his arms to Juzayy.

And there was another notorious incident of distinct inhospitality. Battuta recalled travelling through Sudan and meeting a sultan who warned him about the behaviour of a particular tribe. Having heard that they were a dangerous bunch, the sultan had boldly decided to invite them for dinner. He had dispatched a black slave to carry a formal invitation requesting the pleasure of their company at his table (or rather on his carpet and cushion-strewn floor). Unfortunately, the messenger had met a sticky end: the tribe had killed and eaten him. But there was, added the sultan, a positive side to the situation: Battuta probably did not need to worry about the tribe because the 'infidels will eat men, but they will eat none but blacks, because they say the white are injurious on account of them not being properly matured'.

Such worries and narrow escapes, however, were rare. The norm was what Battuta experienced in, for example, the mountains of Persia: 'I found in every stage a cell with food for the accommodation of travellers and for everyone who arrives there are bread, flesh and sweetmeats.'

Of course, the word 'cells' gives another clue as to why Battuta was able to eat his way across the known world without having to buy dinner. As a religious traveller and a judge of his faith, he was accepted into churches and affiliated institutions. He was fed and shared that food with others, as the prophet Muhammad, the founder of Islam, decreed: 'The best food is that over which there are many hands.'

A remote Christian monastery in Syria fed visitors – including Muslims – with bread, cheese, vinegars and capers.

So it was that Battuta dined on bread, broth and sugary sweets in monasteries, as well as being offered random biscuits by holy men, usually perched on top of remote rocks on epic fasts. One holy man, near the Nile delta in Egypt, provided Battuta with a bed for the night and, on his departure, gave him a package of 'small cakes and a few silver coins'. And a recluse in Yemen, living in a bare cell attached to a monastery, gave Battuta some pieces of dried barley bread with salt and thyme.

He also recorded being impressed by Christians at a large monastery in Syria: 'Every Muslim who stops there is entertained by the Christians; their food is bread, cheese, olives, vinegars and capers.' Had the dough been round and the ingredients placed on top, it could have been a pizza.

In Basra (Iraq), Battuta praised the people, saying that no stranger could feel lonely among them. It was a city of palm groves, and he recalled the most senior religious judge sending him a basket of dates that was so heavy that the porter, carrying it on his head, nearly collapsed under its weight.

In Isfahan, in central Iran, Battuta ate rice cooked in ghee with fried chicken, as well as rice mixed with houmous and seasoned with cinnamon and resin from the mastic tree (a gum still used today in Egypt, Turkey, Greece and Lebanon to flavour everything from drinks and ice cream to cheese and soup). Then there was the watermelon he came across in Khwarizm in central Asia. It had, he described, a green rind and a very sweet red pulp – which sounds familiar. But, unusually, it was dried, he recorded, in the same way dates were back home. And, while it was one of the best melons he had tasted, it did not agree with him. That night, he experienced a 'relaxation' of the bowels, and it was a few days before he felt able to continue his travels.

In Mogadishu, that place of corpulent eaters, the food was particularly elaborate and the people amazingly welcoming. Battuta reported that, when a ship arrived, cohorts of young men came down to the port to greet, welcome and offer themselves as hosts. He was housed in a students' residence, where the floor, he said, was 'spread with carpets and prepared for a feast'. Once they had sat, servants brought out large wooden platters bulging with mounds of rice cooked in ghee. These were surrounded by platters of what he called *kushan* – 'a seasoning made of chicken, meat, fish and vegetables'. In another dish were unripe bananas cooked in fresh milk (an antidote, perhaps, for those dried pieces of watermelon), and there was a dish whereby into curdled milk were placed 'pieces of pickled lemon, bunches of pickled pepper steeped in vinegar and salted, green ginger and mangoes'.

Battuta was shown how to take a mouthful of rice along with some of the pickles. There were mounds of food and the platters were brought out three times a day. It was too much for Battuta, but the locals ate this amount as a matter of habit, which was why, he commented, 'they were fat in the extreme'.

The Mogadishu largesse was a pleasant contrast, however, from what he experienced on arriving in Zaila, today's Somaliland. It was the two main ingredients in the people's diet that were the problem. They appeared to consume nothing but fish and camel. 'The stench of the country is extreme,' he reported, 'as is also its filth from the stink of the fish and the blood of camels, which are slaughtered in its streets.'

Zafar – now Yemen – also seemed to be a vision of hell. He described it as 'a filthy place, and full of flies'. The problem there was a combination of sticky dates and fish sold everywhere in vast quantities – and it was not just the people who ate them. 'They feed their beasts and flocks also with fish, a custom witnessed by me nowhere else,' he commented. It was, however, in Yemen where he first came across a coconut. The fruit, he said, came from a tree that was

> *very rare and valuable. It is something like the palm. The nut is like a man's head; for it has something like two eyes and a mouth; and within when green is like the brains. Upon it, too, is a fibre like hair. From this, they make cords with which they sew their vessels together instead of iron nails. They also make great ropes for their anchors out of it.*

In Anatolia, Battuta found thick soup, but he moaned that there was never any bread. A lot of the soup was a milky mixture in which bits of meat were stewed (an early type of fondue, perhaps), and he complained that 'they do not eat any bread or solid food'. It didn't seem to harm the Anatolians' physiques, though: 'They are powerful and hardy men with sound constitutions.'

While in India, Battuta came across rice, rice and more rice. Every course eaten in Delhi – be it salted peppers, lemons, mangoes, fowl, vegetables or milk dishes – came with ladles of rice. After a period in Delhi, some seven years, he headed south to the Maldives and modern-day Sri Lanka, where, he said, things got worse – he spent 'three years eating nothing but rice'. His constitution could not cope with all the rice and, eventually, he found that he 'could not swallow it except by taking it with water'.

Ibn Battuta came back to his homeland in 1354. But it was to Fez, not his family home in Tangier, that he returned. We know nothing of his homecoming or whether members of his family – the parents he was so sad to leave all those years before – were still alive. He soon came into contact with the sultan, Abu Inan, who, having heard some of the traveller's tales, ordered Battuta to stay in the capital and have his journey chronicled – that narrative possibly commissioned simply for the enjoyment of the royal court.

Ibn Juzayy was selected for the task of writing, as he had a reputation as a poet and a fine calligrapher. Historians believe he took on the assignment enthusiastically, and San Diego State University history professor Ross E. Dunn writes of the likelihood that Juzayy 'developed a warm friendship with the journeyer'. It seems that the pair met regularly for some two years. Their conversations took place in various locations – from the shady courtyard of Battuta's home to the humbler residence of Juzayy, from the gardens and other grand public buildings of Fez to the archways of mosques, where people were apt to sit and meet with friends or discuss business.

While the manuscript was finished by 1356, an illness or accident befell the younger writer and, aged thirty-seven, he died in 1357. Little else is known of him, but, in an introduction to *Rihla*, he suggested that the writing process was deeply satisfying. Battuta's dictation of the narrative was, he wrote, 'entertainment to the mind and delight to the ears and eyes'.

The manuscript finished (and doubtless presented to the sultan), Battuta then appears to have taken up the role of *qadi* in a town somewhere near the capital. And, writes Professor Dunn, 'since he was not yet fifty years old when he ended

Battuta's manuscript was finished in 1356. It took 500 years for a copy to turn up in Europe.

his travels, he very likely married again and sired more children, little half brothers and sisters of the offspring growing up all across the Eastern Hemisphere'.

The book, it seems, languished in the royal court, gathering dust on a shelf somewhere, as scholars have found no mention of it between the fourteenth and nineteenth centuries. The works of Marco Polo, by contrast, had a very great deal of PR.

Five hundred years later, a copy of Battuta's book turned up in Europe – an area Battuta had never made it to. Once translated, not unlike those archaeologists parting the sand and dust to discover bright fragments of tiles glinting in the Italian sunshine, Battuta's work revealed in staggering, colourful detail an ancient world of people, their daily lives, their customs and the food they ate.

In 1369, Ibn Battuta died in the knowledge that he was the greatest traveller of his era. There is an aside in *Rihla* in which he notes that he once met a pious man, who, he said, 'journeyed through the earth, but he never went to China, not the island of Ceylon, not the Maghrib, nor al-Andalus, nor the Negrolands, so that I have outdone him by visiting these regions'.

That's right. He travelled the world and, unknowingly on our grateful behalf, bought – and very possibly ate – the T-shirt.

4

Medieval England

Amid the chaos, smell and dirt of medieval London emerged an altogether smarter dining scene and one thing that transformed the dining experience: a tablecloth.

As we dance merrily through history, exploring the origins of the pizza, pondering on which clever clogs first dreamt up the idea of sharing dishes, and examining the very meaning of the word 'hospitality', sometimes we must stop and ask a question like: when did tablecloths turn up in restaurants? Now even the most deft of scribblers cannot escape such a question – at least not when the history of eating out is being unveiled.

For the tablecloth symbolises culture and civilisation. It shields the diner from the coarseness of wood, or whatever other material might be being used as a table – be it immovable and ancient stone or the plastic top of a modern foldable table. As plaster, paint and wallpaper shield the eye of the beholder from original building blocks, turning a room from functional to stylish, so, too, does a tablecloth – and its accompanying cutlery and crockery – elevate a meal from a feed to an occasion.

But tracking down that moment when an individual unfolded and wafted a cloth across a table – not in the private sphere, but in a public eating house – requires the forensic skills of a sleuth, not to mention a small measure of luck, and a little understanding and acceptance from the reader of some artistic licence.

At which point, out leaps the date 1410. Or rather it is picked from the rubble beneath the dusty floorboards of history.

The year 1410 is when a poem called 'London Lickpenny' was published. The author cannot be confirmed, but some have suggested it might be John Lydgate, a monk and poet from Suffolk.

The poem recounts how a man from Kent who, having been the victim of some scam, losing a number of goods ('defraudyd with great falshed [falsehood]'), goes

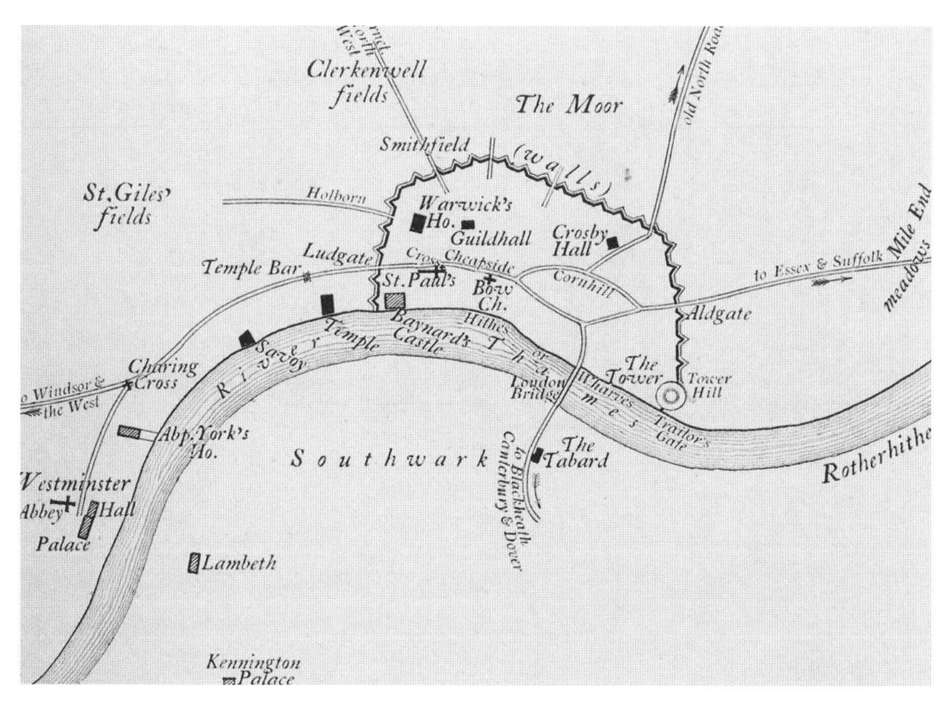

Medieval London was corrupt and uncharitable, but a visitor in 1410 found a tavern in Westminster offering bread, ale, wine, ribs, beef – and a tablecloth.

to London to seek justice, specifically Westminster – firmly the seat of government by that time – and to various districts in what is today the City of London. But his hopes of justice and recompense are dashed as, at every turn, he meets lawyers, judges and clerks whom, he realises, he must pay with bribes. So he returns to Kent, crestfallen. The law seems as corrupt as the people who robbed him and, unless one has money to throw at a problem, one cannot get anywhere. 'For of the law would I medle [meddle] no more,' he says despondently.

Medieval London may have been corrupt and uncharitable, but, as he describes his attempts to seek justice, he leaves a trail of beautiful nuggets for those looking for colour and detail of the city in the early fifteenth century, especially when it comes to eating out. He comes across cook shops in Eastcheap where the cooks – amid the noise of clattering pots and pewter, dancers, and pipes and harps – yell to passers-by the names of dishes they are selling: ribs of beef and pies. And, as he walks through Cornhill, he is poked at and grabbed by the owners of taverns trying to sell him wine by the pint. But then, in Westminster, he comes across an altogether different scenario, a place in style and atmosphere that does not appear to have been seen in England until this point in history.

The morning sun is high in the sky and, near Westminster gate, he finds an establishment where he is neither prodded nor pulled at. It is a place where the cooks pay him respectful attention 'with good entent', offering him bread, ale and wine, along with a meal of beef ribs, which, he notes, are 'both fat and fine'. More crucially, just as sellers of carpets in Turkey might lure one in by unveiling weaves of fine wool and silk and dainty glasses of tea, our man reports that, upon entering the establishment, 'a fayre clothe they began to spread'.

Our unlikely hero, sadly, takes a look around the establishment and then makes a hasty retreat. It appears that, in the same way he had no ready cash to bribe lawyers to help his case, he also does not have enough money to break some fresh bread, sip some wine or get his chops around the decent-looking beef ribs: 'But for lack of money I might not spede [succeed].' He doesn't fancy being forced to do a few hours of pot washing, so walks away.

However, he leaves us with the knowledge that, by the early 1400s, there must have been a few decent dining establishments in Westminster. In which case, Westminster was quite ahead of the game, as there is no evidence of any fancy restaurants anywhere else in London, let alone in other towns or across the countryside.

In fact, there is scant evidence to show that there was anything that could remotely be described as a restaurant in the thirteenth or fourteenth centuries. This is quite disappointing given that, by AD79, the Romans were expanding their empire as far as today's Scottish Borders, bringing smart villas, under-floor heating, straight roads and even gladiators, whereas 1,400 years later, not even an establishment as sophisticated as the Inn of Primus existed (Chapter 1).

That promising start in Europe appears to have stalled in England. Before 1400, dining out in England was simply not a thing. It did not exist. Londoners ate all their meals in the houses of families or friends. And travellers – like Ibn Battuta roaming around Asia Minor (Chapter 3) – more often than not relied upon the hospitality of religious institutions and monasteries.

Sure, there were cook shops and inns (the latter being for travellers, often with stabling for horses, the former serving local trade), but, in the words of history professor Martha Carlin: 'None of these served full, sit-down, restaurant-style meals to the general public. Cook shops served hot food and sometimes ale, but not wine, and they had no seats or tables.' There were, says Carlin, seats in alehouses, too, but no food was served. And, while food was served to guests, taverns were not open to the general public.

The cook shops began as stalls, finding space in the likes of busy markets. The food would be ready to eat: fried fish, boiled poultry, hot pies, cheese flans and cakes. Public records of fines being issued indicate – in Oxford in the 1250s, for example – that cooks were roasting and boiling meat outside the doors of their houses for passers-by. 'No cook should dare boil or roast any food outside his door unless first he have given satisfaction with two or three shillings,' details one record.

Doubtless people were flouting the law, as they had to cook outside since they didn't have kitchens inside. And, if the cooks didn't have kitchens, the poor certainly didn't. For, just as with many Romans, most people had neither cooking facilities nor enough money to buy pots, pans, fuel or ingredients. So workers who wanted hot food took advantage of the stalls and, if one is wondering how or what the poor and their children ate, Professor Carlin adds: 'For the very poor and the homeless, fast food was often their only source of hot food at all.'

Realising this, some authorities – including, in 1379, the authority for the City of London – allowed certain stalls to continue operating into the evening, after local trading had ceased. As the streets grew busy, some stalls, so as not to disrupt the flow of traffic and people, began to set up inside buildings and became actual cook shops. For an idea of what these places might have been like, we can look to Geoffrey Chaucer. In 'The Cook's Tale', written in the 1380s as part of *The Canterbury Tales*, there is mention of reheated food (a pie 'that hath been twies hoot and twies coold') and a lack of hygiene ('for in thy shoppe is many a flye loos').

There is, however, also a much earlier account of some of the public eating offerings in William Fitzstephen's 'Description of London', written in 1170, which contradicts Carlin's assertion that there was no such thing in existence as a public place to sit in and eat. Fitzstephen was a contemporary

Chaucer's 'The Cook's Tale' disparaged unhygienic cook shops.

and friend of Thomas Becket, King Henry II's chancellor who was propelled overnight to the role of Archbishop of Canterbury and subsequently murdered in Canterbury Cathedral, as witnessed by Fitzstephen.

In writing a life of Becket, Fitzstephen produced a picture of late twelfth-century London, a place of almost heartbreaking beauty. It's a city of 'grandeur and magnificence', the climate is 'wholesome', and, as for the ladies, he comments on 'the chastity of its maidens'.

One must imagine the City of London as a small, urban area, surrounded by countryside. Just outside the walls of the city is the Palace of Westminster on the west bank of the Thames – a river that 'abounds with fish' – and, adjoining the palace, 'the gardens of those who dwell in the suburbs, which are well furnished with trees, are spacious and beautiful'. To the north of Westminster 'are cornfields, pastures and delightful meadows, intermixed with pleasant streams, on which stands many a mill ... Beyond them, an immense forest extends itself, beautified with woods and groves, and full of the lairs and coverts of beasts and game, stags, boards and wild bulls.' The land is fertile, 'capable of producing the most luxuriant crops', the wheat of which he compares to the golden sheafs of the Roman goddess Ceres. Across the city are springs, 'whose waters are sweet, salubrious, clear'. The people, meanwhile, are charming: 'The citizens of London everywhere and throughout the whole kingdom are esteemed the politest of all others, in their manners, their dress, and the elegance and splendour of their tables.' In the evenings, boys from rival schools come out to the streets and 'wrangle one another in verse' (a sort of civilised precursor to today's street rap battles). In the winter, they skate on the frozen river.

In the summer, though, there is a place on the banks of the Thames, beside the ships that import wine from France, where the people of the city can come and get food: 'It is a public eating house, and it is both highly convenient and useful to the city, and is a clear proof of its civilisation.'

In an edition published in 1772, the translators of Fitzstephen's Latin work noted that the author mentions 'only one for the whole city', adding in a footnote: 'This is something extraordinary. We have nothing of the kind now, and doubtless it must have been a very large building.'

Inside the building, continues Fitzstephen, 'according to the season, you may find victuals of all kinds, roasted, baked, fried or boiled. Fish large and small, with coarse viands [items of food] for the poorer sort, and more delicate ones for the rich, such as venison, fowls and small birds.' Fitzstephen explains that, if a traveller arrived at a friend's house and was too hungry to wait for the cook to produce dinner, he would head to the public eating house: 'Recourse is immediately had to the bank above-mentioned, where every thing desirable is instantly procured.'

It's quite an institution, apparently. It's open day and night to both knight and stranger, so no one has 'occasion to fast too long, nor these to depart the city without their dinner'.

Sadly, this fabulous canteen doesn't appear to have been mentioned again in any literature, but it sets the seal of perfection on Fitzstephen's musings. For someone who witnessed the murder of a friend on the altar of a church, he seems remarkably chipper. The only hint of negativity in his reportings of London life are what he calls 'the inconveniences of excessive drinking of some foolish people [which the 1772 editor blames on the Danes for introducing 'the custom of hard drinking'] and the frequent fires [amazingly it isn't until almost 500 years later that tragedy unfolds in the timber houses and narrow streets of London in the five-day Great Fire of 1666]'.

If the seeds of seated dining were sown in that great dining hall by the river, they showed no sign of growth until the early fifteenth century, when our man from Kent, or the author of his poem, experienced some tablecloth action in Westminster.

And it's interesting that Westminster is the place to which we can pinpoint the nascent beginnings of fine dining, as it means we can say that the mother of all parliaments gave birth to London restaurants, too. The Latin word *parliamentum* can be translated as 'discussion', and the ancient parliaments of England were just that – gatherings for discussions that were formalised when the crown needed to raise taxes to fund wars. Initially, those who met were barons, but they were then joined by representatives of towns – leading figures or clergymen – who would soon become known as 'commons'. Meeting places were varied. One such assembly, for example, took place in 1290, during the reign of Edward I, at a royal hunting lodge, Clipstone, in Northamptonshire. But, as warfare increased and became an incessant part of life during the Middle Ages, more assemblies were needed as the crown looked to the representatives to raise tax.

Eventually, it made sense for parliaments to be held at Westminster, particularly since, at the end of the eleventh century, a vast hall had been built by William II – son of William the Conqueror – that was apparently the biggest room in England, if not Europe. It is a room that is still (having been rebuilt after a fire in 1834) too large for any practical purpose.

The country knights and landed gentry, along with the 'burgesses' – merchants and lawyers – were then paid for their service to parliament, and so,

Des nouvelles dalbyon
Sil vous en plaist escoute
Mon frere & mon
Ay este dela la mer

Opposite: William Fitzstephen, in 1170, wrote of a London of heartbreaking beauty; he found a rare civilised eating house on the banks of the Thames, a river that 'abounds with fish'.

with that, came administrative personnel. The highest ranking was the chancellor, who spoke on behalf of the king, explained why meetings were being held and answered specific petitions made to the crown. And then there were civil servants. By 1400, parliament was legislating on trade, commerce, defence and more. The official parliament roll recorded more and more meetings and, as the assembly became embedded in the life of the country, so, too, did a professional class grow around it. Of course, that class needed feeding – and not in a fly-infested, seatless cook shop where the pies were reheated.

It was, as Professor Carlin wrote, 'the beginning of the breakthrough that led to the development of genuine public eating houses in the capital'. So, to eating houses that offered chairs, tables and linen tablecloths, came the accoutrements of parliament: lawyers and civil servants; workers from the neighbouring abbey; officials from the palace; visiting merchants and other travellers.

These eating houses thrived because, outside of the walls of the actual city, life was beyond the control of the London mayor and the powerful guilds who regulated, monopolised and protected the trades that operated there. They carefully monitored and regulated everything from shops to eating houses, but did not hinder the development of cook shops, which gradually began to seat people. For, from the same year that the man from Kent supposedly visited London, there is an account of a notorious dinner that occurred in Eastcheap.

The bones of the story can be deduced by analysing the *Chronicle of London*, a document collated in the fifteenth century that contains details of royal letters, records of public events and accounts of certain crimes and misdemeanours between 1089 and 1483. Part of the brief record details that 'in this yere [1410] was a fray made in Estchepe, be the kinges sones Thomas and John with men of the town'. The incumbent on the throne at the time was Henry IV, the first king of England since the Norman conquest whose mother tongue was English rather than French. In late June 1410, two of his six children, twenty-something boys called Thomas and John, decided to visit and dine at a cook shop in Eastcheap with a group of men. They arrived in the evening of Midsummer's Eve, which, by the late fourteenth century, had gained a certain notoriety.

Traditionally, it was an occasion that celebrated the life and martyrdom of St John the Baptist. The day would begin in churches with prayer, contemplation and the lighting of candles, but, as one contemporary, a clergyman called John Mirk, explained: 'At first, men and women came to church with candles and other lights and prayed all night long. In the process of time, however, men left such devotion and used songs and dances and fell into lechery and gluttony, turning the good, holy devotion into sin.'

It seems that the royal boys and their friends did just that. For the 'fray' is described in an additional note in the *Chronicle of London* as a 'hurlyng'. Middle English dictionaries translate this as an 'uproar', a 'tumult', or 'rioting'. Therefore, one can assume that the dinner in the cook shop turned into a party and then got out of control. So much so that the upshot officially recorded was that 'it was ordeyned that neither Tavern ne Cook shuld hold open their hous no more after ix of the clok, vpon payn of enprysonement'. The bad behaviour of a few lads caused the city authorities to insist that cook shops, inns and alehouses close at what we would call 9 p.m.

One wonders if the young princes were given a severe reprimand that added further pain to their hangovers the following day. It may also have been the last time royals and their posh friends attended so humble an abode as a cook shop. Certainly, they would have stood out among the regulars, in dress if not in demeanour.

The royal sons chose a cook shop for their antics, as taverns did not feed non-travellers until later in the fifteenth century. The earliest actual record of this comes in 1461, when churchwardens of a parish church in Southwark noted the expenses of three dinners at a local tavern. Around the same time, there are similar records of an 'audit dinner' in the churchwardens' accounts at St Margaret's in Westminster – which today stands on Parliament Square. And, while we can assume that was not exactly a riotous affair, the expense sheet shows that they drank wine and ate bread and mutton pies. In due course, such humble offerings became a little more sophisticated. Expense records from 1480, for a group of officials arbitrating a dispute between the City of London and St Augustine's in Canterbury, reveal – along with various breakfasts and suppers – a meal in Paternoster Row that included bread, chicken, rabbit and pork, as well as beer and ale.

As more establishments began to offer food, price controls were introduced to protect the poor and the likes of soldiers, who had very little money. In the mid-sixteenth century, for example, the City of York ordered that inn keepers offer soldiers and strangers 'ordinarily boyled & rost beif or motton' for no more than fourpence.

By that time, the word 'ordinary' had become an expression for a cheap set menu, though it later became a colloquial term for a simple type of place across

England that offered cheap ale and food. In 1609, a writer, Thomas Dekker, noted that, upon arrival in an 'ordinary' at around half past eleven in the morning, he was offered a little snuff before being invited to join a table of other young men, with whom he proceeded to share dishes of mutton stew, goose and woodcock, as well as fruit and cheese to finish. Wine was charged as extra – the price was 12 pence – and a poorer group of people sat in the corner eating a humbler meal for threepennce.

In fact, the term would also make its way to the American colonies, where most taverns became known as ordinaries. Back in England, in 1562, a visiting Venetian merchant, Alessandro Magno, wrote of having a fourpence 'ordynarie dynar or suppar' of pottage, a piece of roast meat, a piece of boiled meal, bread and the choice of ale or beer. He also said that the English were 'great meat-eaters', adding that both the quantity and quality of meat consumed were 'extraordinary'. When he visited in the summer of that year, he was obviously gladdened to have found an inn called The Ball, run by an Italian – Master Claudio. The Ball offered 'a choice of two or three kinds of roast meat at a meal, or, as an alternative, meat pies, savouries, fruit tarts, cheese and other things – and excellent wine. Whenever we wanted something else, we had only to say the word and it was provided.'

Menus around town were filled with chicken and other poultry, as well as game, rabbit, venison and swan. Magno was particularly taken with the oysters on offer in London, of which, he wrote, there were great quantities: 'They serve them roasted, stewed, fried with butter and in every possible way; but for preference they eat them raw with barley bread – and they are delicious.'

Sadly, at that time, there was no crisp white Vermentino around – let alone a cool glass of Champagne – to enjoy with his meal, so he had to make do with English beer, which irked him. It was, he said, 'healthy, but sickening to taste. It is cloudy like horse's urine and has husks on top.'

During the reign of Elizabeth I, in 1599, a Swiss visitor, Thomas Platter, wrote that London's taverns offered mainly à la carte menus. This seemed to be a novel concept to him, as he reckoned that ordering individually was rather more expensive then when a party pooled their money for shared dishes and drinks. As he noted: 'One checks up the items and reckons the amount, for they will not serve one for an inclusive charge, indeed, it works out very dear for one person alone desirous of making a good meal and drinking well.'

Such places were well established by the beginning of the sixteenth century, and it appears that the growth of alehouses and taverns was an unintended consequence of Henry VIII's crackdown on what he saw as the corrupt power of the Catholic Church.

The Dissolution of the Monasteries removed an age-old cornerstone of reassurance and comfort for European travellers.

Henry's break from Rome – caused in part by the Pope refusing to grant Henry a divorce from Catherine of Aragon to leave him free to marry Anne Boleyn – and his attempts to become head of the Church of England resulted in the famous Dissolution of the Monasteries. Between 1536 and 1541, various acts and legal processes saw the seizure or disbanding of monasteries, convents, priories and friaries of all shapes and sizes. By 1540, 800 monasteries had been dissolved, and, in doing so, a cornerstone of reassurance and expectation for travellers in England had been removed – one that had existed for centuries across Europe and the wider world. As we saw in Asia Minor (Chapters 2 and 3), the likes of Ibn Battuta were able to explore the known world and beyond by relying on the kindness of religious types who – particularly if you shared their persuasions – offered sanctuary, a bed and food.

Suddenly, this traditional channel of hospitality was gone – abandoned, demolished, burned. Similarly, Protestant reformers were attacking the seemingly constant feasting that occurred in other churches. Every saint's day and religious holiday saw communities piling into church halls or yards and being fed and watered. Indeed, a great quantity of beer was brewed specially for such occasions, and the sight of men downing pints and indulging in revelry amid the tombstones wasn't a great look.

The reformers were reasonably successful in restoring order to sacred events. But this meant that communities had nowhere to go when they felt like a knees-up or a drink – they couldn't look to the church to provide them with a venue and an excuse.

It was the perfect storm. Ex-monastic staff who weren't burnt at the stake needed places to work. Travellers needed places to stay. Communities needed places to relax and socialise. And so human enterprise saw the feeders from monasteries opening taverns, to which locals and passing travellers flocked. The state steadied the ship with price controls.

Unsurprisingly, the sixteenth century saw considerable growth in the alehouse sector. A 1577 survey in England recorded 24,000 alehouses, a ratio of one to every 142 inhabitants. The number doubled in the subsequent fifty years. And, while the country's population was growing (from 2.7 million in 1540 to 5.2 million in 1650), it was outstripped by the growth of drinking hostelries.

As the 1500s drew to a close, the alehouse was a permanent fixture of the English landscape. In other words, we can define the transition from the Middle Ages as the time at which drinking became institutionalised. Indeed, by the seventeenth century, England was represented – and could even be defined – by six key pillars: the private household; the church; the law courts; the royal family; parliament; and the pub.

And the significance of the pub should not be underestimated, because drinking houses (which developed into taverns offering food) gave people common ground. They weren't humbly taking bread and wine from a benevolent monk; they were receiving food and drink, however modest in composition, and paying for it themselves. For an oppressed servant, the ability to pay for a pint in a public space must have felt like freedom. With that right came the chance to socialise with others, as well as a mingling of the sexes. As conversations doubtless moved from the weather to politics, so, too, did a class consciousness grow – a realisation of the inequalities that existed and the feelings of polarisation that must have fermented.

But, if the poorer frequenters of rural alehouses were gnashing their teeth as they poured ale down their throats, the new-moneyed merchants and members of the fashionable classes in the towns and cities of England were avoiding such establishments, shunning the uncivilised and excessive drinking that had begun to concern leading figures of church and state. However, all humans soon discover that eating out is more fun – especially if there's a new and exciting reason to go out, something that is both exotic and non-alcoholic.

For out of the blue came a single mysterious product, an intriguing ingredient. It was a stimulant that you could drink, but it wouldn't get you drunk. It would cause a revolution in the story of eating out and it was one simple word: *coffee*.

5

The Coffee House Revolution

Non-essential for human existence, coffee appeared in Europe and was soon a popular stimulant for mind, body and soul. Coffee houses became social, fashionable and then central for political gatherings.

Early coffee adopters – and we're talking at least eleventh-century early, in Ethiopia – wouldn't have known that the caffeine they ingested, however they drank it (imagine thick, gritty and bitter), sped up the neurons in their body and caused the release of adrenaline. But they doubtless felt a bit perkier. Plus, in order to turn coffee from berry to bean to beverage, they developed a certain degree of ceremony – thus, it appealed to humans. Coffee was diverting and intriguing. One of the many attributes that separates us from animals is that we consume things for more than thirst or hunger. We derive pleasure from what we eat and drink. There is satisfaction in flavour, texture and the wider experience. Indeed, much of the story of eating out is predicated on the fact that it is fundamentally unnecessary. Whatever anyone tells you, we do not need to visit restaurants to survive – but they make survival considerably more enjoyable. The story of coffee is a great example of this distinction from animals: one unnecessary bean went on to build a vast industry, and the apparent 'need' for coffee became indisputable.

If the – also fundamentally unnecessary – unfurling of a tablecloth signposted our emergence from the Middle Ages in around 1410, then the explosion of coffee houses across London in the early 1700s denoted a move from bloody civil war to bloodless revolution.

Attendance at a coffee house became a legitimate status symbol that could once only be attained by attendance at court. The 1689 Bill of Rights – and the so-called Glorious Revolution that brought it about – signified the growing independence of noble society from the personal sphere of the monarch. And, if that coffee house culture was a key driver in the development of civil liberties, then perhaps the coffee bean itself is rather more crucial than its label of 'unnecessary bean' suggests.

Although the first coffee house opened in Oxford in 1652, the coffee bean (as we discovered in Chapter 2) had reached Syria 100 years before and was thriving in Aleppo, according to German botanist Leonhard Rauwolf. By that time, it was also well established in the court of Suleiman the Magnificent, in what is now Turkey. The sultan had apparently been introduced to the drink by a man whom he had dispatched to rule Yemen. But there is also an earlier mention of coffee by the intrepid William Biddulph, in his leaden-titled *The travels of certayne Englishmen in Africa, Asia, etc ... begunne in 1600 and by some of them finished – this yeere 1608*. Biddulph witnessed the sipping of the drink in a Turkish coffee house:

> *Their most common drinke is coffa, which is a blacke kinde of drinke, made of a kind of pulse like pease, called coaua; which being grownd in the mill, and boiled in water, they drinke it as hot as they can suffer it; which they finde to agree very well with them against their crudities, and feeding on hearbs and rawe meates.*

The beverage was less appealing to the poet Sir George Sandys, who came across it in Turkey in 1610. He noted the lack of drinking in the country, as opposed to its prevalence in good old England. 'Although they be destitute of taverns, yet have they their coffa-houses, which something resemble them,' he writes in his sweetly named *Sandys Travels*. 'There sit they chatting most of the day; and sippe of a drinke called coffa (of the berry that it is made of) in little China dishes as hot as they can suffer it: blacke as soote, and tasting not much unlike it.' He also noted that people drank coffee to 'helpeth ... digestion, and procureth alacrity'. But its tummy-soothing, head-clearing benefits were not, it seems, quite enough to pull in customers, so the owners of the coffee houses that Sandys visited came up with another ruse that they knew would bring in local men: 'Many of the coffa-men [were] keeping beautifull boyes, who serve as stales to procure them customers.'

Clearly coffee was established before the sultan's man in Yemen claimed it as his discovery. But the sultan – and the culture and personnel that grew around the drink – made coffee's preparation and consumption fashionable. Before long, it was being made in private houses and in an increasing number of public coffee houses, too.

Gradually, coffee spread to Europe, with written records of it being spotted in Vienna, Venice, Marseilles and Paris in the ensuing decades.

It then made its first recorded appearance in England, the beans travelling in the luggage of a Greek priest called Nathaniel Conopios. Born in Crete, he ended up in Constantinople working as the right-hand man for the senior Greek prelate Cyril Lucaris. But Conopios's boss fell out with the sultan Murad IV, who had him murdered – strangled, in fact – in 1638. Fearing for his own life, Conopios gathered his possessions and his precious coffee beans and escaped across Europe. Thanks to his contacts in the Church of England (William Laud, the Archbishop of Canterbury, no less), he was given sanctuary at Balliol College, Oxford. It was there that the diarist John Evelyn came across him: 'He was the first I ever saw drink coffee.'

Someone else who spotted Conopios was Anthony Wood, the Oxford University aficionado of antiquity, based at Merton College. 'While he continued in Balliol College, he made the drink for his own use called coffey,' Wood later recalled of the Greek, 'and usually drank it every morning, being the first, as the antients of that house have informed me, that was ever drank in Oxon.' The man who gave Conopios save haven, Archbishop Laud, was himself beheaded by Charles I on 10 January 1645. It was a morning, perhaps, when Conopios decided to make his cup a little stronger than usual.

Another found engaging in coffee drinking in Oxford was the English physician Dr William Harvey, who was made warden of Merton College. 'He was wont to drinke coffee,' wrote the biographer John Aubrey, 'which his brother Eliab did, before coffee houses were the fashion in London.' With these pockets of coffee drinking emerging in seventeenth-century Oxford academia, perhaps it is not surprising that the first coffee house in England opened in that same city in 1650.

Wood wrote: 'This year [1650] Jacob the Jew opened a coffey house at the Angel in the Parish of St Peter in the East, Oxon. And there it was by some, who delighted in noveltie drank.' The Angel was an old and well-established coaching inn, so Jacob may have been given a concession there – unless he converted the entire place into a coffee house. The Angel is just half a mile from where the Greek was seen sipping coffee at Balliol.

London wasn't far behind Oxford, its first coffee house appearing in Cornhill in 1652, in an alley opposite St Michael's Church. According to biographer William Oldys, writing in the early eighteenth century, this coffee house came about when a trader called Daniel Edwards was so taken by coffee during his visits to Smyrna (now Turkish Izmir) that he brought back a man named Pasqua Rosée to make the drink for him at his home, in addition to other domestic duties. So good was Rosée's coffee that Edwards' friends started treating his home like a coffee shop. And so, Olys recounted, 'the novelty thereof drawing too much company to him, he allowed the said servant with another of his son-in-law to set up the first coffee house in London at St Michael's Alley, in Cornhill'.

It seems that this coffee house began in a shed at the edge of the churchyard of St Michael's, before moving into a building in the adjacent alley. In the early 1650s, such a street would have been decidedly narrow, dark and dingy. There were several neighbouring taverns whose owners would have felt worried about this new and annoyingly fashionable opposition on their patch. Indeed, possibly concerned about threats from them, Rosée found a business partner in 1654 – a man called Christopher Bowman. Bowman was a grocer and a freeman of the City of London, so his participation would have prevented opposing landlords from disputing the coffee house's right to trade.

Amazingly, an advertisement for this coffee house has survived intact and is today kept at the British Museum, in London's Bloomsbury district. In it, Rosée explains the origins of coffee and how it is made, as well as spelling out its virtues: 'It's very good to help digestion; and therefore of great use to be bout 3 or 4 a clock afternoon, as well as in the morning.' It 'quickens the spirits' and 'makes one fit for business'. Although, he cautions, 'you are not to drink it after supper ... for it will hinder sleep for 3 or 4 hours'. He then, not having an advertising standards authority to worry about for another 310 years, gets a little carried away with health claims. For example, if you hold your head over a steaming cup, it is 'good against sore eys', it can stave off 'consumption' and a bad cough, it can 'prevent and cure the dropsy, gout and scurvy', it is a 'remedy against ...

The Vertue of the *COFFEE* Drink.

First publiquely made and sold in England, by *Pasqua Rosee*.

THE Grain or Berry called *Coffee*, groweth upon little Trees, only in the *Deserts of Arabia*.

It is brought from thence, and drunk generally throughout all the Grand Seigniors Dominions.

It is a simple innocent thing, composed into a Drink, by being dryed in an Oven, and ground to Powder, and boiled up with Spring water, and about half a pint of it to be drunk, fasting an hour before, and not Eating an hour after, and to be taken as hot as possibly can be endured; the which will never fetch the skin off the mouth, or raise any Blisters, by re son of that Heat.

The Turks drink at meals and other times, is usually *Water*, and their Dyet consists much of *Fruit*, the *Crudities* whereof are very much corrected by this Drink.

The quality of this Drink is cold and Dry; and though it be a Dryer, yet it neither *heats*, nor *inflames* more then *hot Posset*.

It forcloseth the Orifice of the Stomack, and fortifies the heat within

it's very good to help digestion, and therefore of great use to be bout 3 or 4 a Clock afternoon, as well as in the morning.

uen quickens the *Spirits*, and makes the Heart *Lightsome*.

Is good against sore Eys, and the better if you hold your Head over it, and take in the Steem that way.

It suppresseth Fumes exceedingly, and therefore good against the *Head-ach*, and will very much stop any *Defluxion of Rheums*, that distil from the *Head* upon the *Stomack*, and so prevent and help *Consumptions*; and the *Cough of the Lungs*.

It is excellent to prevent and cure the *Dropsy*, *Gout*, and *Scurvy*.

It is known by experience to be better then any other Drying Drink for *People in years*, or *Children* that have any *running humors* upon them, as *the Kings Evil*. &c.

It is very good to prevent *Mis-carryings in Child-bearing Women*.

It is a most excellent Remedy against the *Spleen*, *Hypocondriack Winds*, or the like.

It will prevent *Drowsiness*, and make one fit for busines, if one have occasion to *Watch*; and therefore you are not to Drink of it *after Supper*, unless you intend to be *watchful*, for it will hinder sleep for 3 or 4 hours.

It is observed that in Turkey, where this is generally drunk, that they are not trobled with the Stone, Gout, Dropsie, or Scurvey, and that their Skins are exceeding cleer and white.

It is neither Laxative nor *Restringent*.

Made and Sold in St. *Michaels Alley* in *Cornhill*, by *Pasqua Rosee*, at the Signe of his own Head.

Pasqua Rosée's advertisement for his coffee house spelled out the virtues of a new drink that 'makes one fit for business'.

winds', it can steady the old and it can countenance scrofula in children. In addition, those who drink it in Turkey benefit from 'skins [that] are exceedingly clear and white', and it is also 'very good to prevent mis-carryings in child-bearing women'.

No wonder rival businesses dispensing little else but stupefying ale were worried! Indeed, such angst among established inn keepers was seen when one of their ilk, a Fleet Street vendor who sold ale and cut hair, decided to convert his premises

Coffee drinking first emerged in Britain in the colleges of seventeenth-century Oxford University, brought to the city by a Greek priest on the run from Constantinople.

from tavern to coffee house in 1656. James Farr turned off his ale taps, put away his scissors, and started roasting beans at the Rainbow Coffee House – much to the consternation of his neighbouring ale-pourers. On 21 December 1657, they teamed up and collectively filed what was called a wardmote inquest presentment, under a section of law brilliantly titled 'Disorders and Annoys'. It reads, furiously:

> *Item, we pr'sent James Ffarr barber, or makinge and selling of a drink called coffee, whereby in makeing the same, he annoyeth his neighbours by evil smells and for keeping of ffire for most partr of the night and day, whereby his chimney and chambr hath been sett on ffire, to the great danger and affrightment of his neighbours.*

But Farr's opponents failed to shut down the Rainbow Coffee House, and, ironically, in spite of his tendency to accidentally set fire to his building when roasting coffee beans, he and his coffee house managed to escape the Great Fire of London.

As for Pasqua Rosée's Cornhill business, the diarist Samuel Pepys mentioned the place in 1660, so business was still going strong eight years later. Pepys called in one evening in December with a friend, his first visit, remarking: 'I find much pleasure in it through the diversity of company – and discourse.' Pasqua Rosée's place would, however, become an incidental victim of the most infamous of events detailed by the diarist. For, in the Great Fire of London of 1666, St Michael's Alley, like so many of the surrounding streets with their tightly packed timber-framed houses, was engulfed in flames. All that was left in that area of Cornhill was the tower of St Michael's Church.

Back in Oxford, meanwhile, a second coffee house was opened in 1664 by one Cirques Jobson, who, according to Wood, was 'a Jew and Jocobite', his business situated 'in an house between St Edmund Hall and Queen[s] Coll Corner'. This address was opposite Jacob's place and, remarkably, it has been a coffee house ever since; it is now called Queen's Lane Coffee House. Jacob's establishment is also a coffee house today, The Grand Café, having had many guises since the seventeenth century, from hotel to grocer to teddy bear shop. (Jacob himself appeared again in 1671, running a coffee house in Holborn, London. Perhaps he was following the money.)

A year later, in 1655, Wood recorded the opening of a third coffee house, this one run by an apothecary called Arthur Tillyard, who appears to have set up shop in his home, or, as Wood put it, 'sold coffey publickly in his house against All-Souls Coll'.

Wood goes on to explain that Tillyard was encouraged into this enterprise by some young Oxford-based Royalists, presumably students. England at that time was under the control of Oliver Cromwell, with King Charles I having been executed in 1649 following the English Civil War. With England having effectively been a republic since then, Cromwell entered parliament in 1653, dismissed the speaker and members, and declared himself ruler.

Perhaps these Oxford men, with their pro-monarchist views, felt it was too dangerous to meet up and sip coffee at Johnson's or Jacob's, so, knowing that Tillyard had the skills to prepare medicines, reckoned he could provide them with a cup of coffee, and a less public space to discuss politics, in his private home. Among the regulars, who 'esteem'd themselves either virtuous or wits', was the architect Sir Christopher Wren.

Wood notes: 'This coffey house continued 'til His Majestie's returne [the Restoration of the Monarchy] and after, and then they became more frequent and had an excise upon coffee.' Indeed, that frequency not only caught the eye of the tax man (to operate a coffee house, one needed a licence, meaning the authorities definitely knew all about you), but also signified an explosion – a zeitgeist phenomenon that saw coffee houses popping up in cities and towns across the country, nowhere more so than in the capital, London. Coffee houses were places where men – and men only – would congregate and flex the muscles of (male) freedom that the Bill of Rights had conferred. For not only did that act settle the succession of the crown with William and Mary, it also asserted the rights of the individual, spoke of the importance of 'freedom of this realm', and outlawed 'illegal and cruel punishments'.

Coffee houses became an expression of the spirit of liberty that educated men – freed from millennia of grovelling to monarchs – could indulge in. They were, in the words of 21st-century German philosopher Jürgen Habermas (in his text *The Structural Transformation of the Public Sphere*), the places where the 'bourgeois avant-garde of the educated middle class learned the art of critical-rational public debate'. They became clubs for lively discussion, and those who frequented them could reassure their wives (or the local vicar perhaps) that there was nothing to fear in their frequent attendance as they were establishments of refined respectability and sobriety.

Moreover, as coffee houses grew in number, many developed their own character and reputation, largely due to their clientele. As Brian Cowan, author of *The Social Life of Coffee*, put it: 'With so many coffee houses to choose from, Londoners could pick the place whose social or political tenor they found most agreeable.' Some had regional affiliations, some international. A German visitor to London in 1710, Zacharias Conrad von Uffenbach, reported that, having scoured the capital, he found a coffee house to his exact taste. It was filled with his fellow Germans and was run by a Frenchman. Other coffee houses appealed to particular professions – from merchant to physician. And, of course, they were divided by political affiliation, too. In the 1690s, Richard's coffee house was favoured by Whigs, whereas Tories preferred Ozinda's.

Soon, they became places where one could catch up on the news, be it from journalists who gathered there to gossip or from journals and newspapers, which were growing with equal rapidity at the time, with some owners even printing their own. There were pamphlets on the tables, and more salacious writings were distributed in manuscript form. A coffee house keeper in London's Bread Street would meet daily with a clerk from the House of Commons and transcribe (illegally) proceedings from the previous day's parliament. In Oxford, such was the perceived value of knowledge one could get at a coffee house, many establishments started charging people a penny to enter (hence the term 'penny universities'). In London, tokens could be procured to redeem at coffee houses, which took pressure off the serious lack of coins in circulation at the time. Regular customers also began to use their favourite establishments to write and receive letters. The Penny Post system was launched in London in 1680 – a successful operation, which the government took over in 1682 – and it was doubtless easier for a postman to find a coffee house than it was to deliver to a small apartment hidden at the top of an alley.

Indeed, the visibility of coffee houses, whose shop signs were actually regulated, helped them become neighbourhood landmarks. With few, if any, maps in circulation, a coffee house enabled locals – or visitors – to orientate themselves.

Of course, with coffee shops becoming landmarks, post offices, centres of learning, essential meeting grounds for news and gossip, and currency providers, it's hardly surprising that they were watched by the eager eye of that tax man. But therein arose something of

Ultra-Royalist Roger L'Estrange declared that 'coffee houses brew sedition'.

an inter-state tussle. On the one hand, the crown benefited from excise duties levied on coffee: in 1660, a duty of fourpence of every gallon of coffee made and sold was demanded on the maker, and the tax was a key part of the fiscal settlement of the Restoration. On the other hand, the House of Commons deemed that coffee be categorised along with other 'outlandish drinks', and Charles II, ruling from 1660 to 1685, was also suspicious of the places that served it. Given the recently restored monarchy, he was understandably anxious about dissent and how it could be spread – primarily through publications and gatherings. A good few years before the Bill of Rights, coffee houses were already places of lively opinion, and, in 1666, the coffee houses still standing amid the ashes of the Great Fire were proving irksome to the king.

So Charles ventured the idea of banning them with his high chancellor, the Earl of Clarendon, who eagerly agreed with him. Coffee houses, thundered Clarendon, 'allowed the foulest imputations [to be] laid upon the government'. He suggested that spies be sent to coffee houses to monitor conversations, and the ultra-Royalist Roger L'Estrange was appointed licenser of the press. As the official censor, he eagerly scoured the land with a team, hunting illegal presses. The slightest whiff of dissent saw him entering booksellers and printers, and he declared that 'coffee houses brew sedition'.

In the ensuing years, the king made various attempts to curb both news journals and the coffee houses in which they were so often read. Finally, in 1672, he issued a proclamation (one that would make a modern-day US president proud) 'to restrain the spreading of false news [that was helping] to nourish an universal jealousie and dissatisfaction in the minds of all His Majesties good subjects'. Then, in 1675, he attempted to eliminate coffee houses altogether. On 29 December, Charles II issued a 'Proclamation for the Suppression of Coffee-Houses', in which it was written:

> *It is most apparent that the multitude of coffee-houses of late years set up and kept within this kingdom ... have produced very evil and dangerous effects. In such houses, and by occasion of the meetings of such persons therein, diverse false, malitious and scandalous reports are devised and spread abroad, to the defamation of His Majesties government, and to the disturbance of the peace and quiet of the realm; His Majesty hath thought it fit and necessary that the said coffee-houses be (for the future) put down and suppressed.*

All licences issued for the making of coffee were declared void, the making of coffee was banned even in the home, and, while the king was at it, he also outlawed the brewing of tea, chocolate and sherbet. Those who disobeyed the new law did so 'at their utmost peril' and would face 'the severest punishments'.

'God save the king', the proclamation ended. It was printed in the official paper, the *London Gazette*, as well as in manuscript newsletters that were doubtless delivered to, and read with astonishment in, coffee houses. Posters were put up, and Royalist vicars lectured their Sunday congregations about the evils of coffee houses, quoting from the new edict.

The king may have rested well that late December night in the belief that he had warded off a potential long avenue of sedition – but the law was very unpopular. In the words of Sir Ralph Verney, coffee house regular and occasional MP:

> *Noe Englishman will long endure to bee forbid meeting together, soe long as they doe nothing contrary to law. I beleeve the meetings will bee as greate, and as constant as ever, and ... they will rather drink sage, betony, and rosemary drinkes rather than tea, or coffee, because those native commodities pay neither excize, nor customes, soe the crowne will bee the only looser by this new needlesse prohibition.*

While individuals could switch to other drinks and meet elsewhere, it was the coffee house owners who had the most to lose. A great many came together to petition the king, and a group of representatives was met in Whitehall on 6 January, just seven days after the proclamation was issued. The men explained the significant investments made – in buildings, stock and staff – and how many livelihoods of those associated with the business would be ruined.

The king met again with his Privy Council, and a six-month reprieve was announced. Just eleven days after the proclamation, it was effectively repealed. Charles never gave up, however. From time to time, he issued various proclamations – but coffee houses remained open. The next monarch, James II, also had a go at them, demanding, for example, that coffee house licences be refused to those who would not guarantee to forbid the circulation of unlicensed publications on their premises. But, after his reign crumbled, successors William and Mary did not attack coffee houses (though they did issue injunctions against what they saw as seditious false news). By then, with the Bill of Rights following the bloodless Glorious Revolution, coffee houses – in particular, the new and grander ones built in the years after the Great Fire – were firmly entrenched in English towns and cities.

But, back in the 1660s, grumbling about coffee houses also emerged from various elements of the economy that had been negatively affected by its success. As one contemporary economist put it: 'The growth of coffee houses has greatly hindered the sale of oats, malt, wheat, and other home[-grown] products. Our farmers are being ruined because they cannot sell their grain and with them the landowners because they can no longer collect their rents.'

While the men who used coffee houses as their second homes shut the door on whinging farmers and pesky monarchs (as well as on the dirt and noise of the streets), they faced another threat – one that, for many, was a rather more delicate problem: women.

Perhaps men thought that, by going to coffee houses, they could persuade their wives that they were occupying their time in a place of utmost propriety, engaging in vital discussions about the future of their country, the coffee doing nothing untoward but clearing their minds for lucid and essential discussion. However, women were having none of it. In 1674, possibly after one lonely night too many, a group of London wives did a little pamphleteering of their own. These pamphlets' arrival on the tables of the likes of the Sultaness Head coffee house near London's Royal Exchange, where Samuel Pepys could sometimes be found, would probably have been met by the clientele with as much astonishment as the king's bid to outlaw their 'clubs'.

The front cover of their pamphlet introduced in bold capitals: 'The Women's Petition Against Coffee'.

It was, it went on, 'representing to public consideration the grand inconveniences accruing to their sex from the excessive use of the drying and enfeebling liquor'. Across several pages of flowery prose, these coffee house widows said that the drink had made their men mere 'cock-sparrows' and, worse, that the drink had 'Frenchified' them. Coffee apparently rendered men impotent – a woman approaching her husband could only 'hug a meagre useless corpse' – and nonsensical: 'Like so many frogs in a puddle, they sup muddy water, and murmur insignificant notes 'til half a dozen of them out-babble an equal number of us at a gossipping.' Men were also accused of spending all their money in the coffee house, leaving them so poor that they could only feed their children bread. And, as for their claims of discussing vital matters of state, the pamphlet reckoned that 'they frequently have hot contests about most important subjects; as what colour the Red Sea is'. Moreover, coffee houses may have been a place of sobriety, but they actually made men drink more, too. It was, the women wrote, a 'retrograde

Insurance company Lloyd's of London began in Lloyd's Coffee House, where a pulpit was installed so that customers could hear announcements about auction prices and shipping news.

motion', as, once drunk, the men would 'stagger back to soberize themselves with coffee', before returning to the inn. Even those who managed to stay sober all day, full of virtue, would nip to the inn on the way home, while 'we poor souls sit mopeing all alone 'til twelve at night ... when at last they come to bed, smoakt like a Westphalia hogs-head'.

The men read and digested the leaflet and then printed a riposte ('The Men's Answer to the Women's Petition Against Coffee'), which wasn't half as well written or amusing. The women's pamphlet was described as 'scandalising': coffee had 'incomparable effects in preventing and curing most diseases incident to humane bodies'.

Such is the language of the original female attack that some historians have questioned whether the pamphlet was actually the work of men. Was it solicited by the crown to stir up discontent about the institution? Or was it more of a satire to be enjoyed by the men who used such establishments, to have a good chuckle at their own expense? Indeed, at the time Pepys was visiting coffee houses, there were several written satires circulating based on the supposed antics in such places, as well as comic illustrations: the debates that slipped into fights; the sipping of coffee interspersed with something a little stronger. However, questioning the authenticity of the document is not a suggestion that a woman could not have written such a piece of wit, but more that no woman could have been bothered.

Despite this, coffee houses continued to grow. By 1700, London had a coffee house for every 1,000 members of the population (as one writer has pointed out, that is forty times the proportion of coffee houses in New York today!). And Lloyd's of London, the insurance company, famously has its origins in Lloyd's Coffee House in the city. When it moved premises in 1691, a pulpit was installed so that auction prices and shipping news could be announced.

While coffee houses had effectively evolved from the original cook shops, those were still going strong, too. They were popular with those whose class precluded them from entering a coffee house, but they were also frequented by a smarter set looking for more casual drinking and dining. French writer Francis Maximilian Misson described one such place in his 1698 book, *Mémoires et observations faites par un voyageur en Angleterre*:

> *Generally four spits, one over another, carry round each five or six pieces of butcher-meat, beef, mutton, veal, pork, and lamb; and you have what quantity you please cut off, fat, lean, much or little done; with this a little salt and mustard upon the side of a plate, a bottle of beer and a roll and there is your whole feast.*

As every fashion has its peak, the dwindling number of coffee houses in the late eighteenth century had a lot to do with tea. However, the gentlemen who had turned coffee houses into clubs then decided to go one step further. They pooled funds to create serious establishments, grand buildings where they could meet with like-minded individuals, edifices whose rooms mimicked the grand houses of London and the stately homes of English counties. And there they could, of course, drink coffee, but also enjoy wine, good food and the firm exclusion of women – their pamphlets could no longer interfere with the serious pursuit of pleasure. Many such clubs still exist today, on Mayfair's St James's Street. Some still exclude women and, occasionally, some women attempt to invade – if they can be bothered.

6

The French Revolution

With his loathing of the aristocracy and its lavish accoutrements, Robespierre dispatched the heads of France's wealthy elite with the efficient use of Madame Guillotine. But, if he cast an eye into the future, he would not have expected smart restaurants to be a lasting, if unintended, legacy of his.

It was in the English coffee house of the eighteenth century that the nascent middle classes gathered. It was a place that provided a salon for men without drawing rooms – those who were educated, newly moneyed and often well travelled, especially if they were merchants, wide-eyed from their journeys to the likes of the Levant. Without ownership of land, they may not have been entitled to vote (they would need to wait until the Great Reform Act of 1832 for that), but they were certainly political. They conversed, debated, shared pamphlets and joisted with their monarchs and womenfolk (Chapter 5).

But the coffee house wasn't the exclusive domain of civil servants, successful traders and new money. Titled Englishmen would pop in, as would aspiring members of the working classes – at least those who managed to brush up with a borrowed frock coat and wig.

In general, conduct in coffee houses was cordial, Hogarth's depiction of a fight breaking out at the seedy Tom King's Coffee House in Covent Garden being rather an exception to the rule. The joisting was more intellectual and satirical; raised voices rather than fists. Even the most ferocious of pamphlets were written with wit.

Across the English Channel, in towns and cities in France, their middle-class counterparts were a little different. They were the bourgeoisie. Dictionaries may translate this word as 'middle class', but it is a more politically charged term. Its etymology is of the burghers, the mercantile class of medieval days, eagerly on the make for several hundred years until they get a little more lively at the

Robespierre unwittingly ushered in an era of fine dining.

end of the eighteenth century. So, while their distant English cousins scorned a fellow into submission with some pugilistic wit, before heading home from the coffee house with a minor diversion to an inn for a skinful, the French were getting cross. Very cross.

Occupying the ground between aristocrat and peasant, they wanted more than coffee, tea, chocolate, sherbet and a chat. And what would grow from this was nothing less than violent, ugly, bloody revolution; a decimation of the old order, the destruction of the aristocracy. What the protagonists of the French Revolution never realised – and, of course, never intended to happen – was that, while the bourgeoisie would bring down the nobility, they would also usher in an age of fine dining. This is an unintended consequence for which we, with more than 200 years to get over the harsh realities of the efficient Madame Guillotine, are extremely grateful.

One such Frenchman who wouldn't waste his time talking political shop in a coffee house was Maximilien Robespierre. A definitive and fully paid-up member of the bourgeoisie, a lawyer, politician, revolutionary and number-one fan of that guillotine, Robespierre made a speech on 5 February 1794 to the National Convention. This assembly of the French Revolution met in the grand – and almost unfeasibly enormous – setting of the Salle des Machines. It was a vast theatre, capable of seating up to 8,000 people – testament to the openness of the new regime – and Robespierre rose to his feet, resplendent as ever in his silken frock coat, breeches and silver-buckled shoes. His grey wig was a further accoutrement, both in fashion and in keeping with the times, but also conferring on him the respect of regime seniority. He spoke his words long and loud; he wanted those in the gallery who often came to listen (as well as to heckle and jeer) to hear every one of them.

Robespierre had been one of the main protagonists in a revolution that had gone from aggravated thought among the intelligentsia to aggravated assault from the mob, as some 1,000 people stormed the medieval prison and armoury that was the Bastille on 14 July 1789. And, some seven years on, Robespierre was addressing the now well-established alternative government, the National Convention, speaking in the wake of what would become known as the Reign of Terror. With much encouragement from him, that efficient tool of death, the guillotine, had been busy cutting off the heads of some 17,000 people.

Robespierre's speech would, in part, be his justification for the judicial slaughter. 'Up to the very moment when I am speaking, it must be agreed that we have been guided, amid such stormy circumstances, by the love of good and by the awareness of our country's needs, rather than by an exact theory and precise rules of conduct, which we did not have even leisure to lay out,' he decried. This was his way of saying that, to be honest, up until that point, they'd been making it up as they went along.

The goal towards which they were heading, he continued, was 'the peaceful enjoyment of liberty and equality'. Robespierre spoke of a land where there would be a substitution of 'morality for egotism ... the rule of reason for the tyranny of fashion ... love of glory for the love of money ... genius for wit, truth for glamour ... which is to say all the virtues and miracles of the republic in place of all of the vices of monarchy'.

Robespierre saved special ire for what he saw as the greedy, selfish and frivolous aristocracy. He decried the 'monstrous opulence of a few families'; it was not right that a 'tiny fraction of the people ... decide the fate of the whole of society'. They and their supporters needed getting rid of. Their heads, as well as their accoutrements, their houses, their furniture, their good living, their drink and their food – all of it needed to be sliced into dust by the guillotine and its sister, the political machine.

The aristocracy's seemingly ostentatious living – with their private chefs, their fancy dishes and their expensive wines, eased gently into their bodies by priceless crockery and glassware – particularly grated on Robespierre. While he drank coffee and had a passion for fruit, he, according to one historian, 'seems not to have cared what he ate'. At dinner, he 'confined himself to a single glass of wine, heavily cut with water'. An egalitarian and fair society would not feature unnecessary luxuries. 'All tyrants in league against the republic will be vanquished,' he declared.

At the end of the eighteenth century, the aristocracy of France was pre-eminent. It had been thus since medieval times, when the only form of wealth was land: those who owned it exercised total power and rights over those who worked on it and depended upon it for survival.

But emerging from the Middle Ages were new technology, new trade routes and new opportunities. The cart became a carriage, boats became ships, trading opportunities brought other means of exchange. Those who dared to leave their village, town or city and venture overseas became merchants. Others became ship owners or manufacturers. They had new aspirations and new money. Looking around at society, in France, for example, they saw an embedded social structure that was at odds with their awakened purpose.

There was no existing position between the feudal classes of aristocracy and peasant. This new group didn't fit in; moreover, the class system was in their way, blocking their capitalist enterprise. And, worse still, the things they were making and importing were being used by the aristocracy – clothes, food, machinery – yet the aristocrats had nothing to do with the creation of such items.

But the aristocrats were immovable. They had to retain their rights to land and workers. The master/servant order could never be broken. The new class of bourgeoisie merchants and traders could see that the aristocrats were actually holding back the advent of progress, retarding the advent of a new era of industry. In the words of French historian Albert Soboul: 'The essential cause of the revolution was the power of a bourgeoisie arrived at its maturity and confronted by a decadent aristocracy holding tenaciously to its privileges.'

But the bourgeoisie could not bring down the aristocracy on its own. It had to galvanise the rural peasants and the urban labourers. And an inefficient network of transportation, coupled with a series of poor wheat harvests in the early 1770s, added hunger to the argument. Peasants lived on bread; without it, they would starve. It was the fuel that Robespierre needed to set France on fire.

In 1792, King Louis XVI was seized and beheaded. His wife, Marie Antoinette, suffered the same fate nine months later. The aristocracy was brought down; its economic base was destroyed. But, as the tentacles of terror slipped in through the doors of palaces and châteaux to grab those preening miscreants, it wasn't just the toffs who were dragged to the guillotine: 40,000 people met their fate there.

Take Gabriel-Charles Doyen, for example, private chef to Marie Antoinette. After the queen's trip to the guillotine, Doyen found himself without a job, so he went to Robespierre six months later and protested. He demanded employment and even back-pay. But Doyen did not get the response he was looking for. He was accused of 'favouring the degradation of constituted authority, the destruction of the republic and the return of despotism'. His skills as a chef were not required by the revolution, so he was executed, too.

Similarly, cook Eugène-Eléonore Gervais gathered together domestic employees no longer in work following the fate of their aristo bosses. They lobbied the government and demanded fresh employment. They were immediately arrested and sentenced to nine years in the galleys.

Across France, chefs, along with butlers, maids and their ilk, the domestic staff of the former aristocracy, lost their jobs. It was a just consequence as far as Robespierre was concerned. Except, however, that one cannot ever immaculately control the market. Chefs and butlers had skills, and, whatever Robespierre's personal preferences, French people liked to eat – and eat well at that.

On the day of the storming of the Bastille (the occasion many see as the start of the French Revolution), it is estimated that there were some 2 million servants in France. With a total population of 28 million, that meant one in every twelve men or women was in domestic service.

So these disenfranchised workers looked for employment in the public sphere. With the kitchens of rural châteaux redundant, many of the unemployed travelled to Paris to find jobs. And, in doing so, a revolution of a culinary nature took place. It was the unintended consequence of the political and social upheaval. Soon after these formerly private chefs arrived in the capital city, a number of restaurants opened.

There was, for example, the man who was in charge of the kitchens of Louis Joseph de Bourbon, Prince of Condé, one of France's senior aristocrats. The man's name was Robert (his surname is lost in the echo of history) and, as the family's executive chef, he had sight over culinary operations at both the family's Paris home and their château in Chantilly.

The vast home in Paris, Hotel de Condé, was a building that occupied almost the entire sixth arrondissement of Paris. There a large number of servants worked between the various wings of the house, the courtyards and intricately manicured gardens with neat hedgerows, rose gardens and small areas of herbs providing a quiet haven in the middle of the bustling metropolis.

Robert, as senior staff, was dressed in livery – the colours and buttons reflecting the family's coat of arms – and he was well accustomed to acute grandeur. Outside of the kitchens and pantries, he operated in ornate rooms with

Staff from abandoned palaces (such as Château de Chantilly, north of Paris) found work in smart restaurants and hotels in the French capital.

tall painted ceilings, walls hung with tapestries and old-master paintings, and a library filled with rare books and even rarer hand-drawn maps.

He would also be sent ahead to the family's country pile to ensure all was in order for an impending visit. The Château de Chantilly – some 30 miles north of Paris – was another giant house, a large, three-floored rectangular building, adjacent to a two-storey annexe, both with blue-grey leaded roofs. The house was abandoned during the revolution and much of it destroyed.

Twenty years later, the prince came back from exile and visited the house. All that was left was an empty, dilapidated, dusty void, an echo chamber of sadness. Remarkably, a few old retainers were still at the house and saw him return. 'He re-entered the château and wept,' wrote a mid-nineteenth-century author. The prince came across his old groom and the son of his former woodman. The latter told the prince, with a little embarrassment, that the woods where he used to poach hares as a child with his father now belonged to him, but that the prince would be most welcome to hunt hares there himself – 'as many hares as were poached by my father'. Louis Joseph de Bourbon was 'agitated' at the news of this transfer of land ownership, and replied: 'Thanks for your offer, my friend, but I never hunt on any person's ground but my own.' The loss of property, status and a twenty-year exile had failed to stamp out his aristocratic sensibilities.

The household that Robert oversaw was complex and, from food and laundry to salaries and maintenance, it was run like a business, with positions including: the *homme de confiance*, a secretary and accountant; the *gens de livrée*, in charge of guests, their transportation and admission to the house; the *portier*, for non-family visitors and deliveries; the *femme de charge*, a housekeeper; the *maître d'hôtel*, in charge of food preparation and service; and the *officier*, who took care of the wine cellar, linen and silver.

On 19 July 1789, the Prince of Condé, having assessed his chances with the new regime, made a hasty escape to England. Before the year was out, Robert, with his knowledge of suppliers and the business of food, had opened a restaurant on the Rue de Richelieu. His chefs, rôtisseurs, sauciers and pâtissiers were in the kitchen, and front of house were as many butlers and footmen as he could assemble, working as impeccable waiting staff. Perhaps they chose not to wear their livery for fear of affronting their customers, the dastardly revolutionaries.

In the chaos of revolution, his restaurant seemed an ordered vessel, and so, fresh-faced from school, others came, who would work at the restaurant for a few years before moving on to open their own establishments. It's hardly surprising that the new grand restaurants of the nineteenth century were very well organised – their patrons had been looking after guests to a high standard for generations.

As well as the revolutionaries, these restaurants had another type of customer – individuals they were well used to, whom they had once served in great luxury. At the height of the terror, there was only so much work the guillotine could do each day, so lingering in the city's jails, very well aware of their impending fate, were hundreds of dispossessed aristocrats, their clothes – silk waistcoats and long white shirts – fraying and filthy. They needed feeding, so they ordered take-outs.

According to contemporary French dramatist Louis-Sébastien Mercier: 'The victims in the prisons worshipped their stomachs, and the most exquisite victuals were seen passing through the narrow wicket-gate destined for men who were about to eat their last meal on earth.' The guards made no attempt to hinder the passage of food, possibly in exchange for a gold cufflink here and there. Mercier continued: 'From the depths of a dungeon, arrangements were made with a restaurant and the contract signed by both parties with specific clauses as to the seasonal vegetables and fresh fruits.' Apparently no visitor to an aristocratic prisoner came without a bottle of Bordeaux, some exotic liqueurs or delicate pâté.

And the local pâtissiers were also quick not to miss a trick. 'The pastrycook, who knows perfectly well that sweet things are always desirable, sent his pricelists down into the bowels of the prison,' records Mercier.

Thus, the revolution flooded the market with staff, and gave it order, talent and impetus. But there had been some restaurants in existence before the bourgeoisie had decided to start slicing the heads off toffs.

There was, for example, a man called Boulanger who had opened an establishment in 1765 and called it a restaurant. The word came from the restoratives he offered, displaying his metier for soups and hot broths. As well as his pick-me-up bouillons, he also sold more solid dishes, including one of sheep's feet in a white sauce. This agitated the guild of 'traiteurs', the caterers who had established themselves a monopoly; they had exclusive rights to sell cooked meat dishes. Boulanger spotted that a bouillon was outside of their control, but the traiteurs nevertheless watched him with suspicion. They felt he was taunting them when he put a sign above the door that proclaimed: *Boulanger débite des restaurants divins* (Boulanger sells restoratives fit for the gods). If they understood Latin, another sign goaded them further: *Venite ad me omnes qui stomacho laboratis et ego vos restauro* (Come to me, those who are famished, and I will give you sustenance).

Then, when the sheep's feet hit the menu in 1765, they took Boulanger to court. Sheep's feet in a white sauce was, in the traiteurs' eyes, a ragout, a stew, and that was their domain. But the courts decided Boulanger's dish was not a ragout, and so, while the Parisian food guilds lost the case, Boulanger's menu expanded further.

Some scholars see this case as being a turning point in the evolution of restaurants, the loss of power of small traders and their exclusive rights to sell meat, cakes, bread and more. Others are more sceptical. Indeed, London-based historian Rebecca Sprang claims to have scoured contemporary sources and, aside from a small mention in a 1782 book entitled *The Private Life of the French in Other Times*, says there is no evidence for the Boulanger legend: 'These legends just get passed on by hearsay and then spiral out of control.' Which is interesting, given how detailed the story has become. Reports survive, for example, of Boulanger winning his case by convincing the courts that his separate preparation of the egg-yolk-enriched sauce, made on the side before being poured over the cooked mutton, meant he was not stepping into the traiteurs' territory of slowly cooking a number of ingredients together in the stew.

Whether or not it was a man called Boulanger who broke the food guilds' power on the eve of the French Revolution, there were restaurants run by other names of French legend who are yet to be knocked down by Sprang. There was Beauvilliers, Robert, Bancelin, Méot and the Trois Frères Provençaux, all of whom as 'restaurateurs' were supplanting the traiteurs. And, extraordinarily, doubtless to the huge irritation of a modern-day French gastronome, inspiration came from England.

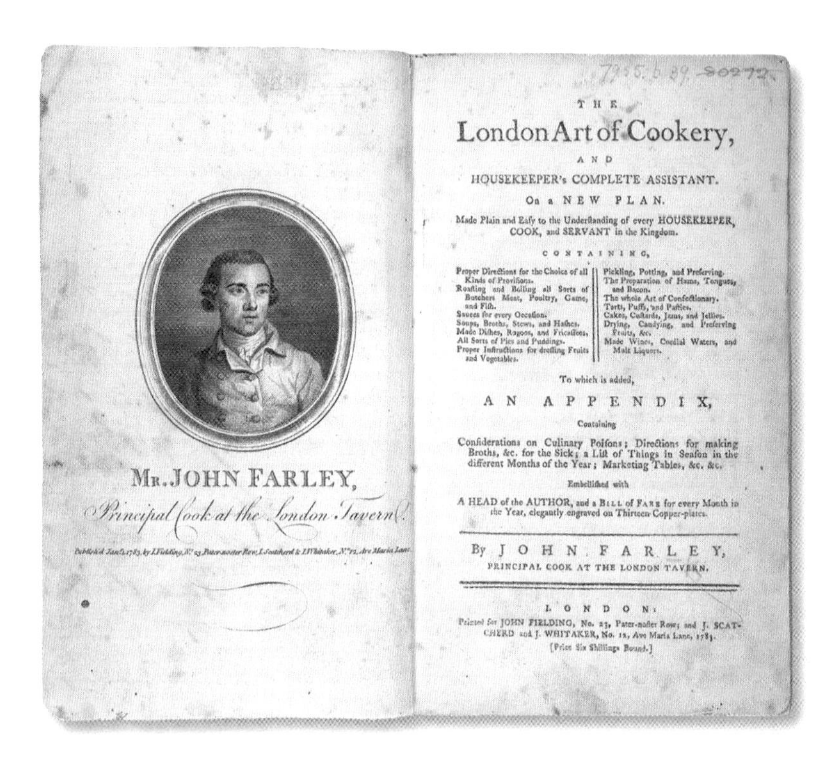

Mr. JOHN FARLEY,
Principal Cook at the London Tavern.

THE
London Art of Cookery,
AND
HOUSEKEEPER's COMPLETE ASSISTANT.
On a NEW PLAN.
Made Plain and Easy to the Understanding of every HOUSEKEEPER, COOK, and SERVANT in the Kingdom.

CONTAINING,

Proper Directions for the Choice of all Kinds of Provisions.
Roasting and Boiling all Sorts of Butchers Meat, Poultry, Game, and Fish.
Sauces for every Occasion.
Soups, Broths, Stews, and Hashes.
Made Dishes, Ragoos, and Fricassees.
All Sorts of Pies and Puddings.
Proper Instructions for dressing Fruits and Vegetables.
Pickling, Potting, and Preserving.
The Preparation of Hams, Tongues, and Bacon.
The whole Art of Confectionary.
Tarts, Puffs, and Pasties.
Cakes, Custards, Jams, and Jellies.
Drying, Candying, and Preserving Fruits, &c.
Made Wines, Cordial Waters, and Malt Liquors.

To which is added,
AN APPENDIX,
Containing
Considerations on Culinary Poisons; Directions for making Broths, &c. for the Sick; a List of Things in Season in the different Months of the Year; Marketing Tables, &c. &c.

Embellished with
A HEAD of the AUTHOR, and a BILL of FARE for every Month in the Year, elegantly engraved on Thirteen Copper-plates.

By JOHN FARLEY,
PRINCIPAL COOK AT THE LONDON TAVERN.

LONDON:
Printed for JOHN FIELDING, No. 23, Pater-noster Row; and J. SCATCHERD and J. WHITAKER, No. 12, Ave Maria Lane, 1783.
[Price Six Shillings Bound.]

Chef John Farley's The London Art of Cookery *featured recipes cooked at the London Tavern in Bishopsgate.*

While a political revolution took hold in France, there had long been another rage: English fashion. The French aristocrats looked to their English counterparts for a stylish sense of dress, but also noted how many of them took their meals in taverns. So, although France may have taken the lead gastronomically, for the ensuing 200 years, London was actually ahead of Paris.

The English taverns – where one could buy wine, as opposed to the alehouses that sold beer – were more refined and socially superior. By the middle of the eighteenth century, taverns had progressed to serving food and, unlike inns, establishments in London were beginning to offer choice. (Inns would continue to offer humble fare for many years to come; having tethered your horse, you ate whatever came out of the kitchen.)

The London Tavern in Bishopsgate had a fine reputation and a famous chef called John Farley. Two chefs named Francis Collingwood and John Woollams cooked at the Crown & Anchor Tavern on the Strand. A man called Richard Briggs cheffed at the Globe Tavern on Fleet Street, the White Hart Tavern in Holborn and the Temple Coffee House. And we know this because they all produced cookbooks. Farley's tome, *The London Art of Cookery*, was published in 1787. It featured recipes for stews, hashes, ragouts, fricassees, sauces, soups, broths, vegetables, puddings, pies, pancakes and fritters. He discussed techniques for boiling, roasting, baking, broiling, frying, pickling, preserving, collaring, potting and candying, as well as how to make wines, cordials and liquors. He intended his book to be an essential guide for 'every housekeeper, cook and servant in the kingdom'. It is still in print.

Such places were saluted by the writer Samuel Johnson, who, in 1791, wrote: 'There is no private house in which people can enjoy themselves so well as at a capital inn.' At home, he continued:

> *The master of the house is anxious to entertain his guests – the guests are anxious to be agreeable to him; and no man, but a very impudent dog indeed, can as freely command what is in another man's house, as it were his own. Whereas, at a tavern, there is freedom from anxiety. You are sure of a welcome ... there is nothing which has yet been contrived by man, by which so much happiness is produced by a good tavern or inn.*

A French writer visiting London, meanwhile, noted with some consternation that the English ate better out than in. 'It is there [the tavern] that they often take a visiting friend,' wrote Louis-Antoine Caraccioli, adding: 'Is that how a gentleman should live?' In time, of course, his fellow Frenchmen would live exactly like that.

Then, famously, one of the largest and smartest restaurants in France opened in the 1780s and paid very clear homage to its inspiration. Antoine Beauvilliers' establishment on Rue de Richelieu – with its mahogany tables, fine linen tablecloths, crystal chandeliers, menu of grilled veal chops in buttered paper and impressive wine cellar – was named La Grande Taverne de Londres.

Beauvilliers appears to be one of the early chefs who worked the room as well as the kitchen. A contemporary English writer, Dudley Costello, recorded a conversation with a Frenchman who said of the chef: 'Look at his portly figure, his triple chin, his broad, joyous face, and the light that sparkles in his large grey eye.' He had begun his career as a kitchen boy in the royal kitchens, rising to become what Costello's friend called 'the idol of the court of Marie Antoinette ... obscured only for a moment during the Reign of Terror, but beaming forth with fresh lustre when patriotism and cookery revived'.

In fact, Beauvilliers quickly exiled himself to England during the revolution once he saw others associated with the nobility being detained. Returning later

Antoine Beauvilliers' La Grande Taverne de Londres, on Rue de Richelieu, featured fine linen, crystal chandeliers and an impressive wine cellar.

when the dust had settled, he wrote his famous *The Art of Cookery* in 1814, its exhaustive instructions including: 'They [chefs] ought to have a thorough knowledge of every necessary for the kitchen, such as the qualities of the meat, the age, the healthy appearance, the best mode of keeping.' It also advised that chefs spend their spare time wisely, assisting in other kitchens, for example: 'If a cook has to turn over a receipt book continually, the labour is immense, and the time lost is incalculable.' And Beauvilliers wrote of how the more humble staff should be treated, too: while measures should be adopted to prevent them from gambling and getting drunk in their spare time, 'servants ought to be well fed and well treated'.

Across France, but particularly in Paris, restaurants grew in number and were met with considerable demand. In the capital, there was an influx of revolutionary deputies from the provinces. While they lodged in boarding houses, they ate out at the increasing number of restaurants around the Palais-Royal and Rue de Richelieu. It's likely that they brought or suggested menus to cater for their regional tastes, such as Provençal dishes like *brandade de morue* (a comforting dish of cod and gratin) and *bouillabaisse* (a rich fish stew).

But it seems that the grandest establishment of Paris was Méot, on the corner of the Rue de Valois. It was opened by one of Robert's protégés and, in 1793, it offered what French food historian Jean-Paul Aron described as 'an extraordinary nightly spectacle'. (All the more extraordinary because, in that year, following food shortages, the revolutionary National Convention passed a law against hoarding and had men searching warehouses and cellars.) A French historian writing in 1854 described the scene at Méot as: 'The halls of Apollo, where Lucullus [the Roman politician whose name became a byword for lavish banquets] himself would feel at home! Superlative wines, novel and exquisite refinement, a land of enchantment for the gourmet!' Guests were offered little bowls to wash their hands in and, on special occasions, 'suddenly, the ceiling opens to release a flock of thrushes'.

These new Parisian establishments, with their grand cuisine created for pleasure not survival, emerged at the same time as another very un-revolutionary phenomenon: the bourgeois gastronome. Moving between the smartest restaurants was an individual who was not a cook, but an expert in cuisine – a stylish person skilled in matters of taste and an expert in the art of eating. Some saw it as art, others greed. In the words of writer and sometime harpist Madame de Genlis, a noblewoman who kept a low profile during the Reign of Terror: 'The Jacobins [members of a notorious pro-revolution club], who abolished the properties in France and did away with good manners and gallantry, started the fashion for gluttony, and this was just what one would have expected of them.'

It wasn't exactly the sort of thing Robespierre and the revolution had in mind. Indeed, 1795 saw the publication of *La Cuisinière Républicaine* (The Republican Cookbook) in which the virtues of vegetables were placed front and centre, particularly the potato. 'The vegetable kingdom offers no plant more healthful, more convenient and less expensive,' wrote the authors.

History does not record what Robespierre thought of this travesty of his political works and dreams. Five months after he addressed the National Convention, his autocratic terror policy fell out of favour and he himself faced execution. He was taken to the scaffold, placed in the frame and, unusually, as the executioner secured his body with locks, he was turned to face upwards, so that his last view of this earth would be of his beloved, exacting and exquisite blade as it hurtled towards his neck.

The architect of the revolution had fallen from grace. As so often occurs, the innovators recede and become bankrupt – sometimes morally as well as financially – and others sweep in to gain the prize. In the words of Albert Soboul: 'History is a dialectical movement. The bourgeoisie that started the revolution was not the same as the bourgeoisie that profited from it.' Indeed, Jean-Paul Aron writes that, wanting somewhere to plan and rewrite the new constitution in 1795, the revolutionaries found a private room at restaurant Méot. Doubtless the opulent ceilings and frescoes, fine food and wine helped stir them to suitable ire as they wrote a document that savaged the licentiousness of their opponents.

Thus, as Robespierre was being sliced into oblivion, diners, in that growing band of smart restaurants across Paris, had reason to toast his rise as much as his demise.

7

The British Industrial Revolution

As the Industrial Revolution (between circa 1760 and 1840) took hold across the United Kingdom, new opportunities arose that meant many found themselves eating away from home, by necessity. This precursor of eating out formed the foundation of future restaurants. Across the country, the offering was decidedly mixed. Among the many requiring food and drink while on the road was Scottish geologist John MacCulloch. However, while researching and mapping the Highlands and Western Isles, he found the hospitality more akin to the Stone Age. He may have been a geologist, but, through his writings, he became an accidental critic.

It had been a long day in and around Callander, a village on the River Teith in Scotland's Perthshire county. Just north were the Callander Crags. Geologist John MacCulloch, in his diligent work to collect, analyse, record and describe the geology and minerals of the region, had hiked to the top of the trail, just over 1,000ft high at its cairn.

If it was spring, there was little evidence of it. Through low cloud, mist and drizzle, MacCulloch had picked his way through bracken and woven between birch and pine trees, unable to discern an actual path. While some of it was a gentle slope, he also found himself clambering up what

Nineteenth-century accidental food critic John MacCulloch.

appeared to be more Scottish burn than walkway. Having paused occasionally on his hike to look down and see if a view was emerging through the mist, he could see virtually nothing upon reaching the top.

Somehow retracing his steps in reverse for a couple of hours, he reached Callander and headed for one of the two inns he had heard could provide him with rest and shelter.

Being a geologist had made him a fit man. For years, he had walked across remote Scottish hills and mountains, and even more remote islands. But now, aged fifty-one, the wet weather and damp, the brooding skies and dark hills, were beginning to lose their charm. 'Cloudy, grey, cold and dreary chaos,' he called it. Finally, he spotted the inn ahead and allowed himself to imagine that soon he could remove his wet clothes, have a drink and a hot meal, and enjoy the warmth returning to his body.

The ensuing stay – the food and the drink he consumed, the kind of night he had and the sort of breakfast he ate – is something we have recorded in great detail. For MacCulloch was not just a fastidious expert on rocks ('that great man of mica, trap and granite', as Victorian writer 'Frederick Fag' described him), he also gave in-depth critiques of so much that he encountered on his journey through the Highlands and Western Isles of Scotland. Essentially, he wrote down his experiences as a series of very long letters to his friend Sir Walter Scott. But they were later published as a collection, forming a brilliantly detailed and atmospheric guide. And, in style and colour, his musings on the food, drink and hospitality he encountered render him as fine and useful a source as the best travel or restaurant critics.

Upon entering the inn, run by a Mrs Maclarty, MacCulloch was asked to wait by the landlady herself, who called for a girl named Peggy. '*Peeeggy*,' she cried again and again. Finally, the answer came similarly, '*I'm cooooming*.'

'You must not prepare to be impatient,' MacCulloch noted. Indeed, the necessity of forbearance turned out to be essential.

'If you are wet, the fire will be lighted by the time you are dry,' he continued, 'at least if the peat is not wet, too.' As he sat and waited for dinner by the cold fire in his wet clothes, he looked around for a poker in case there were some embers he could stir. He used an umbrella instead.

In due course, Peggy emerged and fanned the fire with her petticoat, which did the trick of stirring the flames, but also of filling the room with thick smoke.

As MacCulloch's coughing fit receded, Peggy ushered him to a table where he waited for ages before she brought out some food. 'In time comes mutton, called chops, then mustard,' he wrote. 'By and bye, a knife and fork; successfully, a plate, a candle and salt.' He asked for some pepper, which arrived 'when the mutton [was] cold', and was then brought some bread and a glass of whisky. All of these things were spread haphazardly across the table, wrote MacCulloch, to serve a certain purpose: 'They conceal the defects of Mrs Maclarty's tablecloth.'

After dinner, he waited a long time for his room to be ready and then found it damp. The blankets over him were heavy, but had 'the property of weight without warmth'. He woke in the middle of night, freezing cold, to find all his bedding has slipped onto the floor. He tried to pull the covers back over him, but, in the darkness and confusion, 'by dint of kicking and pulling', everything became 'irremediably entangled, sheets and all'.

He got up at 5 a.m., tried to wash, but couldn't find any soap, and struggled to shave, as the mirror was so old and distorting that he cut his face. The only towel he could find was wet and dirty, so he dried his face with the curtains.

Later, waiting for breakfast, he went into the kitchen to see if he could find a kettle to speed things up. He cautioned his readers that entering the kitchen 'will not accelerate this', as he spotted a thick kettle nestling over smoke, 'not on the fire, likely to boil tomorrow'.

He cast an eye around the kitchen. Some oat cakes were sitting in ash by the fire, and he thought he spied a herring, heaps of bedclothes on the floor, some dead chickens, what looked like bits of a pig, and a cat sleeping. There was a pot full of potatoes next to a bagpipe and a bucket of water, and then, from some 'unintelligible recess', he noticed 'two or three naked children' peeping at him.

Breakfast, he concluded, 'will probably be ready in two hours'. He reckoned the reader could 'have no inclination to partake with me of the breakfast', so made a sharp exit.

Mrs Maclarty's establishment was, however, a little more advanced than the scene MacCulloch encountered further north, towards Stornoway and Skye. This was an area of Scotland so sparsely populated that, for 100 miles around, 'everyone knows of his neighbours' births, whether of calves or children, and of his business, and of his wife's tea drinking'.

And things were considerably more claustrophobic and prehistoric on the remote Scottish island of Rona, situated in the North Atlantic, 44 miles north of Cape Wrath – the most northerly point of mainland Scotland.

The population, having been wiped out at the end of the seventeenth century by an infestation of rats, was once again very much in evidence. Five families lived in underground, troglodyte dwellings – meaning their walls couldn't be blown away by the vicious ocean storms – with roofs that were a mixture of turf and straw.

MacCulloch found these five families living there with six children in each family. Irrespective of who their parents were, 'the children were divided equally among the families', wrote MacCulloch, 'and, when the number exceeded 30, the surplus were sent off to Lewis [a nearby island]'.

They grew barley, oats and potatoes, ate a diet of potatoes, oatmeal, milk (from a cow brought to the island when she was in lactation) and dried, salted fish, which they caught off the rocks, but never ate fresh.

MacCulloch was invited to dine by the leader of the clan, Kenneth MacCagie ('a good-humoured fellow'), and his family – most of whom, at least the men and children, 'were fat'. They were well fed, MacCulloch said, or – as a comparison might go in a similarly ancient culture – rich, because they had all the food they wanted and, although many of them barely had clothing, they were comfortable enough and content.

Apart from the women, that is. The 'wife and mother looked as wretched and melancholy as Highland wives and mothers generally do,' wrote MacCulloch.

The cheerful Kenneth MacCagie ushered the visitor in. Ahead was 'a long tortuous passage, somewhat resembling the galley of a mine, but without a door, which conducted us into the penetralia of this cavern'. Inside, he could make out areas used as beds, covered not with straw, but with ash. And in the centre was the 'ancient grandmother', nursing an infant beside a fire of smouldering peat.

It was a wretched scene, 'a variety in human life worth studying', he commented, with heroic understatement. Outside was 'a climate where winter never dies' the 'rain and storm' endless, and beneath it, in 'a smoky subterranean cavern', were 'a deaf octogenarian grandmother; the wife and children half naked; and, to add to all of this, solitude, and a prison from which there was no escape'.

MacCulloch was offered thick barley cakes, the kind he had seen before on St Kilda, where he had described them as 'heavy and unpalatable'. He looked at the unappetising cake and listened to the wind outside, then muttered a saying he knew to himself: 'But the weary wind began to rise, and the sea began to rout.' He later wrote: 'It was time to think of leaving a place where a few hours of neglect might have detained us the whole winter.' So he made his excuses, declined the local delicacies, and got the hell out of there.

Some time later, MacCulloch found himself in the confines of London's Portman Square – that fashionable part of the city. He was in an elegant drawing room, '[a]round which were arranged some twenty ladies, and their white muslins, and feathers and all other things befitting, like flowers in a greenhouse, breathing sweats'. As he took in this scene, he thought back to that dark, dirty underground hovel that others in Victorian Britain called home. He thought of the contrast, writing: 'Only imagine my utter confusion of mind and body ... to emerge from a coal pit into the sunshine could not be more dazzling.'

A few years later, in the 1830s, the community on Rona again dissipated. Perhaps, once his grandmother had died, Kenneth had had enough. The island has been deserted ever since. Maybe Kenneth moved to nearby Lewis, where the landowners would pay him the equivalent of £2 a year in clothing to tend sheep and grow crops on the island. Or, alternatively, maybe he heard about what was happening in the towns and cities across the country, revving up on account of the Industrial Revolution, and, like so many others, sought new prospects and new dreams.

This period was a major turning point for western culture. The Industrial Revolution, which, for example, saw the production of textiles move from home to factory, created jobs that led to workers straying further than the confines of their villages and towns. They no longer toiled in local fields and they could no longer travel home for lunch.

Historically, their lives had been intertwined with agriculture, the perpetual cycle of ploughing, sowing and harvesting, and their existences at the mercy of the weather and their employers. Getting food had been a constant concern, hence the people of Rona salting their fish: you couldn't be certain when there would be another catch.

But the Industrial Revolution brought about a huge shift. The British historian Emma Griffin wrote that, since *Homo sapiens* emerged as a sub-species 200,000 years ago, no collection of human society had 'succeeded in decisively and permanently protecting every one of its members from the threat of an empty belly prior to our own industrial era. The onset of Britain's Industrial Revolution inaugurated an extraordinary divergence from the established parameters of past experience.' And this change is acutely exemplified in our experience of eating away and eating out. By 1840, England and Wales had some 15,500 hotel and inn keepers, almost 38,000 publicans, and 5,500 beer-shop keepers.

Indeed, the nineteenth century saw an extraordinary shift in the way people in Britain lived. In particular, the function of the home changed. In simple terms, the pre-industrial era saw the home as a base from which its inhabitants, the kin and nucleus of a family, didn't stray too far. In a classic rural setting, work was found in and around the village, and the home itself was what economic historian

Joel Mokyr described as a 'basic unit of production'. It was a world so entirely different to ours today. Food was not just cooked, it was grown and harvested. Certainly, it was rarely purchased, although it might have been traded for other goods. Domestically, food would have been preserved – salted, pickled, dried... – and beer would have been brewed in a larger house in the village with enough space for a bread oven and a brewing room.

The Industrial Revolution saw the demise of this domestic economy, as traditional household activities took place elsewhere. Work was found further from home, and, consequently, social activities also took place elsewhere – from drinking to entertainment. In the words of Mokyr: 'The household of Britain was subjected to considerable shock. The most dramatic was its change from a producing unit to a primarily consuming entity.'

Another activity that took place outside of the home was education. A good example can been seen at the joined south Northamptonshire villages of Weston and Lois Weedon. Previously, willing parents could take their children to classes in the rectory or, in the summer months, on benches in the porch of St Mary & St Peter Church. But, in 1848, Rev. Samuel Smith, the village priest, and local squire Col. Hon. Henry Hely Hutchinson founded St Loys School, which was available for all, rich or poor. This transformative action, seen across the country, improved literacy, of course, but also expectation.

Long working hours gradually shortened and enforceable bank holidays were introduced. Leisure moved from being a much-needed rest from work to an activity in its own right; and leisure activities themselves changed from the medieval to the modern. Part of the impetus for this came from emerging groups of moralists: evangelicals and Christian socialists; Methodists and those from the temperance movement. Their campaigns led to the restriction of drinking hours and the end of arcane amusements, including public executions (finally abolished in 1868) and rat- and bull-baiting. Activities such as going to church, exercising and reading were encouraged. Clearly not everyone was gripped by the idea of swapping a gory hanging for a good book, but the general effect was great change, particularly in cities like London.

As industries like magazine and newspaper publishing expanded, thousands of new jobs were created. Similarly, hotels – a new concept for the nineteenth century – were constructed, as were music halls and, crucially, restaurants. But, in the words of economic historian Professor Michael Ball: 'The most time-consuming non-work activity ... was not religious observance, but drinking.'

The nineteenth-century British temperance movement campaigned to end public executions and encouraged church-going and reading. But, stubbornly, drinking remained the most popular non-work activity.

After all, it was marginally less enjoyable than a hanging, but a hell of a lot more fun than reading.

Gin drinking was still popular in the nineteenth century, although regulation had eased the excesses witnessed in the latter part of the eighteenth century. Instead, beer had become the beverage of choice, with 34 gallons per head drunk annually in England and Wales in the early 1800s. The working classes saw a

third of their income spent on beer – it was safer to drink than water, and many drinking holes were warmer and more comfortable than the drinkers' homes.

In the early part of the nineteenth century, urban pubs became multifaceted, with some used as meeting places for trade unions and societies, others as singing saloons, and a few, such as pubs in London's Borough High Street and Piccadilly, used as ticket offices for travel on horse-drawn coaches and stabling for the horses.

Hotels also multiplied around coaching stations, adding to the multitude of private lodgings that were available across the capital. Contemporary guides show a large number of hotels in the West End of London – near Oxford Street and Covent Garden – and, as to the quality of food offered, an upbeat assessment was made by John Feltham in his 1818 work *Picture of London* (a book that presents a vivid description of the capital's entertainment, post offices, churches, prisons, galleries, hospitals and more): 'Perhaps no city exists in the world where the labouring people and certainly none where the middle classes enjoy so large a share in the necessary and inferior [trivial] comforts of life, as in this metropolis.'

The meat commonly eaten was beef, lamb or pork, with Feltham noting that 'poultry is seldom at the tables of any but the wealthy, the supply being, owing to the state of agriculture, inadequate to a general consumption and the price exorbitant'.

The English capital had also benefited from the French Revolution (Chapter 6) in the same way Paris had, with a number of French chefs operating in London kitchens. Like their colleagues in Paris, they were often former private cooks from households that had literally been cut down to size. Their customers were rich Englishmen after a taste of how the French aristocracy lived. A former butler front of house and a chef in the kitchen proved a tantalising and novel combination of considerable quality.

There was Alexander Grillon, for example, who opened Grillon's Hotel on Mayfair's Albermarle Street in 1802. Having fled France, he found work with an English family and then established his hotel in London. Given his pedigree, it's perhaps not surprising that the exiled King Louis XVIII used the hotel as a London base before returning to France in 1814. Decades later, the hotel was still operating and featured in *Black's Guide* under the section 'First Class Family Hotels for the Aristocracy and Foreigners of Distinction'.

The Industrial Revolution kick-started huge change, with the wealthier consistently eating well. But perhaps Feltham's view of London was through a set of rose-tinted glasses, as the improvements were far from universal. You didn't have to live in remote Rona to note that the trickle-down effect of progress and success seemed to defy gravity. This is the surmise of economic historian Charles Feinstein in his less-than-cheery essay entitled 'Pessimism Perpetuated':

> *For the majority of the working class, the historical reality was that they had to endure almost a century of hard toil with little or no advance from a low base before they really began to share in any of the benefits of the economic transformation they had helped to create.*

There is actually considerable debate among academics about the living standards of the British working class between the decades of 1770 and 1830. Some records suggest that salaries increased, and even doubled, for many. Average heights rose, too, indicating improvements in food and more protein in diets. Infant mortality rates also reduced. But did the move from rural peasant to city slicker really improve one's standard of living?

Technological innovation, such as the invention of threshing machines for wheat, led to a glut of farm workers. Those workers soon found jobs in cities and factories and, in due course, on the railways. This urban living and organised labour improved access to education, as society ordered itself and realised that an educated child meant a better worker.

However, living standards differed across the country, and abnormal weather at the start of the nineteenth century saw several failed harvests. Living standards were also affected by war and by international trade disruption, which pushed up prices and created a credit crunch. In the latter part of the eighteenth century and into the early nineteenth, there was almost two times as much war as there was peace.

As to the 'new' homes in the cities, many were simply slums. Salaries may have risen, but so did the size of families, which meant that, with more dependents, there was actually less to go around. And all of this heavy work, of course, made people hungrier! Indeed, that is a point made by a woman employed in agriculture who spoke to the early Victorian writer Henry Phelps: 'Working in the fields makes people eat so much more.'

There are also the accounts written by Friedrich Engels in his *The Condition of the Working Classes in England* in 1845. He poked about in homes in cities and towns, reporting that 'the dwellings of workers are everywhere badly planned, badly built, and kept in the worst condition, badly ventilated, damp and unwholesome'. He talked of 'great multitudes in rags' and, as to what they ate, claimed that 'the food of the labourer, indigestible enough in itself, is utterly unfit for children'. He also wrote of inebriated parents giving their children spirits and even opium. At the end of the day, 'the working man comes from his work tired, exhausted, finds his home uncomfortable, damp, dirty, repulsive ... liquor is almost their only pleasure, and all things conspire to make it accessible to them'.

Every study seemed to report the most extraordinary hardship in most of the new factories of the Industrial Revolution, too.

The moneyed classes, of course, were enjoying increasingly interesting food and hospitality, and their social lives were getting more and more lively as entertainment, such as racing and dancing, became smarter and more fashionable. Indeed, fashion went into a frenzy that had to be supported. Dresses needed making

Young girls employed in dress-making factories worked eighteen hours a day and 'food was served them ready cut up in order to require them the least possible time for swallowing'.

– lots of them. 'The personal adornment of the ladies of the bourgeoisie involves the saddest consequences of the health of the workers,' wrote Engels. Accounts of mid-nineteenth-century dressmaking in London reported some 15,000 young girls leaving the countryside to be employed in factories. They would eat and sleeep on the premises, and walk home after shifts that lasted days, which, for some, meant a walk of up to 60 miles per week. Little rest was afforded to these girls. They worked around eighteen hours a day and sometimes had only two hours' sleep a night. There were even cases in which the girls didn't undress or change clothes for nine consecutive days – 'these unfortunate girls are kept by the means of the moral whip of the modern slave driver'. As to what they ate, Engels found that 'food was served them ready cut up in order to require them the least possible time for swallowing'.

Parliamentary papers in 1833 recorded factories in which

> *detached rooms are fitted for the work people in which to wash, clean and eat ... sometimes the school room in which the children are taught in the evening is appropriated as a dressing and eating room for the adults during the day. But in many cases there is no washing, dressing or cooking rooms.*

Unregulated factory owners often provided the bare minimum of food for their workers, be they men, women or children. Engels quoted some of the children he met, who worked in the pottery business around Stoke, central England. 'Don't get enough to eat, get mostly potatoes with salt, never meat, never bread, don't go to school, haven't got no clothes,' said one. Another added: 'Haven't got nothin' to eat today for dinner, don't never have dinner at home...'

The food that was provided – in areas such as Wolverhampton, Staffordshire, the centre of the iron district – was, according to Engels, 'almost exclusively meat from diseased animals or such as have died a natural death, or tainted meat, or fish to eat, with veal from calves killed too young, and pork from swine smothered during transportation'. The result? Frequent bowel complaints and illness.

At the water-powered mill in Cromford, Derbyshire, built by Sir Richard Arkwright in 1771 for spinning cotton, a large number of children were employed – as well as women and some men. (Generally, women and children were seen as easier, more pliant employees, and more docile than men, who, in the early years of the Industrial Revolution, having gone from being big fish working domestically, were often ill disciplined and frequently drunk.) In the second decade of the 1800s, Arkwright's son, Richard junior, who had followed in his father's footsteps and managed to make even more money than him, recorded the living and eating pattern at the mill.

It was a twelve-hour day for the workers, beginning at 7 a.m. in the summer and 8 a.m. in the winter. The machinery only ever stopped while dinner was being served. 'As to breakfast, it is very irregular,' wrote Arkwright. A bell would ring at half past eight, and all but the actual spinners would eat for half an hour. He continued:

> *There is a room called the dinner-house, in which there is a range of hot plates or stoves, much as the same as in gentlemens [*sic*] kitchens; the mothers or the younger sisters of the hands employed [often whole families would be working at a factory] bring the breakfasts into this room. As soon as the bell rings, a number of boys carry those breakfasts into the different rooms in the factory.*

It was then a system of first come, first served. Many workers felt they couldn't leave their stations and, according to Arkwright, 'very few have their refreshment, probably not one in five'. Quite how they worked on empty stomachs is a mystery, but, given Arkwright's success, the workers presumably did somehow find enough sustenance, however basic.

The Industrial Revolution also saw routes across the country opening up, as more people travelled for work, and businesses took advantage of this.

There had, in fact, been much development in the mid-eighteenth century, criss-crossing England with coach routes. The first horse-drawn stage coaches had been advertised in 1667 – 'flying machines' travelling between London and Bath. An advertisement placed on the walls of two inns in the respective cities made the announcement:

> *All those desirous to pass from London to Bath, or any other place on their road, let them repair to the 'Bell Savage' on Ludgate Hill in London, and the 'White Lion' at Bath, at both which places they may be received in a stage coach every Monday, Wednesday and Friday, which performs the whole journey in three days (if God permit), and sets forth at five o'clock in the morning.*

Travelling was treacherous, the makeshift routes strewn with branches and precarious holes that were as dangerous as the highwaymen – or -women – who stalked them. Mail coaches began in 1784 and, to make the journeys more tolerable, inns cropped up along the routes. Horses could be changed or rested, and there was food and drink for the weary travellers. By the mid-eighteenth century, there were inns every 7–10 miles. They were most prolific along the Great North Road, which stretched from London to Durham and is today's A1.

One of the busiest inns was The George in Stamford, Lincolnshire. If you were starting a journey from there, you could wait in either of the two waiting rooms once you had your ticket: one was marked 'London'; the other 'York'.

Such inns served simple food and, of course, there was no choice. The growth of inns was particularly prevalent in Scotland, specifically in the Highlands and Islands between 1790 and 1840. There was a vast increase in the number of travellers to that region, many of whom were searching for the wilds of Scotland that they had encountered in contemporary fiction, the writings of James Boswell or the poems of James Macpherson. They all romanticised the landscape – boundless oceans, vast and gloomy skies, huge mountains – and so did Dorothy Wordsworth, sister of William, who travelled through the Highlands, writing of eerie mists, stormy promontories, solitary huts, ghostly ruins and land stretching out into dark infinity. Tourists wanted to retrace the steps of these literary heroes – or travel as far away as possible from the warring continent – and a new array of inns was only too happy to furnish their needs.

According to Canadian academic Theresa Mackay, a large proportion of the inns were run by women. Mackay found evidence of some sixty female

The romantic Scottish highlands of the early 1800s offered travellers vast and gloomy landscapes, huge mountains, perpetually bad weather – and dismal food.

inn keepers, many of whom were single or widowed, and one such inn keeper was a Mrs Maclarty, at whose shambolic inn John MacCulloch suffered that dismal night.

How MacCulloch relished the knowledge that he had: the unique and rare insight of different lives and landscapes he had witnessed. His glistening prose illuminated page after page in the letters he wrote to his friend Sir Walter. He had seen and experienced the discomfort of the poor and the vast inequalities that existed in – and seemed to be perpetuated by – the new machine age. But he wasn't so churlish as to sniff at the new refinement.

Indeed, if he'd ventured south from London, he might have been even more amazed at what was happening in the kitchens of Paris – particularly in the domain of a man called Marie-Antoine Carême...

8

Carême and the New Paris Guide

With the French Revolution becoming a distant memory, the aristocrats back in town, and new money eager to splash the cash, the fine-dining restaurant boom in Paris took off like never before.

As we have seen, the eighteenth century saw a vast increase in the number of people eating out. But, because it was broadly a functional undertaking, one is minded to describe it as 'eating away'. It was mostly an activity of necessity. While some pleasure may have occasionally come of it, that was not the primary intention. And, thus, the food consumed outside of the home was not vastly different from that consumed inside. A meal comprising a bowl of soup, a piece of mutton served with pepper and mustard, and some bread – washed down with beer, wine or whisky – filled the stomach and was comforting in its familiarity.

Choice was not on the menu. For example, one of the ways in which the French government-controlled inns was by giving them licences that insisted they buy specific produce from specific caterers – pastry makers and butchers that were controlled by the all-powerful guilds.

When soup maker Boulanger successfully challenged this power (Chapter 6), he unwittingly paved the way for a more modern food service. The private chefs of the French Revolution, in entering the public domain, injected creativity and finesse into the dining scene. And, although that revolution did not create the restaurant concept, it did put fire in its belly. There were around fifty restaurants in Paris in 1789. Ten years later, there were 500.

By the 1820s, freed from the restraints of revolution, and with aristocrats returning and attempting to reclaim their properties and royalty back in town, Paris became fashionable. The restoration of the Bourbon royal family after Napoleon was vanquished created a more peaceful era. Post-revolutionary France was more egalitarian: the middle class grew; successful merchants bought the

Parisian Marie-Antoine Carême brought cooking out of the Middle Ages.

grand apartments that were once only the domain of nobles; and people had money to spend. Covered arcades were built with luxury shops, offering sanctity from the dangerous, dirty and pavement-free streets. Those shops sold jewellery, furs and paintings. There were hair salons and, of course, there were restaurants.

Many restaurants took inspiration from a man who cooked in the private sector; a man who codified French cuisine, turned it into gastronomy, and remains an influence on chefs even to this day.

His name was Marie-Antoine Carême. Born in 1784, he was one of the most significant culinary figures of the early nineteenth century, not because he catered weddings, where he would display food as art in his extraordinary architectural sugar sculptures and ice carvings, but because he created a difference between home and professional cooking. As the American chef, teacher and food writer Wayne Gisslen reflected in 1999: 'It was Carême's practical and theoretical work as an author and an inventor of recipes that was responsible … for bringing cooking out of the Middle Ages and into the modern period.'

The emergence in the late eighteenth century of the stove gave cooks the opportunity to control heat in a way that was impossible with open fire. Commercial kitchens were also developing a new order. As Gisslen explained, they were divided into three departments: a meat chef (*rôtisseur*) controlled the rotisserie; a pastry chef (*pâtissier*) was in charge of the oven; and a cook (*cuisinier*) looked after the stove.

But Carême added procedure and order to this. And he added lightness. Since the Middle Ages, the grand cuisine of the aristocracy was all about complexity and scale: the larger the better. But Carême believed in the simplicity of presentation, however complex the work behind the scene. His sauces were made to enhance great ingredients, not hide poor ones.

And, while he never actually ran a kitchen for a restaurant, his influence can still be seen in his invention of the chef's hat and his classification and creation of sauces. He is also credited with refining the order in which food is presented to the table – from all at the same time (traditionally called *service à la française*) to a succession of courses, as mapped out on a menu (*service à la russe*). He also wrote a series of books that remained a bible of restaurant service for more than 150 years.

Carême was a man confident of his talents, convinced about the superiority of French cuisine, and assured of its place in the future. He produced a seminal tome entitled *The Royal Parisian Pastrycook and Confectioner*, as well as writing *L'Art de la Cuisine Française*, in which he recorded, exhaustively, what he saw as perfected French cooking. It was a book to which various volumes were added after his death. His culinary output was ground-breaking and historic.

'This work … is absolutely new,' he wrote proudly, 'and will throw additional lustre on our national cookery, so long and so justly esteemed by foreigners.' The food of his nation was, he continued, 'always valued and encouraged by the French nobility, the delicacy of whose taste rendered them truly capable of appreciating fine-flavoured and excellent dishes. Our modern cookery has become the model of whatever is really beautiful in the culinary art.' The epicentre of great cooking was in his own kitchen. He concluded, with great conviction: 'The art of French cookery, as practiced in the nineteenth century, will be the pattern for future ages.'

Carême's books were radical in that they were unashamedly for professionals. Their titles featured the word 'art', and some were literally 'architectural projects'. His idea of modern cooking was complicated, challenging and not for the faint-hearted. The craft was diligent, time-consuming and very serious. But, for the diner, the effect was awe, wonder and pleasure.

Meanwhile, among Carême's contemporary cooks in England were the likes of Eliza Acton. Her *Modern Cookery in All Its Branches* was very firmly domestic. While Mrs Acton was teaching about suet, Carême was making brioche. Acton had a recipe for 'boiled pigeon'; Carême offered 'timbales of pigeons, with truffles'. On the fine-dining front, the English had a little catching up to do.

What also separated Carême from cooks of the past – and many of the future – is that he cooked not according to tradition, but developed methods to produce the best results instead. It's why he could genuinely state that his work was new. The only tradition he clung on to was a belief that the French palate was without rival. And he felt no shame in the fact that the people he fed were the richest and most noble. Indeed, he would have felt content that, when his career was at its peak, the French Revolution was a thing of the past. The mouths he was proud to feed were no longer threatened by the guillotine. But, like so many chefs, his background was starkly different to the people who were lucky enough to taste his food.

One of sixteen children, his father was a hard-drinking labourer and little is known of his mother. He was turned out onto the streets of Paris at the age of eight by his father, who perhaps felt – quite correctly, as it turned out – that his son would have a better chance if he left the squalor of their home.

Having found work and lodging at a humble restaurant – the type travellers would frequent – by one of the gates of Paris, he ended up serving a six-year apprenticeship there. Then, at fifteen, he found work with a leading pastry chef of the day, Sylvain Bailly, whose bakery was in a fashionable and more prosperous area of Paris. This precipitated Carême's extraordinary rise. He thrived there and his experiments in pastry impressed Bailly, who rewarded Carême by encouraging him to read, write and spend time in a local – and rather magnificent – library, the Bibliothèque Nationale. (Its collection had swelled during the revolution, as books were seized from the homes of aristocrats and stored there.)

In time, Carême's opulent confectioneries, which might depict the ruins of ancient Greece or the most famous buildings of France, attracted the attention

Carême's books were unashamedly produced for professionals; his recipes and ideas were not for the faint-hearted.

Dinner SERVED AT The Royal Pavilion AT Brighton

To HIS ROYAL HIGHNESS THE PRINCE REGENT and GRAND DUKE NICOLAS OF RUSSIA
By Chef Antonin Carême on 18th January 1817

Eight Soups

Chicken and mixed vegetables
Clear consommé
Soup of mutton with capers
Rice soup with carrot
Curried chicken soup
Consommé with chicken quenelles
Celery soup – fowl consommé

Eight Removes of Fish

Perch in hollandaise sauce
Salmon trout served with sponges
Cod in mornay sauce
Pike garnished with its roes
Breaded sole with truffle garnish
Turbot in shrimp sauce
Fried whiting with diced vegetables
The head of a great sturgeon in Champagne

Forty Entrées served around the Fish

Spring chickens
Glazed veal with chicory
Tart of thrushes au gratin
Chicken à la Chevry
Young rabbit cutlet
Quenelles of young fowl in cockscomb and mushroom sauce
Quail with diced vegetables
Jellied partridge with mayonnaise
Sliced tongue with cabbage and chestnuts
Diced chicken in ham and mushroom sauce
Fillets of game fowl in white sauce
Sliced duck in bitter orange sauce
Salmon steaks in Montpelier butter
Mousse of game fowl with cream and truffles
Fillet of lamb garnished with kidneys and sweetbreads
Rabbit pie on a bed of laurel
Spring chicken in creamed mushroom sauce
Rice casserole with truffle and foie gras
Braised ducklings with lettuce
Sautéed pheasant in foie gras sauce
Supremes of pheasant in white sauce
A crown fashioned of chicken on tomato sauce
Timbale of pasta with boiled egg and asparagus
Escalope of venison with fried onions and tomatoes
Stuffed partridges in tomato sauce
Spit-roasted woodcock
Chicken in aspic
Fillets of sole in warmed aspic
Fried veal brains with a parmesan crust
Escalopes of grouse in game sauce
Pheasant sausage with braised lettuce and mushrooms
Glazed small fowl with cucumbers
Chicken salad with onions
Cushion of ham on a bed of spinach
Risotto of chicken wings and white truffle
Pigeons in crayfish butter
Chicken in a gypsy style
Pastry nests in white sauce
Mutton chops with creamed potatoes
Poached chicken in aspic glaze

Platters after the Fish

Chicken vol-au-vent
Terrine of larks
Custard rissoles
Ducklings Luxembourg
Battered fried fish in tomato sauce

Eight Great Pieces

Marinaded haunch of boar
Pullets with diced vegetables
Fillets of beef with horseradish, ham and Madeira
Pheasant in truffle and wine sauce
A turkey, garnished with kidney, sweetbreads and vegetables
Loin of veal with truffle, foie gras and pickled tongue
Partridges encased in pastry with glazed roots
Roast beef and sliced mutton

Eight Centrepieces Patisserie

ARCHITECTURES IN SPUN SUGAR, FONDANT AND MARZIPAN

An Italian pavilion
A Swiss hermitage
Great Parisian meringue
Tower of caramelised profiteroles with pistachios
A Welsh hermitage
The Royal Pavilion, rendered in pastry
A great nougat in the French style
Tower of profiteroles with aniseed

Eight Roasts

Woodcock larded with bacon
Turkey
Spiced pheasants
Chicken with watercress
Teal dressed with lemons
Chicken with truffle tartlets
Grouse
Quails larded with bacon

Thirty two Desserts and Savoury Entremets

Stuffed cucumber in white sauce
Conserve of gooseberries
Greek raisin waffles
Buttered spinach
A pyramid of lobsters with fried parsley
Apricot and almond tartlets
Upside-down lemon jelly
Scrambled egg with truffle shavings
Turnips in tarragon sauce
Apple and rum pudding
Spun sugar diadems
Choux pastry flowers
Truffles in warm linen
Chicken, chicory and hazelnut salad
Maraschino jelly with whipped cream

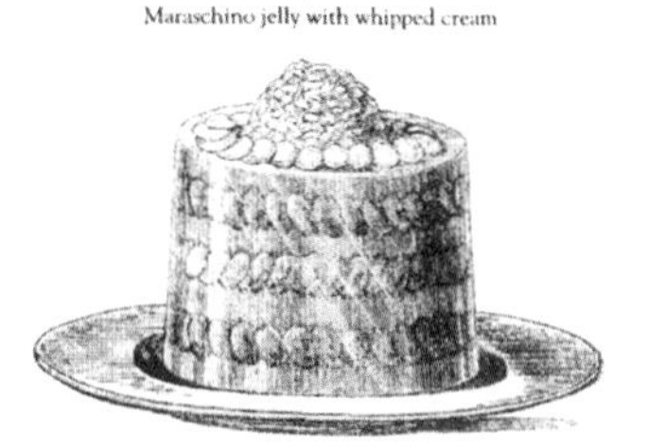

Mushroom tart
Sardines with tomato and onions
Conserve of strawberries
Pyramid of shrimp
Upside-down cakes with caramel glaze
Salsify salad
Dauphine cream cake
Apricot blancmange
Lettuce in ham liquor
Grilled mushrooms with sherry
Pancakes with Chantilly cream
Almond loaf
Sautéed potatoes with parsley
Almond cakes
Rose ice cream
Orange liqueur jelly
Braised celery

Twelve Great Rounds

Four apple soufflés
Four vanilla soufflés
Four fondues

Afterword

The Prince Regent gave this extraordinary dinner to symbolise British supremacy in Europe, regarding the defeat of Napoleon as a personal triumph. He ascended to the throne as King George IV in 1820, but his lavish dining habits and excessive drinking led to morbid obesity, and he was crippled by gout. Having once remarked to Carême, "You will kill me with a surfeit of food", he died in 1830 of 'fat on the heart'.

Chef Antonin Carême, 'King of Cooks and Cook of Kings' was the greatest chef of his, and some would say all, time. He left the Prince's service later in 1817. Though he was to work for the Tsar and the fabulously wealthy Rothschilds, this dinner at the Royal Pavilion was the service of his career. He died in 1833, it is thought of carbon-monoxide poisoning – from years of cooking over charcoal in the great kitchens of Europe.

In 1825 Grand Duke Nicolas, the Prince Regent's honoured guest, became Tsar Nicolas I. A reactionary and autocrat, he was dedicated to the maintenance of a Russian Empire under the Tsars. He died, possibly by his own hand, of poisoning in 1855 - as Russia slipped towards defeat in the Crimean War.

of Napoleon, whose wedding cake Carême designed for the emperor's marriage to Marie Louise of Austria in 1810.

Demand saw Carême cook for Prince Regent George IV and Tsar Alexander I, too. He famously created a 120-dish feast at the Brighton Pavilion on 18 January 1817, hosted by the prince regent, to celebrate the visit from Russia of Grand Duke Nicholas.

Carême made a fortune and recorded for posterity, in a number of books, the designs for his most famous creations. Having set in stone what he saw as the four fundamental sauces – béchamel, velouté, espagnole and allemande – he also believed passionately in the importance of presentation. He once wrote: 'I want order and taste. A well-displayed meal is enhanced 100 per cent in my eyes.'

For centuries, the human necessity for food had never afforded a cook the luxury of focusing so much on appearance – notwithstanding superior flavour and texture – but Carême changed that for ever. He was also not afraid to put himself centre stage. Alongside illustrations of his creations, he included sketches of himself dressed in what would become the uniform of the grandest head chefs to this day: the double-breasted white chef's jacket and the tall white hat (toque).

Carême died in 1834 from lung disease, aged just fifty – the result of working in unventilated kitchens – and, with hindsight, we can safely say that he was the first modern-day celebrity chef. He was, wrote the turn-of-the-twentieth-century French poet Laurent Tailhade, 'burnt out by the flame of genius, and the charcoal of the roasting spit'.

But Carême did not operate in isolation; he was not the only famous cook in Paris. While his private work was appreciated behind the closed doors of the palaces and grand houses of Europe, the dining scene in his city had also been set alight.

A key moment was 1827, for this was the year that the fifteenth edition of Galignani's *New Paris Guide* appeared, heralding the proliferation of good restaurants in the capital. The guide – also titled *Stranger's Companion Through the French Metropolis* and published by two Italian brothers whose bookshop still exists on the Rue de Rivoli in Paris – was intended for those with the wealth and wherewithal to travel to the French capital. (These were the days when a passport could be requested by calling at the French ambassador's residence at 50 Portland Place, London, a week before travel. One would return the following day to pick up the passport, which would have been signed by the ambassador himself.)

Opposite: Carême's feast for the prince regent and Russian tsar was a 120-dish extravaganza, the menu a monumental culinary achievement.

The guide announced that, in Paris, 'the gourmand may dine much more luxuriously than he can in London for the same charge'. The number of cafés also astonished the writer. They 'abound', he wrote, 'in no other city is there anything to resemble them'. Indeed, he reckoned there were some 2,000 in total, and remarked that 'there are Parisians, and many strangers, that lounge nearly the whole of the day in cafés'. It was in these cafés that another significant difference could be noted between the English and the French: 'In Paris, all classes mix together, strangers converse with each other, some play at dominoes, some read newspapers and periodical publications.'

Most cafés also employed a well-dressed lady who managed the place and ran it from a vantage point near the entrance. It would be sacrilege to arrive or depart without taking off one's hat and bowing to her. 'Attired in a most elegant costume and frequently adorned with jewels, she occupies an elevated seat,' reported the guide, 'where, amidst the fulsome compliments of dandies and the gaze of vulgar eyes, she directs the service and receives the money.'

Whereas restaurants and coffee houses in London at the time were generally designed with seating divided into discreet booths, Parisian establishments were open plan and usually cluttered with tables, lamps, statues, columns with vases on top, and plenty of mirrors. There was a great deal of noise – the confluence of talk and laughter – but the *New Paris Guide*, possibly mindful that the French Revolution was still a distant memory, warned visitors: 'In frequenting such places, it is advisable to avoid political matters.'

As to the restaurants, the inference is that London establishments also lagged behind in not offering as much choice of dishes. The novelty of Paris was that, as the guide explained, 'in the restaurants, there is generally presented a bill of fare called *la carte*, with the price of every article, and some of these bills contain upwards of 300 dishes'. And, when it came to wine, the recommendation was to order the *vin ordinaire*, as it seemed just as good as the pricier bottles. Overall, it was felt that 'luxury and economy may be combined in this capital'.

Dinner in a smart restaurant cost around 2 francs. In simpler establishments that offered fixed-price menus – a meal of bread, soup, a choice of three main courses, dessert and wine – the cost was 22 sous (about a franc). That would be around £10 in today's money, so it did combine luxury and economy rather well.

Writer Francis Coghlan, in his *A Guide to France*, written in 1830, also mentioned a cheaper echelon of restaurant, of which there were many across the capital, but he advised his readers to avoid them: 'There are many houses in Paris which profess to furnish four dishes, half a bottle of wine, a dessert, and bread for 30 sous, 1s 3d, but those who have the least regard for cleanliness should avoid these abodes of filthy splendour.'

While Galignani said that there were as many restaurants as cafés, there were sixteen he specifically listed – his guide's pick of the best. One of the names included was Boissier at the Palais Royal.

Louis Boissier's restaurant was in the grand and ornate setting of the former royal palace. The establishment is still operating today and is called Le Grand Véfour (the name of Boissier's predecessor). Originally opened in 1784, the restaurant was bought by Boissier in 1823, and it became part of a fashionable covered arcade described in the *New Paris Guide* as 'the central point of Parisian amusements'. In addition to luxurious shops, it was a district of up-market gaming houses and rooms, where those new-moneyed merchants could play dice, cards and roulette. But there was another side to the Palais Royal. It was, confided that delectable guide book, 'the *ne plus ultra* [ultimate] of pleasure and vice, of delight and depravity … it is a place in which those who live for animal enjoyment only … might pass their life with ample gratification'.

Boissier's restaurant was a picture of opulence; a ceiling of dainty plasterwork with frescoes of garlanded women and roses, and walls clad with gilded mirrors. The food was equally sumptuous: dishes like *Marengo au poulet*, topped with truffle (a sautéed chicken dish that celebrated a Napoleonic victory of 1800), or simpler fare, beautifully presented, like *côtelettes de mouton* (lamb chops) or *merlan* (whiting).

Fancy pastry desserts, such as those paraded by Carême, were still only served at private events, but at restaurants came biscuits, macaroons, meringues and exotic fruits, as well as gooseberries, grapes from Fontainebleau (south of Paris), and pineapples grown in the greenhouses of Sarcelles (north of the capital).

Another smart establishment lay on the corner of Rue Montorgueil and Rue Greneta, in the second arrondissement of Paris. There chef Borrel had his restaurant, Au Rocher de Cancale – an institution selling oysters and seafood that is also still operating today. Borrel was, reflected the editor of London's *Harper's Magazine* a few decades later, 'a great man in the kitchen', but he 'had a wife, prettier than she was wise … [who] spent more than Borrel earned'. He went bust, and his wife 'ran away with a vagrant Russian'.

The story then goes that, some years later, a Russian arrived in Paris looking for the famed chef Borrel and a dinner at his restaurant. Upon hearing that the place had closed down, he searched for the chef at other restaurants in the city,

Chef Borrel's restaurant, in Paris's second arrondissement, sold oysters and seafood. It is one of several nineteenth-century restaurants in the French capital still operating today.

until a waiter at the Café de Paris pointed the Russian towards Borrel's now very humble quarters. The Russian found the chef, gave him money and clothes, and persuaded him to come to Russia. There he installed Borrel in the kitchens of a restaurant in St Petersburg.

Once again, Borrel's fortunes rose and he became a new culinary star of the city. He knew little of his patron's background, but, visiting his house one day and finding him not there, Borrel got chatting to the Russian's housekeeper. She told him that her boss had been to Paris on a previous occasion and had returned home with a Frenchwoman, who, she gathered, had been married to a famous chef at the time...

Borrel stayed at the house and later confronted both the Russian and the former Mrs Borrel. But they managed to settle the affair. The Russian felt of the Frenchwoman – in the words of the *Harper's* editor – that 'the heyday of her youth was gone', so he gave her up and took another mistress. Borrel then remarried his wife, who, unnerved by her potential notoriety, became significantly less spendthrift with her husband's money!

Another establishment in the *New Paris Guide* was Grignon's, on the Rue Neuve-des-Petits-Champs, opposite the Palais Royal. Writing in *Fraser's Magazine for Town and Country* in 1860, a writer, whose nom de plume was 'A Man on the Shady Side of Fifty', cast his mind back some forty years to the 1820s, when, he wrote, 'Grignon's ... was the most crowded restaurant in Paris'. He reflected that one could have an excellent dinner of three or four dishes and a bottle of Mâcon for about 4 francs. He had even kept a few old receipts that recorded a dinner of *perdreau rouge farci aux truffes* (red partridge stuffed with truffles), another of roasted woodcock, and a third of *sole au vin de Champagne* (sole in a Champagne sauce), washed down with a bottle of Clos Vougeot. This was a wine from a vineyard in Burgundy founded by monks in the twelfth century. While wines from this vineyard have traditionally been red, from the pinot noir grape, if the wine were chosen to go with his fish, rather than an undisclosed meat course, then it may have been a more suitable white Burgundian Chardonnay from that château.

Other great restaurants of the day included Lemardelay, at 100 Rue de Richelieu, frequented in the late 1820s by the composer Hector Berlioz. And novelist Honoré de Balzac was a regular at chef Martin's Veau qui Tete (Suckling Calf) on Place du Châtelet.

The guide also mentions two restaurants run by Englishmen: Dunn's, on the Rue Vivienne; and Tilbrook's, on the Rue Lepelletier. The latter, described by Coghlan, provided an 'English style of cookery'. Little else is recorded, so one can only guess as to what the restaurant might have been like, but it was honoured with inclusion on the list of the best that Paris had to offer. Doubtless such establishments came as a relief to travellers faced with the rich and intricate menus that abounded the city. Indeed, some dishes clearly unnerved the English, so the *New Paris Guide* felt moved to defend certain French habits, including the eating of frogs. There was, it was written, an

> *absurd prejudice still prevalent in England against the natives of France, for eating frogs, which is deemed by the English to be a mark of poverty and wretchedness. The truth is that the French do eat fricasseed frogs, which are of a peculiar kind, fattened in a particular manner, and of which it requires a great number to make a small dish as the thighs are used only for that purpose. They are an acknowledged and exquisite luxury and are rarely to be met with, on account of the excessively high price.*

But Parisian restaurants would not have to rely solely on English writers to celebrate their magnificence or explain why the French capital was becoming pre-eminent in its cuisine, seemingly without rival across the world. Towards the end of the 1820s, an American woman in her late twenties made an extraordinary journey from her home in Massachusetts, USA, to France and Spain. She recorded her trip in a long series of letters to her father, which were later collected and published.

Though Caroline Elizabeth Wilde Cushing was an adventurous and independent woman, she nevertheless missed her parents and spoke of 'the wide expanse of ocean [that] separated us'. She returned from her travels wiser and increasingly determined that women be taken more seriously and not be constrained by society to avoid business and public life. She was particularly inspired by the women she came across in Paris, who, she wrote, took 'an active part, sometimes the chief command, in extensive mercantile establishments, or very large hotels'. They were 'perfectly capable of undertaking the entire management of their husband's business, upon the occasion of his illness, absence or death'.

Some such women she came across in restaurants. As in many hotels, they seemed to be running the business. She also noticed the ladies who sat on those high chairs at the entrances to some of the smarter establishments. She 'presides over the whole', Cushing wrote, 'and receives the money after you have dined; and also serves out the fruit, which makes a very fine show upon a large table near her'. Though Cushing did concede: 'She is generally selected for her beauty, in order to attract persons, as one of the ornaments of the saloon.'

As well as noting the unusual presence of women dining together at restaurants, Cushing also spotted gentlemen eating alone and noticed a large number of couples lunching and dining. Moreover, she heralded how Parisian restaurants did something still unheard of back home in America: they combined function with pleasure. They didn't just open when it suited the chef or inn keeper, and they offered considerably more food than any place she had ever experienced.

Every restaurant she visited provided soup to start ('the indispensable commencement of a dinner in France') and then – even at the more humble establishments – came 'three different dishes, besides wine, fruit, bread, and a small cup of coffee, without milk, but with a plentiful allowance of sugar, with which your repast finishes'. The restaurants she saw at the Palais Royal 'give you the luxuries of the country, prepared in the highest perfection of gastronomic art'. And all of these places were full, so she soon realised 'the convenience of being able to obtain a good dinner at a moment's warning'.

The restaurants of Paris represented a new modernity. They thrived in a city that, a few decades after bloody revolution, seemed comfortable in its own skin: open, accessible, democratic. Cushing noted 'the ease with which a person may have access to everything worthy of being seen in Paris'. Exhibitions, public and private institutions 'granted free admission, to strangers particularly ... In no other city whatever can be found equal advantages, either for study or amusement, and in no other are these so easy of access as in Paris.'

Two years after she returned home, at the tender age of thirty, Caroline Cushing died. A few months later, her letters were published. Read today, they give an insight into what it was about Paris that enabled restaurants to thrive – and eating out to become pleasurable. But, more crucially, they show that restaurants had become as important a part of culture as art, museums, buildings, paintings and music.

Talented individuals alone were not enough to create a magnificent dining scene. A spirit of openness and freedom was also needed. As the world would see in the twentieth century, nothing destroys food culture like communism. But, similarly, nothing restricts its growth like a society controlled solely by rich nobles. To thrive and prosper, an economy needs new money – vulgar merchants splashing their cash in fashionable eateries.

Paris of the 1820s cemented its reputation as having the finest restaurants on earth, a crown that would not be challenged for over 100 years. Indeed, there would be little competition from across the English Channel, where the British were relishing the new Victorian age – an era in which a young man or woman wishing to progress upwards through society most certainly did not choose food as a topic of conversation. Even expressing pleasure at the consumption of pudding was considered almost sinful, and eating out became a thing of glorious Dickensian gloom.

But there were some fabulous exceptions...

9

The Victorian Era

The start of Queen Victoria's long reign saw Britain in for a long period of significant transformation, from culture to industry. But, while the spirit of Victorianism did not manifest in restaurants, another institution emerged that would, in time, have a great effect on eating out: clubs – for aristocrats and working men.

The Victorian era saw huge change across England. But it didn't just start when Queen Victoria's reign did, on 20 June 1837, nor did it end when she died on 22 January 1901.

There was change, precipitated and embedded by the effects of the Industrial Revolution. There was political reform. There was peace and prosperity. And there was also considerable poverty. The background to developments in the story of the restaurant and food is complex. A lot happened between 1800 and the turn of the twentieth century.

Sport was codified; rules were published for rugby, cricket and croquet. Railways were built, as were steam ships. Anaesthetic transformed medicine. Photography went from an art form to a profession in the world of news-gathering, whereby newspapers such as the *Telegraph* and [*Manchester*] *Guardian* were founded. The Reform Act widened the franchise of democracy. The circus boomed, as did bands and bandstands. Tinned meat arrived from the US and Australia; helpfully, the tin-opener was invented, too. Factories that made cheese opened, as did the Suez Canal, which enabled imports from India and Asia to ship to Britain faster and safer. Refrigeration helped preserve the food on those ships. Bananas arrived from the Canary Islands. Public soup kitchens began serving food to the poor. The Adulteration of Food and Drink and Drugs Act promoted health and safety. And, in 1902, the creation of the Metropolitan Water Board ensured water flowed across the capital.

Slowly but surely, England moved from agrarian to industrial. British food historian Colin Spencer highlighted the extraordinary statistic that, in 1800, 80 per cent of the British population lived in rural areas and small towns, but, by 1900, that figure was reversed: 80 per cent of the population lived in major towns and cities. Only 12 per cent of men worked in agriculture.

That shift had profound implications for the world of food. The rural pre-industrial era was a time when most people had access to land, even if very few of them owned it. As we have seen (Chapter 7), agrarian life saw workers living near home, often making a living from the land, growing and harvesting veg, and preserving the excess. They tended livestock, they raised pigs and they shared the sausages and hams with their family and neighbours. They ate cabbage, carrots, turnips, cucumbers and peas. They didn't eat chickens. Most people, rich or poor, tended to have a similar diet domestically. It was varied and there was plenty of protein. In the words of Andrea Broomfield, author of *Food and Cooking in Victorian England*:

> *Most Englishmen and women, irrespective of their class and breeding, would have enjoyed a spit-roasted joint of beef or mutton accompanied with a brown gravy and a boiled plum pudding made rich with spices and dried fruits. They would have gladly washed down such a meal with mugs of ale.*

The move to the city was not necessarily a voluntary one. Many families realised that the factories had taken their livelihoods; the cottage industry of spinning thread, for example, was decimated once machines could do it faster and cheaper. Even when they found work in the cities such as Manchester or Birmingham – the latter's population swelled to five times its original size between 1800 and 1850 – they didn't have the job security that the land offered, with its constancy of sewing, harvesting, preserving...

There was often less space, which didn't just mean smaller rooms for families, but also no room for the tools they once used to make and preserve food. No room for the butter churn or the wooden barrel to keep the salted meat. Many diets suffered as a result. An extraordinary number of people appeared to exist on little more than potatoes and weak tea.

The slum dwellings of many workers were stifling, too – shared beds, little space in which to relax, not the most appealing of places to return home to after a hard day's graft. Often, single men were only allowed into their lodgings to sleep.

It's not surprising, therefore, that many men chose to repair to the inn after work, or gather in a new kind of institution: a club. This was a place for working men, like-minded souls whose self-respect, dignity and humour would be greatly enhanced if they could gather somewhere that suited their outlook on life. Unlike a pub, a club's existence was not for its owner's profit, and it was free of raggedy children and nagging wives.

The earliest known working men's club was started in 1850 in Reddish, an area of Stockport in what is now Greater Manchester. This was an area that developed quickly during the Industrial Revolution; the cotton mills needed workers, and terraced houses spread across the town to house the workers and their families.

The Reddish Working Men's Club was a place where men could socialise and relax after work. In fact, it was started as a mechanics institute by a local mill owner, Robert Hyde Greg. Greg had taken over control of his father Samuel's business on his death in 1834. It was an extremely successful enterprise that, by 1831, had five factories, employed 2,000 people and turned 4 million lbs of cotton into cloth each year. In the ensuing twenty years, he doubled the size of the business. He was a man who battled legislation to curb the employment of children, and, though he was said to be thoroughly unpleasant and argumentative, he made sure his workers were educated and went to chapel.

The club he built included a library, and soon many more workers, not just mechanics, were welcome. The club was located within the confines of Greg's mill and provided the comfort and warmth that most of the workers would not have had at home.

Similar clubs were then built and opened around the country. Many were in the northern towns and cities that served as the powerhouses of the Industrial Revolution, but it was actually the Midlands and Home Counties that saw the early growth.

A club opened in Hertfordshire in 1855, one in Cheltenham in 1849, and Walthamstow and Coventry both saw working men's clubs open in 1860. It was boom time in Northamptonshire as clubs opened in a number of towns in this period. Cheshire had one in 1875, Godley in Greater Manchester in 1872, and Rochdale in 1877. Then, further north, clubs opened in Northumberland and Scotland in the 1880s. In 1868, there were some seventy-two working men's clubs. By 1901, there were more than a thousand.

While food was not a priority, many did offer meals. However, few of them had very elaborate kitchens, and some used travelling caterers.

One such provider, at the turn of the twentieth century, was Bob Ludlam's business, which offered its services across London and advertised in the working men's club journal. An advertisement Ludlam placed in 1911 promised 'excellent dinners, teas, suppers, &c., at prices to suit all pockets'. Several clubs also encouraged men to join allotments, so that they could grow food and then share some of it at the club.

But, of course, these clubs weren't built or funded by the men who joined them. As with Greg's institution in Reddish, many were created by the owners of the industries in which the men worked. They were not free houses like the pubs the men visited, and there was usually a very crucial difference between the two: clubs didn't serve booze.

So was the spread of these clean, roomy environments actually a carefully managed form of social engineering? After all, the working classes, for considerable time now, had gained a reputation for sipping alcohol on an industrial scale. Whether this reputation was unfounded, or whether men really were drinking as much as their wages would allow during the week and then going mental when they received their pay packets on Friday night, a large number of people in the Victorian era perceived it to be a problem and decided to do something about it. One of them was London-born Henry Sully. Having succeeded in business in the railways, he entered the Unitarian ministry and became a very firm believer in the advancement of the working class. But one thing was holding it back: what Sully described as the 'wretched and degrading bondage to the public house'.

Seeing that these clubs were manifesting around the country, Sully decided to get in on the act. In 1862, he set up the Working Men's Club and Institute Union. He established an office on the Strand in London and recruited peers and MPs to support him. He rallied them to his cause, which was a combination of the social idea of a club and the educational hues of an institute. He even published a prospectus setting out his plans and ideals in order to help him raise interest and money.

The headline of his objectives was that working men 'can meet for conversation, business, and mental improvement, with the means of recreation and refreshment, free from intoxicating drinks', and stated: 'Notwithstanding all efforts made to improve the character and condition of the working classes in this country, intemperance, ignorance, improvidence, and religious indifference still abound among them to a deplorable extent.'

He praised the temperance movement – by now well established in recruiting folk to its teetotal cause – for the good it had accomplished, although, he noted, ‘it often fails to retain those whom it has reclaimed from intemperance, in not supplying something to occupy the leisure hours formerly spent at the public house’. He added that, when men used pubs for work-related meetings, even if no alcohol was involved, they all tended to repair to the bar afterwards, ‘especially the younger men’.

Sully encouraged clubs to have the idea of education written into their constitution, so you might have seen men gathering to play cards, dominoes or cribbage in one corner, quietly reading the newspapers or magazines provided (which they wouldn’t otherwise have been able to afford) in another, or even taking discreet lessons in literacy. Typically, a club had a room that served refreshments; other rooms might have included a billiards table, a reading room and a main hall, often with a stage at one end, so that the room could be used for debates and talks.

According to records, suitable addresses doing the rounds at the clubs included one by a J. T. A. Haines of University College on ‘The Reformation’, and another delivered by Rev. E. M. Walker of All Souls College on ‘Peasant Partnership’.

Thirteen clubs were created in the first year of Sully’s cause, and another thirteen organisations – such as Greg’s mechanics institute – were amalgamated. The following couple of years saw some 300 clubs pop up across the country under Sully’s auspices.

But, while his constitution suggested that 50 per cent of committees should comprise working men themselves, there was a growing feeling among both members and patrons that Sully’s hand was somewhat supercilious. Indeed, one such patron was the Scottish aristocrat Lord Rosebery, who said that working men ‘are to be raised by their own endeavours and are not to be patronised, and fostered and dandled’. And a bricklaying member of the Scarborough Working Men’s Club even stirred up a revolt against the benefactors, forming a new committee composed solely of working men. Speaking on that new committee, he talked of ‘the patronising spirit, which was too much shown towards the working classes’. This feeling spread among the clubs, and, by the late 1860s, according to historian John Taylor, writing 100 years later, ‘a revolt against patronage was well under way’.

Clubs moved to evict non-members from their boards, and then they voted to dismiss their patrons altogether. Of course, they needed to fund their clubs, since previously their work managers or posh patrons had provided the money. So the members did two things: they introduced a small and affordable membership fee and they raised further funds of their own – by selling alcohol.

The economically shrewd quickly realised that, because they were clubs, they could sell beer without the need to make a profit, thus undercutting pubs and attracting more members. And they were further cheered in this cause by Lord Rosebery, who announced that clubs 'should be free from all vexatious, infantile restrictions on the consumption of intoxicating drinks'.

Sully also suffered attacks from another peer. Lord Stanley wrote in *The Times* about Sully's high-minded, Unitarian interference. He said that working men wanted social clubs 'not schools in disguise'. There was also a disparaging letter from a Lord Lyttelton in the *Saturday Review*. The peer had written that the best thing Sully and his counterparts could do was 'withdraw themselves utterly and for ever away from the concern, and leave the artisans to manage their own affairs', since they were 'hovering crushingly' over the clubs and their members.

So, in July 1868, Sully sat down and wrote a long – and furious – public statement, correcting what he saw as untruths circulating about his beloved network of clubs. It was entitled 'Facts and Fallacies connected with Working Men's Clubs and Institutes'. In it, he defended the charge that he and his ilk had patronised members. 'We have pre-eminently aimed at inducing working men to establish these clubs by and for themselves,' he wrote, adding crossly: 'We only wanted to help working men to help themselves, not to do the thing *for* them.' He also addressed the attacks in the press. '*The Times*, Lord Stanley, and the *Saturday Review* do not maintain that consummate ability … to dispense with accurate information,' he stormed.

The men who joined these clubs needed him, he argued: 'They cannot either establish or work a club without some help (*not merely in money, remember*) from middle-class people.' And many of these men required his help because of the resistance they faced from their own ilk, who scoffed at the idea of meeting in a club rather than a pub, and mocked those who encouraged it:

> *There are always plenty of working men … who have no relish for the rational amusements and quiet social intercourse that the clubs afford and a great relish for the fun of chaffing those who have higher or more orderly tastes than their own. But there are few things the British workman fears one tithe as much as ridicule.*

They would rather face death in battle, he continued, than suffer 'persecution … when they attempt to lead their mates in a more civilised way'.

So it was up to men like him, who had 'public spirit and good social position', to help members through this maze of mockery, financial angst and administrative complexity. And, he added, when he was actually among the men, the mockery stopped and they all behaved themselves. He even quoted one man as telling him: 'Why, Mr Sully, we treat one another so much better when there's a gentleman among us.'

As for Lyttelton's attack in the *Saturday Review*: it was preposterous, railed Sully. 'You might as well expect an army to conquer without officers.'

Sully was proud, he concluded, to have offered 'working men a substitute for the street-corner or the tap-room'. But one suspects that what really irked him was the tone of the attacks and the fact that they were coming not from well-to-do middle-class men like himself, but from members of the aristocracy – toffs whom he clearly despised. Perhaps he assumed that they gathered to concoct their attacks on him in another institution, one that he was also unwelcome in: the gentlemen's club.

For the growth of working men's clubs mirrored the expansion of this other type of establishment, one peculiar only to the English. It was an institution that, at the end of the eighteenth century, emerged from the culture of the coffee house (Chapter 5). Like the working men's clubs, there were billiards tables, shelves of literature, and food. And there was most definitely – and unashamedly – alcohol. Plenty of it.

Due to the generosity of the benefactors, many of the working men's clubs were in pretty decent buildings – new constructions that we would today classify as typically 'Victorian', often redbrick and Gothic Revival in style. But the gentlemen's clubs were, of course, significantly grander. Indeed, many of them mimicked the rural stately homes owned by a large number of their members.

As coffee houses widened their customer base, the gents had looked around at some of the people languishing at the fringes of their company – and sometimes listening in – and had decided that they were getting a little too close for comfort. While some coffee houses had the feel of a club, there was never any official barrier to entry. So, as gentlemen found themselves increasingly drawn to London, either for business or social reasons, they wanted a place that was conducive to their tastes – rooms that felt like their own libraries, studies and dining rooms. Thus, the gentlemen's clubs were built and furnished in a similar style, and the men who served in them dressed like the butlers and footmen in private homes. Moreover, while the gentlemen might have wished for their own libraries and studies to be

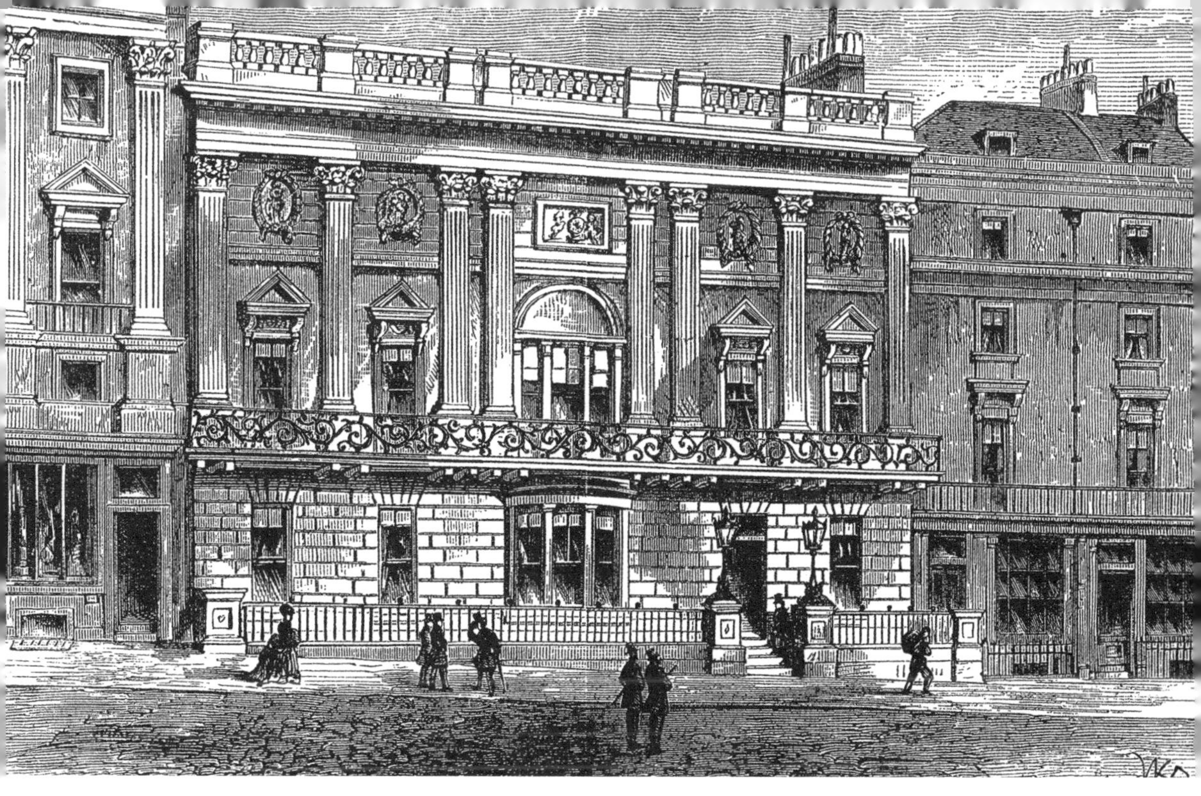

White's club on London's St James's Street began as a chocolate house in Mayfair and became a refuge for aristocrats who disliked the mixed company of coffee houses.

free of the fairer sex, in London, at their clubs, women were banned from joining. Indeed, if women ever tried to enter a club, they would be physically prevented from doing so.

Some gentlemen's clubs were in existence in the seventeenth century, but they grew fast in the latter part of the nineteenth century. In 1850, there were thirty-two listed in *The British Almanac* (with thirty of them in the West End of London, mostly along Pall Mall and up St James's Street). By 1910, that number had grown to eighty-one.

The oldest club was – and remains – White's. According to London clubs historian Amy Milne-Smith, 'White's is the archetype of clubland.' It began as a club within a chocolate (rather than coffee) house, just off Curzon Street in Mayfair, opened in 1693 by an Italian called Francesco Bianco. He decided that he would better attract customers if he gave his place a name with softer, more English connotations. So he called it Mrs White's Chocolate House.

A group of men met regularly at White's to gamble. And, as happened in other coffee houses, they segregated themselves from the rest of the customers, as they wished to gamble with their own kind, whom they could trust to honour any debts. Records of White's say that the men inaugurated themselves as a club in 1697. In the words of Milne-Smith: 'The club at White's was created, and for many years existed, within the larger chocolate house, before taking over the whole; this process was repeated at several other coffee houses and taverns.'

Some ninety years later, and with a reputation as a gaming house for racy aristocratic members, it moved to St James's Street, where a building was refit in the Palladian style. The tall-ceilinged dining room, with its portraits of royalty hanging against its striking crimson wallpaper, was called the Coffee Room.

The club became the unofficial HQ of the Tory Party and morphed into a discreet haunt for friends. White's membership committee took a very dim view on anyone attempting to join or on any members who used the place for business – values the club still holds dear to this day.

More clubs were built as men sought their privacy and seclusion and began to identify with their particular establishment; 'clubman' became a new word for 'gentleman'. The clubs enabled members of the upper classes who might not

The Bombay Yacht Club: one of a number of gentlemen's clubs whose concept originated in London and then spread across the British Empire to offer reassuring sanctuaries for army officers overseas.

have had their own aristocratic pile in the country to dwell within one while in London. As clubs opened across the town – places like Boodle's and Brooks's, and then, in the early nineteenth century, the Reform Club, the Travellers Club and the Athenaeum Club – so, too, did they spread across the empire.

Serving officers could retreat from the heat and dust of Bangalore or Bombay and seek the reassuring English style of comfort in the clubs there, many of which were founded in the second half of the nineteenth century. They could regroup over a drink, in their sanctuary and with their own kind, away from the pesky locals. The reinforcement of this entitled privilege formed part of the backbone of how the empire was ruled. It was a spirit that came directly from the exclusive heart of St James's. The dominating structures of those clubs symbolised the part of London in which they stood – a mere few hundred yards from Queen Victoria's Buckingham Palace – as the centre of wealth and influence. Thus, bearing in mind the expanse of the empire, you could say it was in fact the centre of the world.

But not everyone was impressed. Decades later, as recalled in his book *A Wanderer in London*, Edward Lucas found himself walking down Pall Mall on a wet day. Born in Kent to a humble family of Quakers, he visited the street in 1905 and felt hemmed in, claustrophobic even, with such vast austere edifices on either side, shielding the street from light. He returned another day when the sun was shining, but found little improvement. 'There is something chilling about these huge, sombre, material monasteries called clubs, solemn temples of the best masculine form, compounded of gentlemen and waiters, dignity and servility,' he wrote. 'They oppress me. Pall Mall has no sweet shade; its shade is gloomy.'

Lucas, in due course, became a successful writer and publisher, and it seems he got over his initial angst about these seemingly impenetrable fortresses, as an obituary appearing after his death in 1938 revealed his membership of four such places: the Athenaeum, the Beefsteak, Buck's and the Garrick.

But, a few decades prior, behind the facades of the buildings that were rattling Lucas, there was something more than just gambling, conversation and drinking being indulged in. There was food. And some of it was very good indeed.

In fact, several of the most legendary chefs of nineteenth-century London emerged from clubland. There was Alexis Soyer, for example. His kitchens were in the Reform Club and they were probably the finest in London.

Soyer's story somewhat mirrors Carême's (Chapter 8). He was a working-class Frenchman who became an extraordinary chef, some of his talents

Alexis Soyer, who created the most influential working kitchen in Europe at the Reform Club.

manifesting in vast culinary feats, from 10ft-high desserts to thirty-course banquets. He was the author of bestselling cookbooks and the inventor of ingenious kitchen gadgets. But he was a man whose death was not marked by any tributes from the establishment figures whose bellies he indulged. The day after his funeral at Kensal Green cemetery on 11 August, the *Morning Chronicle* newspaper, a Whig-supporting organ, reported that 'none great and noble stood around his grave'.

Born in 1810, north-east of Paris, in Meaux, a town famous for its Brie cheese, he moved to the capital as a teenager and spent his formative years at Rignon's restaurant on Rue Vivienne. He was then engaged as a private chef to some smart Parisian families before being employed full-time as number two in the kitchen of France's prime minister.

But political turmoil in July 1930 rattled him, so he left for London, where his skills were snapped up by the Duke of Cambridge. He then worked for a number of aristocrats, before arriving at the Reform Club.

The start of his career at the Reform coincided with a major building project for the club. It was a three-year construction and its renaissance grandeur would eclipse all other clubs. If the Italianate saloon and column-lined gallery were to impress members of rival clubs, then the staff of the likes of Boodle's or Brooks's would hardly have believed what went on behind the scenes, in the kitchen. Having wowed with his coronation banquet in 1838, which fed 2,000 members of the aristocracy, Soyer was given carte blanche to design a kitchen with architect Charles Barry.

His ideas included: ovens with new state-of-the-art temperature-controlled flames; fish slabs cooled by running iced water; mechanical spits driven by steam; and small lifts to get food from the kitchen to the dining room servery, two floors up. As Ruth Cowen wrote in her biography of Soyer, *Relish*: 'Over the next three years, the fertile genius of the architect and the practical ingenuity of the young chef would combine to produce the most famous and influential working kitchen in Europe.'

When the building opened on 24 April 1841, the members, open-mouthed, toured their magnificent new facilities. And then they did something that was unheard of at the time: they went down to the basement and visited the kitchen. Soyer's domain was a series of interconnecting chambers with no doors, so that he, forever in his red velvet beret, could move nimbly from room to room. Two huge ranges dominated the roasting room – one could even take a whole sheep – and, in other rooms, there were small ovens dedicated to soufflés, charcoal grates, hotplates, steam ovens and boiling stoves. A vast tin-plated screen on wheels protected the cooks – and visitors – from the intense heat of the flames. 'Soyer often used them as a party piece,' wrote Cowen, 'flinging them open so that his visitors would jump in shock, entirely unaware that they had been standing so close to such an intense fire.'

Another fireplace was devoted to the roasting of game and poultry, and there were large bain-maries for soups and sauces. There was a separate butcher's room, kept to a constant temperature of 35 degrees, in which whole carcasses were broken down and game was cleaned and prepped. A cool room housed pastry and confectionery, and another was dedicated to veg.

There were rooms for staff, a butler's room, a staff dining room, and a room in which a kitchen clerk would use a system of speaking tubes to oversee deliveries at ground level.

But it was Soyer's gas stoves that were his greatest accomplishment. They were clean, smoke-free and controllable. Moreover, fed by the world's first public gasworks, they were a perfect example of how the Industrial Revolution, reaching into the Victorian era, transformed civilised living.

It was, Soyer wrote, 'the greatest comfort ever introduced in any culinary arrangement'. Carême, Soyer's hero, had suffered an early death because of his exposure to fumes and the bad ventilation of kitchens. Soyer could create culinary art and still breathe properly. 'You obtain the same heat as from charcoal the moment it is lit, it is a fire that never requires making up, it is free from carbonic acid, which is so pernicious and creates neither dust nor smell.'

Soyer's kitchen became a talking point in London's clubland and there was coverage of it in newspapers and magazines. *The Spectator* wrote of 'matchless culinary arrangements'; another magazine said that 'Soyer is the glory of this edifice'.

In creating a matchless kitchen, Alexis Soyer achieved something no one might have thought possible in the Victorian era: he got the smart set talking about food.

Soyer's kitchen achieved something unthinkable in the Victorian era: it got the smart set talking about food.

Out of his kitchen came consommés and soups, lightly poached fish – from turbot to salmon – with delicate sauces, lobster, platters of baby turkeys, hares in all kinds of sauce, from redcurrant to watercress, complex dishes of pastry, flourishes of truffle here and there, roasted and stuffed chickens, and glazed sweetbreads. There were cakes and meringues, pastries and chocolate, fruits cut and displayed as art. And everything was brought from the kitchen to the table on glistening salvers, under cloches of all sizes, and served onto beautiful china plates.

The visit of Ibrahim Pasha of Egypt to the Reform in 1846 saw what Milne-Smith called 'the most sumptuous and impressive meal ever served in England'. Its pièce de résistance was a 2.5ft-tall pyramid of meringue coated with spun sugar and filled with pineapple cream.

But it wasn't such fantastical banquets that had the greatest impact. Soyer also set a new standard. Now that they could see the possibilities – that the food at lunch could be as much pleasure as the company and the wine – culinary ordinariness would no longer be tolerated in clubs.

It soon seeped out of clubland. And so did Soyer. Having funded his masterpiece, the Reform was keen to maximise its income and therefore increased the number of covers and meals. Soyer felt he couldn't maintain his quality at that volume, so, in 1850, he quit. A year later, he opened Gore House, a restaurant in Kensington, hoping that visitors to that year's Great Exhibition would flock to him. But the kitchens would never live up to his expectations and, a better chef than he was businessman, the restaurant, although popular, lost money and soon closed.

Having fed the well-healed, he turned his attentions to feeding the British Army, funding a trip to Crimea himself. He teamed up with Florence Nightingale and reorganised the provision of food in the field hospitals. Later returning in 1857, he spent his remaining years advising the army on catering, as well as delivering occasional lectures.

He had forever changed the London dining scene, but none of those aristocratic bellies showed themselves at his funeral. Because, while food is key to the success of a great meal, for the British, it was not the most important thing. The Victorian upper classes weren't ready to fully champion a chef and his food, and make him the overriding topic of conversation. That would take at least another 100 years.

10

Britannia & Co. Opens in Bombay

One restaurant became a story of immigration, loyalty, identity, amalgamation and longevity, and, ultimately, how a restaurant can provide a space shared by people of all classes, sexes and religions.

In the year 2019, one February lunchtime, the 93-year-old co-owner of Britannia & Co., on Sprott Road in South Bombay, does his party piece to a table of English tourists.

'Please give your queen our love,' says the gap-toothed, round-spectacled Boman Kohinoor. 'This restaurant, like the city of Bombay, is short on space, but please tell her that we will do our best to fit her in.'

He then brandishes a laminated photograph of himself with the current Duke and Duchess of Cambridge. 'When I met them, I was awestruck. The prince was so charming. Princess Kate was so pretty and beautiful. They asked me how long I have worked in my restaurant and the kind of dishes I have been serving.' He also shares a newspaper cutting – a letter to the *Times of India* – entitled 'Let's bring back the Brits'.

To a modern, right-on millennial Brit, this kind of slavish loyalty to a regime of once brutal colonialism might feel awkward, not even offset by the tasty flavours of the restaurant's most popular modern dish, berry pulao (a basmati rice dish scented with zereshk – barberry – berries).

Yet the restaurant is a living symbol of an establishment that is a union of class, sex, religion, taste and imagery. A portrait of Queen Elizabeth II wearing the Imperial State Crown and royal regalia – a living representative of what was once the world's greatest coloniser – hangs proudly next to one of Mahatma Gandhi, leader of the Independence Movement, who fought – with non-violence – against British rule.

The restaurant itself is filled with men and women, people of differing classes and religions. The menu is a mixture of traditional Parsi pulavs (rice dishes) and

Boman Kohinoor in Britannia & Co. The Iranian café, opened by his father in 1923, originally served clean and simple food that appealed to the cautious British palate.

dhansaks (lentil-based dishes), Muslim biryanis, south Asian masalas, Indian kheema, and a decidedly English egg sandwich.

The flags of India and Iran are framed adjacent to each other. Vast signs are written in English, but are decidedly Indian in tone. 'THIS EATING HOUSE PREMISES IS FIRE COMPLIANT', reads one. 'PLEASE DO NOT ARGUE WITH MANAGEMENT', says another.

At the top of the menu is the image of a chicken, encircled with the words: 'There is no love greater than the love of eating – since 1923'. That was the date Boman's father opened the place. It was a restaurant that showed how an immigrant community had become entrenched in the fabric of Bombay, and yet, through its menu, also showed forceful loyalty to the British rulers: it was continental. In the words of Boman: 'The British did not want spicy food, so we catered for their palates.'

The restaurant also catered for British architectural tastes, which were on display as the empire extended its colonial tentacles, for it was designed by the same man who built the Gateway of India. Scottish-born architect George Wittet constructed the vast arch to commemorate the 1911 arrival in Bombay of King and Emperor George V of Britain and his wife, Queen and Empress Mary. The finishing of the monument and the opening of the restaurant coincided in the early 1920s. Two years after the restaurant opened, Wittet contracted dysentery, though probably not from dining at Britannia & Co., whose approach to cleanliness, as well as non-spicy food, was also intended to appeal to the local British residents. The dysentery became acute. Wittet suffered severe abdominal pains and a very high fever. As he lay sweating on his bed, the punkah wallah's fan doing little to ease his discomfort, perhaps he thought back to his childhood spent in Blair Atholl, a small village in Perthshire in a valley of the Grampian Mountains, in the shadow of the Duke of Atholl's vast and stately Blair Castle. Maybe he contemplated the cool waters of the River Garry, which flowed by the village and powered the local mill that produced oats for his family's porridge. How he would have missed the fresh air, rain and simple food of Scotland as he lay sweltering in the Indian heat, before finally succumbing to his dreadful ailment.

Britannia & Co. is part of the Ballard Estate, an Edwardian neoclassical block that, locals say (few of whom rely on hands-on experience), thanks to Willet, feels like London.

The name of the restaurant itself is, of course, the personification of the United Kingdom. Britannia & Co. shows the power of symbolism that can derive from a restaurant.

To describe its founder Rashid Kohinoor as a migrant is a little disingenuous. He was a Parsi; his ancestors fled Iran – or Persia – at various stages during the Arab conquest of that country, partly to avoid having their religion extinguished by Islam between AD636 and 651. The Parsis are also termed Zoroastrians, because those particular Persian immigrants

The Parsis settled across India and became skilled at integrating themselves with incumbent rulers.

were fleeing the persecution of their religion, which was a complex blend of an ancient tradition of spirits and divine beings, songs, poems and the thoughts of the prophet known by the Greeks as Zoroaster, who was born around 1500 BC.

The Parsis came to India and gradually settled in various cities and towns, until a number of them moved to Bombay in the nineteenth century. There they grew in size and stature. To the scattered communities of Parsis across India, this became the principal community – the Parsi leaders – whose priests inherited the mantle.

They integrated into Bombay life and became part of the political culture of the city. But they tended to be loyal to whichever regime was ruling. Parsi tradition favours the constant improvement of life – the logic of which persuades followers to support whomever is in power.

So, over time, they showed loyalty to the Hindu rulers, the Moghul emperors, and then the British. This may have made them unpopular with locals – those put down or diminished by the incumbent rulers – but it suited the Parsis. Experience taught them that this was the best way of remaining intact themselves and preserving their own identity. To rebel could have resulted in them being wiped out, which wouldn't help continuity. As the historian Jesse S. Palsetia wrote in *The Parsis of India: Preservation of Identity in Bombay City*: 'They remained ever conscious of the need to safeguard and distinguish their minority community identity.'

British power was well entrenched by the time Rashid opened his restaurant. The British had been gradually extending their hold over the subcontinent ever since the East India Company was founded in 1600. As it traded, so it waged war on locals who got in the way of its businesses – from silk to tea, spices to salt. Power was consolidated after various key battles, and then – following the Indian Mutiny in 1857 – the British conceived an act imposing direct rule on the country from London, commencing the era known as the British Raj. This rule of India by the British crown existed until India gained independence in 1947.

The Parsis had incorporated themselves into the world of British economic and political power from the late eighteenth century, which had stood them in good stead. As Palsetia noted, this 'evinced the successful transformation the Parsis effected from minority community in the provincial setting to influential colonial elite in the new urban setting of Bombay'.

The Parsis saw an opportunity if they assimilated British values, and this, writes Palsetia, 'both competed and functioned alongside the Parsis' commitment to traditional identity'.

It was into this atmosphere of collaboration and opportunity that Rashid Kohinoor emerged. The food business was in his blood. His father had owned a restaurant in the city, near Bombay's General Post Office, named simply Kohinoor.

Kohinoor might have evolved – as other Parsi cafés had – from a bakery business. The Portuguese had introduced Bombay to using yeast in bread-making in the nineteenth century, and many Parsis embraced the practice and opened bakeries. *The Imperial Gazetteer of India*, a detailed chronicle of the likes of business, administration and economics, states that there were 1,400 bakeries in Bombay in 1901. The Parsi bakers then opened cafés as a means to sell their products.

For whatever reason, Kohinoor senior's place was sold, but, retiring from the business, he was still happy to encourage his son, and so gave him funds from the proceeds enabling him to open his own establishment.

Rashid searched for a site before coming across the Ballard Estate development, which was owned by the Port Trust. It was new and clean – unlike so many buildings in the city – and the area housed a large number of British, who worked for the Raj in everything from banking to trade, politics and the army. He started negotiations for a lease, but first he had to obtain a licence from the local British administrator.

Bombay in the 1920s was the city of a million people, where the buildings, constructed in the Victorian era, were still pristine and glistening. Victorian gothic structures – such as the High Court, the Victoria Terminus train station and Crawford market – lent a grand air to the city, although several such buildings were still flanked by slums, which irritated the British. From time to time, they cleared the slums and erected new developments, such as Ballard Estate. A few blocks away was also the grand Taj Mahal Palace Hotel, which had opened twenty years previously, built by Jamsetji Tata, founder of today's vast Indian conglomerate the Tata Group. It was the first hotel in India to have electricity, its lifts were constructed in Germany, its fans came from America, and the grandest suites were staffed by English butlers.

The streets teemed with locals, many dressed in white kurta pyjamas and wearing little circular white hats. Young Indian civil servants, cogs in the British Raj, wore dark jackets over their traditional dress and carried books and files. Men pushed or pulled long carts; other wagons were dragged slowly by pairs of oxen, and small carriages passed drawn by ponies. A few cars drove along, weaving their way past stationary cows resting in the heat of the day in the middle

Bombay in the 1920s was a city of gleaming buildings and a melting pot of global culture.

of the street and raggedy children walking arm in arm. Men washed using taps that spouted water from carved stone monuments, and, lining the streets, women sat on their haunches selling herbs and spices from wide circular baskets.

'The fifteenth century is constantly rubbing shoulders with the twentieth,' said American James Fitzpatrick in his travelogue film of the city in the 1920s. Fitzpatrick also noted the Parsis he saw at the Bombay racecourse: 'They are regarded as the wealthiest class in India and they are obviously the most progressive.' They were part of what he felt was an extraordinary mix of people. He saw 'Parsi merchants, Arab traders, Afghans and Sikhs, Chinese, Japanese, Malayans, Americans and British'.

Through Bombay, the Gateway of India, surmised Fitzpatrick, 'flows the commerce of an empire; great commercial houses, stately public buildings and educational institutions flank its broad thoroughfares; railways converge here from every state in India and steamship routes diverge to the ends of the earth'.

In the midst of this were British administrators, working in buildings free of the heat and dust of the city, who managed the vast bureaucracy that had grown to maintain Bombay. It was to one such office that Rashid walked and, as he went, wondered what the easiest way would be to get that licence to operate. It may have been the height of empire, but rumblings about British rule were well under way. Mahatma Gandhi had emerged as an activist at the end of the 1910s; Bombay was the centre of his operations and, in separate protests about pay and conditions, 1919 had seen the first major strike by textile workers.

Rashid's answer was, in fact, obvious; it was all around him. He would abandon the family name and flatter the local administrator instead. And, according to Priya Bala and Jayanth Narayanan, chroniclers of the great restaurants of India, Rashid had 'heard the local administrator had a thing for names associated with the British Raj'.

Having queued for the appropriate documents, Rashid then filled out a long form outlining his proposal, and finally added the name of this new place that would serve clean and simple food to the British: Britannia & Co.

He left the paperwork there and went home to wait for news. Rashid knew that licences for such businesses could take months. But, within days, he was summoned back and watched with bated breath as the British bureaucrat approved and then stamped his licence. The owners of the Ballard Estate – the Port Trust – then agreed a 99-year lease, and Rashid Kohinoor was in business.

Britannia & Co. was immediately popular with the local British, who felt at home in the tall-ceilinged dining room with its whirring fans, chiming pendulum wall clock, and a menu of food that they not only recognised, but might also allow them to get through the rest of their day without having to repair in haste to an unsavoury lavatory.

There were sandwiches, bread and butter, mutton cutlets, roasted legs of chicken, and even chocolate mousse. Soon, some of the city's wealthier Indians started to visit. They would have seen, among the waiting staff, a number of young boys and girls helping to clear tables, ferrying plates and glasses to the kitchen porter. These were some of owner Rashid's nine children, one of whom was Boman, who, aged sixteen in 1939, went from occasional helper to full-time member of staff.

He has worked at the restaurant ever since. One of his younger brothers, Merwan, joined him in the early 2000s, having closed another restaurant that Boman also had a share in. But, while younger than Boman, Merwan was more frail and naturally more reserved, so he sat quietly on a high chair by the front of the restaurant, watching the comings and goings. He died in 2018 at the age of eighty-seven.

Merwan's restaurant was also a Parsi café, named Bastani & Co. There was only one big sign in this place, but it made Britannia & Co.'s demand that there be no arguing with management look mild. Indeed, there wasn't just a single rule, there were twenty-one, and they are all worth noting:

> *No talking to cashier / No smoking / No fighting / No credit / No outside food / No sitting long / No talking loud / No spitting / No bargaining / No water to outsiders / No change / No telephone / No match sticks / No discussing gambling / No newspaper / No combing / No beef / No leg on chair / No hard liquor allowed / No address enquiry / — By order.*

Bastani & Co. was also a longstanding establishment in the city, founded in the late 1930s. Like its sister restaurant, it attracted a wide clientele. 'Everyone comes to Bastani's,' reported *Business India* in 1995, 'lawyers from the municipal courts, moviegoers from the Metro cinema, Parsis from the agiary [temple] next door, students from the St Xavier's College, journalists...' This Irani restaurant was 'part of Bombay's fabric'. When it closed in 2004, a letter-writer to Indian newspaper *The Telegraph* howled that 'part of our life has been lost'.

The regulars would miss its traditional bentwood chairs, chipped teacups, checked tablecloths, mirror-clad wooden pillars, and the huge glass jars that held biscuits and stood proudly on its shelves. They could then only imagine the café's mava cakes (made with milk and flavoured with cardamom), bun-maska (a bun sandwich crammed with butter), chicken biryani (mixed rice) or kheema-pau (spiced, minced lamb).

Kheema-pau could, however, still be enjoyed at another Iranian café, New Excelsior. And there were baked goodies served at Kyani & Co. Dozens of Iranian cafés had opened in the early stages of the twentieth century, many of which offered a variety of food familiar to Parsis.

In more recent years, the most popular dish at Britannia & Co. has been that berry pulao, created by Boman's wife, Bacha. She made a firm impression on the menu that Boman described as Indo-Iranian – dishes that were Iranian in origin, but that would suit the Indian palate.

Because, of course, after 1947, after independence, Indians didn't need to worry so much about the British palate. The British Army had actually requisitioned the restaurant during the Second World War, but, when Boman got his establishment back, Bacha got her hands on the menu.

'Gradually, once the British left, we did away with the continental dishes and started to serve Parsi food,' said Boman. A small selection of those mild dishes remained – as they do today (the sandwiches and the bread and butter) – but it was pulaos, dansaks, biryanis and dals that now shimmered on the menu.

Today, such cafés find themselves threatened by the modern world of Mumbai. A property boom in the 1990s, for example, pitted developers against the ancient restaurateurs. These humble places were suddenly slap bang in the middle of the most valuable real estate in India. If the owners refused to be bought out, they ended up in court. One famous victim was the Parsi café New Empire, for so many years perfectly perched opposite the Victoria Terminus. It's now a McDonald's.

New chains of coffee shops eroded profits, and that the cafés were often the locations for Bollywood movies counted for nothing. While many establishments had started to serve beer on a mezzanine level, a new band of licences – affordable by new bars, backed by new money – were too costly for them.

When Bombay's Bastani & Co. – founded in the 1930s – closed in 2004, one writer lamented that 'part of our life has been lost'.

At ninety-three, Boman continued working regularly at Britannia & Co., even though his own son took over as manager. 'I am ninety-three years old, but I still come daily to the restaurant for five to six hours,' he said. 'I go round and speak to my customers and I enjoy it. People say I should retire, but I don't like staying at home. I get up in the morning and, after I've refreshed myself, I feel restless. I just want to come to the restaurant.'

In 2004, the owner of Kyani & Co., Farhad Ottovari, looked wistfully over the road at the closed and shuttered windows and doors of his former rival, Bastani & Co. Their loss was his gain. 'Time is the destroyer and time is the greatest healer,' he said.

According to Indian author Sharada Dwivedi, the closure of places like Bastani was 'a huge loss to our cultural and culinary heritage. Irani cafés symbolise Mumbai's communal harmony like nothing else does.'

Any modern British visitor, embarrassed by Boman's slavish love of their royals, should see Britannia & Co. in the context of the unifying power of such places. As a new wave of establishments, whose culture isn't even skin deep, take over, Britannia & Co. should be cherished. It represents a message of harmony constructed over hundreds of years.

But time is also a looming problem for Boman Kohinoor. That 99-year lease is up in 2022...

11

The Invention of the Taco Machine

The postwar growth of suburbia and car ownership in the US helped to precipitate a revolution in fast food. Entrepreneurs took inspiration from the automobile assembly lines for the building of homes and the cooking of food. Hamburger shacks opened, and an appetite for a new kind of dining spread across the country. Some recipes were inspired by immigrants, and the invention of a taco machine in New York City, by a Mexican, precipitated an avalanche of cultural confusion.

It is most vexing for the racist anti-immigrant who bridles at the sight of brown faces obscuring his horizon to then find himself gleefully slobbering over their curries, fried rice, chows or tacos.

What history shows is that the belittled immigrant, having fed furious citizens of his host nation, sees his dishes grasped from under him, assimilated to better suit those citizens' palates – bastardised so they become economical to sell, and then given a label that shrouds and masks their original, foreign origins.

Future diners perceive such dishes as local – sold on the street corner, even delivered to one's door. It's not just that they don't know of the dishes' origins, but, because they like the food, as do their family and friends, the people with whom they identify, they now feel that it is *their* dish, representative of *their* nation.

The story of the cultural appropriation of food is as current as it is old, and just as complex. But globalisation, the efficiency and speed of transportation and logistics, means that today it is more widespread than ever. Some are perturbed and angry about it. Others lick their lips. Some happily nurse their bank accounts as a result.

The sharing of recipes – that appropriation for good or ill – occurs because of history's intrepid travellers, including colonialists and conquistadors. Hernán Cortés revolutionised the western world in the sixteenth century when he returned from South America bearing the likes of cocoa beans, tomatoes and turkeys.

Italian immigrants in early twentieth-century New York, keen to taste the food of their home country, bastardised their own iconic culinary traditions.

Cortés followed in the wake of the voyage to the Americas by Christopher Columbus in 1492. The ensuing years then saw what is now called the Columbian exchange. This was not the swapping of a bundle of notes for a small packet of white powder, but rather the interchange of food, people, ideas and disease that occurred between the Old World and the New. Europe, the Old World, seemed to get the better end of the deal, receiving maize, sugar cane and potatoes, as well as tobacco for cigarettes, vanilla for ice cream and quinine for gin and tonics. The Old World returned the favour by dispatching Europeans to the Native Americans and giving them smallpox, measles and cholera. The New World did at least send the Europeans back with syphilis.

However, many of history's travellers were not conquering but fleeing, forced to abandon their homes, and, in doing so in haste, stuffing their pockets with seeds and beans that might remind them of home. Recipes were not needed because they were ingrained in the travellers' minds, as culturally significant as religion, songs and memories.

Early twentieth-century Jewish refugees from Russia arrived in New York, for example, with poppy seeds in their pockets, with which they made mohn cookies. It gave them a simple taste of home in a new and very foreign environment.

Tom Bernardin used to give tours of Ellis Island, the historic entry point for New York. On collating *The Ellis Island Immigrant Cookbook*, he noted: 'I became aware of how important food was to [the immigrants'] experience, not just on a nutritional level, but as a means of bringing with them, and preserving, this part of their earlier lives.'

Elsewhere, some farmers who fled the Congo in the 1990s took long-term shelter in refugee camps in Namibia and were able to grow aubergines from the seeds they brought in their pockets. And others escaping the Cambodian genocide of 1975 took seeds to refugee camps in Thailand. One such refugee, Voeun Tath, later moved to Dallas, Texas, where she still grows Cambodian bunching onions from those original seeds. As people like her fled civil wars and genocide, they managed to take a little bit of home with them. Don Lambert, who, in 2018, was managing a programme in east Dallas to encourage community gardens, said: 'Most people, as they move from one country to another, have often brought little samples of seeds, maybe hidden away in pockets here and there.'

The food cultures of certain countries also developed in other countries as a result of the general exportation of crops and animals. For example, the late nineteenth century saw the US states of California and Florida developing orchards for fruits, nuts and citrus. The soil and climate suited these products, and Italian peasants seeking new horizons migrated to those states to make their skills available on farms there.

Between 1870 and 1970, according to Donna Gabaccia, professor of history at the University of Minnesota: 'Over 26 million individuals departed from Italy as migrants, typically in search of work. The residents of Italy had long been poor, but only in the late nineteenth century did their poverty motivate them to travel such long distances.'

A third of those migrants went to North America, a quarter to South America and 40 per cent migrated to other European countries.

By 1920, there were 5 million Italian immigrants in New York alone. Many of these Italians worked in food businesses and created a demand for the exports of tomatoes, olive oil and pasta from areas such as Sicily and Palma. But meat was too expensive a product for export, so many relied on cheap beef, which, when minced, could disguise the onset of decay. This was used in Italian cafés in New York to make meatballs, which were served with tomato sauce in spaghetti.

In Buenos Aires, Argentina, the poorer Italian migrants pounded beef to resemble Milanese veal cutlets, which they cooked with tomatoes from cans that had been packed in Naples. In rustic Italian restaurants in the city, the dish was called *milanesa alla napolitana*. Neither the New York nor the Buenos Aires dishes would have been familiar to an Italian on the streets of Naples. Constrained by their own circumstances, but keen to create the food of their home country, migrants were bastardising their own dishes.

Given the high import costs, producers in the US started to make cheeses that approximated the hard ones of Parma, and growers in California cultivated plum-shaped tomatoes that resembled the varieties of Naples.

The Italian immigrant Hector Boiardi then took US-produced pasta, mixed it with the new home-grown tomatoes, and canned it, releasing his new 'Chef Boyardee' brand. Boiardi had owned a restaurant in Ohio, and so many customers had asked him if he could supply his spaghetti sauce that he had begun to make and sell it in used milk bottles. His upbeat and simple product attracted the attention of one of the major suppliers to the US Army, who, with 15 million soldiers to feed in the Second World War, found this an incredibly handy product. Boiardi's Pennsylvania factory had to operate twenty-four hours a day.

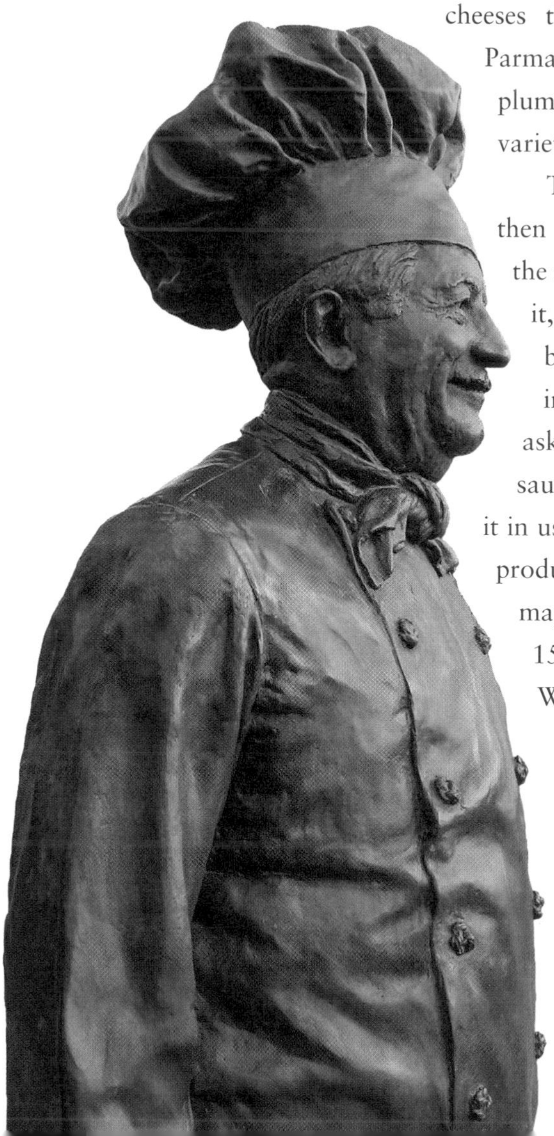

Hector Boiardi, of the Chef Boyardee brand, created a spaghetti sauce that helped to feed 15 million US soldiers.

The pizzas sold at the first Pizza Hut in Kansas in 1958 would have affronted a purist of Italian cuisine.

The army boys loved it, even the sons of Italian immigrants, and word then spread across the States about this Italian meal in a can. Today, the makers of Chef Boyardee products, the enormous Chicago-based American packaged foods manufacturer Conagra, distribute a dozen Italian-style foods, from ravioli and macaroni to pizza sauce and tortellini.

Is this Italian food, though? And what of Pizza Hut, which sold its first 'Italian' pizza in Wichita, Kansas, in 1958? It would surely affront an Italian purist, who would no doubt exclaim 'mamma mia!', if real Italians actually said that.

This is a universal story of angst and complexity, but no more is it exemplified than with the food of Mexico.

In 1951, a man called Glen Bell, who had been operating a business selling burgers in San Bernardino, east of Los Angeles in California, hung a new sign outside his shop that read: 'Tacos nine-teen cents'.

Bell's hamburger stand was 4 miles down the road from another burger joint, run by brothers Richard and Maurice: the original McDonald's (which had opened in 1940). This was three years before a man called Ray

Kroc partnered with the brothers and began to expand the business across the US.

The genius of McDonald's was its remodelling in 1948. In particular, unlike other burger stands in the city, its menu was much smaller. The offer was limited to hamburgers, fries and shakes; it didn't sell any food that needed a utensil to get said food into one's face. The kitchen was designed with heat lamps, so the burgers could be made in advance and customers didn't have to wait for anything to cook. The only extras were garnishes – ketchup, onions and pickle – and, with no plates, everything was delivered in a paper bag or cup, so there was no need for a kitchen porter to wash up returned crockery.

These economies enabled McDonald's to reduce the price of its burgers to 15 cents – half the price of its rivals. This was extraordinary and revolutionary, and queues – fast-moving ones – formed out of the door and down the street. Kroc then bought the franchise rights in 1954. By the end of 2018, there were some 37,855 outlets, in over 100 countries, serving 69 million customers.

Bell had watched with envy as the McDonald brothers' business flourished in those early days. 'You could look in the carport behind the restaurant and see their new Cadillacs,' he once said. The pair also owned and shared a mansion with twenty-five bedrooms.

Bell was having no such luck. His tiny shack, with a cubbyhole for selling, had been built by his own hands – and looked like it – and people were turned off by having to queue for their orders for fifteen minutes. Then, in 1948, a storm hit the city that proved the jerry-built state of his joint. The 80mph winds completely destroyed his building.

But, with a loan from the Bank of America to rebuild, he re-opened two months later and added hot dogs and root beer to the menu. He started work at 5 a.m. and served the last customer at eleven o'clock in the evening. It was a schedule his wife, Dorothy, couldn't cope with. On the birth of their child, she persuaded him to quit the business and get a job in a local gas station.

He did just that, but couldn't get his own ideas out of his head. He worked hard at the station, but, as he filled customers' cars with petrol, he kept gazing opposite to an empty piece of land. Then, without his wife's knowledge, he went ahead and leased that small patch of barren ground and built a new stand there. His wife found out and reluctantly agreed to let him quit the gas station job.

Meanwhile, his continued spying on McDonald's consistently showed him he was behind the curve. The brothers' constant innovations – from paper cups to

The remodelled McDonald's of 1948 had a simple menu, all the food was made in advance, no utensils were needed and the burgers cost just 15 cents.

modern sauce dispensers – frustrated him. And he also concluded that there were too many other burger stands in the city.

He needed another idea. Having dined at a number of Mexican restaurants (in particular, a neighbouring establishment called Mitla Café), he reckoned that, if he could copy their tacos, but produce them in an assembly-line fashion, he might be on to something.

'If you wanted a dozen [tacos] … you were in for a wait,' he later recollected. 'They stuffed them first, quickly fried them and stuck them together with a toothpick. I thought they were delicious, but something had to be done about the method of preparation.'

He explained his idea to Dorothy, who was still recovering from her discovery that he had opened a new burger stand. 'Tacos could be the new thing,' he told her over dinner at home, 'they'll make our place different from all the rest. I just need to figure out a way to make them quickly.'

She said something about their son, Rex, and how it wasn't her idea of a life to spend the rest of their days struggling in a poor Hispanic neighbourhood while he kept on dreaming. But Glen didn't hear her pleas. His mind was on the small wire form he had persuaded a man who made chicken coups to create. With this, he could dip the tacos into the oil and, as the shells crisped, they would hold their shape. The wires were made. Glen could then dip six at a time. Next, he invented a pre-fabricated taco shell that didn't have to be fried, only filled to order. His tacos were less messy than burgers and every order was gloriously identical – no extra onions or cheese.

Sales were small to start, but people needed to cotton on to the idea. 'Business is good,' he told Dorothy, 'slow but good. Tacos are the future.'

Maybe, thought Dorothy. *But you aren't.*

In 1953, she filed for divorce. Glen conceded and gave her everything he had: his house, his bank account and his restaurant business. Then he moved 70 miles away and started all over again. He dropped burgers and focused only on tacos.

Today, Taco Bell displays the awesome power of the restaurant franchise model. There are over 7,000 such eateries, with almost $2 billion of global revenue in countries across the world, from Russia to the Middle East, South America to Finland.

The growth of Bell's business was part of the postwar consumerism roller-coaster. In the US, between 1954 and 1967, sales of restaurant food doubled. This went alongside the growth in the food-processing industry. TV dinners became a national habit, and there was money to be made. Bell's experiment became a huge success story – particularly as middle-class white America warmed to ethnic foods, especially those nicely bastardised to suit their palates – but among other experiments were numerous failures.

The trail of fast-food flops is as doleful as a litter of discarded wrappers, burger boxes and drinks containers. Some never made it beyond a first store; others fell by the wayside. Many – those occupying prime retail sites, for example – were bought up and swallowed by big brands. US fast-food aficionados may feel a tug on their heart strings at names such as Chicken George, VIPs, Doggie Diner, Red Barn, Bennigan's, G. D. Ritzy's, Pup 'N' Taco, and Howard Johnson's. The stories of these restaurants are a tangy mixture of passion, hope, endeavour, success and failure, with plenty of finger-wagging Dorothies along the way, most of whom were proved right.

Meanwhile, well into his taco-empire journey, Bell had fallen in love again and married Martha, with whom he had two more children. He was once asked what had first attracted him to Martha. 'Her interest in tacos,' he replied.

However, what Bell sold as tacos, under his business's early guise as Taco-Tia, were completely different to what a Mexican – in Mexico – might consider a taco to be. Bell's tacos were hard. In Mexico, the hard shells were – and are – for tostados, which are flat. Bell's fillings had cold cuts of beef and salad, nothing else. A Mexican might tell you that a taco is a flat, floured tortilla, warmed on a grill, and, before the meat is ready, has diced onion and coriander added to it. Then can come sizzling, juicy strips of beef (*carne asada*), marinated, before being freshly grilled. Glen wasn't grilling meat – that was the beauty. He certainly didn't sprinkle any coriander leaves.

How the Mexican taco makers got the idea from which Bell then developed his tacos is a book in itself – indeed, there is more than one – and it's a story of cultural complexity, of New World meeting Old, and of common sense. People have been using flour or maize-based products to hold together bits of meat or veg for quite some time. However, in the words of Jeffrey Pilcher, author of *Planet Taco: A Global History of Mexican Food*, 'the taco achieved national hegemony only in the twentieth century'.

But was it Bell's legendary mechanisation of the taco's production that precipitated its leap to being a cornerstone of fast food? For the legend that Bell invented the first machine to make hard tacos is disputed by those who say he got his ideas from other Mexican entrepreneurs, and certainly his propensity to examine the activities of competitors suggests this is not unlikely.

Indeed, while Bell's first's taco was sold in 1951, a patent exists for a machine invented in New York, a year earlier, by Mexican-born restaurateur Juvencio Maldonado.

Maldonado had arrived in New York in 1924, at the age of twenty-six, possibly as a former soldier looking for a new life in the wake of civil war in Mexico. His girlfriend, Paz, joined him four years later; they married and started a Mexican grocery store on New York's Upper West Side. This was not to cater for a local Mexican population – there wasn't one – but just because the couple felt that their foods, the likes of salsa, tortillas and chocolate, would be popular with the neighbourhood. This was the era of the motor car, cigarettes, trams, wide streets and modernity. New Yorkers were up for the novel and the exotic. The couple worked long days and charmed the locals, but it was too hard. The ingredients were too unusual; the idea of cooking with items whose names people couldn't even remember by the time they got them home was just too much. So, in 1938, the Maldonados, still convinced that Mexican food could charm New Yorkers, resolved to make it easier. They shut the grocery store and, finding a small site in the West 46th Street theatre district, opened a restaurant called Xochitl, the word for flower in their native tongue.

The stout Maldonado decorated the place with sombreros and wooden American Indian heads, and at the centre of the restaurant was a large and vulgar painting of an Aztec eagle and serpent. This related the classic legend of the Aztec gods telling their people to build a city – Mexico City – on the spot where they saw an eagle consuming a rattlesnake.

The menu offered chilaquiles (corn tortillas), salad made with cactus, and that rich Mexican sauce, mole. The tortillas were made fresh every day, and from them came tacos (hard and soft), enchiladas (soft tortillas stuffed with meat, veg, beans or salad and covered in chilli sauce), and tostadas (crispy tortillas covered with various goodies, but invariably tomatoes, salad, refried beans and grated cheese).

Finally, the New Yorkers got it and flocked to Xochitl. They particularly enjoyed the crunch of his fried tacos. So much so that Maldonado – an electrician by trade – spent his spare time inventing a machine that would fry a large number of tacos mechanically. In 1947, he filed a patent for a 'form for frying tortillas to make fried tacos'. The application contained five elegant technical drawings on one page and a detailed explanation on another. It showed a hand-held device with a number of shelves that would contain the tortillas, which would then be dipped in the fryer. The drawings identify Juvencio Maldonado as the 'inventor'; he attested that the device was 'new', and the application was granted in 1950. (The patent finally expired on 11 July 2019, on the day this very sentence was written!) Not only did the device considerably increase the number of tacos that could be fried at one time, it also maintained some peace in the kitchen. While the customers loved tacos, the chefs hated their creation. The constant splattering of hot oil marked them with little burns on exposed bits of their skin and made their aprons filthy, and, even in their sleep, they never seemed to be able to escape the smell. When Maldonado unveiled the device to his team, they cheered. His invention, he later said, had restored 'peace after open mutiny among the cooks, who dreaded handling the fried taco orders'.

In the ensuing years, Maldonado sold his tacos 'to go', as an addition to his restaurant business. His invention saw tacos grow in popularity.

Perhaps it was a coincidence – innovation needed to solve the same problem at the same time – but the contraption that Glen Bell introduced to his taco shop in San Bernardino was virtually identical.

Yet, if Bell was guilty of the sin of plagiarism, was Maldonado guilty of a worse crime? Pandering to the sensibilities of New Yorkers by frying tacos and thus abusing his culinary roots? Was his adulterating of tradition, his hand in the Americanisation of Mexican food, an act of cultural treachery? According to the late Mexican poet Octavio Paz, 'the melting pot is a social idea that, when applied to culinary art, produces abomination'.

But another contemporary Mexican writer, Gustavo Arellano, defended the likes of Maldonado and even Bell's taco empire. 'We must consider the infinite varieties of Mexican food in the United States a part of the Mexican family; not a fraud, not a lesser sibling, but an equal.' Arellano felt that, 'wherever there is something even minutely Mexican, whether it's people, food, language or rituals, even centuries removed from the mestizo sauce, it remains Mexican'.

And Pilcher concluded that the struggle to define Mexican food 'has been going on for 200 years'. Indeed, he mentioned that even the definition of Mexico itself is questionable. After all, national borders, which change according to wars or diplomacy, do not weigh up considerations of food tradition when they are implemented. The Treaty of Guadalupe Hidalgo, imposed by the US after the invasion of Mexico in 1848, annexed South Texas, turning a part of Mexico into the US. 'A dish served on the south bank of the [Lower Rio Grande] river is the national cuisine,' wrote Pilcher, 'on the north bank, it is ethnic food. For families on both sides, it is simply home cooking.'

Pilcher, in his mission to get to the heart of authentic Mexican cuisine, went in search of the ultimate original style of taco. He travelled to Hermosillo. This is a city in the north-west Mexican state of Sonora. It is a city of flowers, of nature, of sport and of gastronomy. Its food is almost sacred. The city's tourist office states proudly that UNESCO dubbed its Mexican food an 'intangible heritage of humanity'. If you want authentic Mexican food, it's worth the journey. Indeed, it was quite a journey for Pilcher to make from his home in Minneapolis, especially when the fare in his own local Mexican joint on Lake Street – the tacos de barbacoa enlivened by a fresh tomatillo salsa – was fantastic.

In Hermosillo, Pilcher was put in touch with the local librarian, who, a cookery teacher as well as an authority on authentic Mexican cuisine, promised him the best tacos in town.

The place they went to was a Chinese restaurant.

Today, when the US is encouraged to disparage Mexicans, even by its president, who has pledged to build a wall to protect citizens from Mexico's dastardly crime and drugs, the most popular fast food – after the American classics of Subway, McDonald's, Burger King, Dunkin' Donuts and Pizza Hut – is Taco Bell.

12

Postwar Britain

Italian-born restaurateur Charles Forte won a contract to provide the catering for the UK's Festival of Britain: a chance for the country to show its booming postwar recovery to the rest of the world. Forte's high-speed catering operation fuelled his mission to build an enormous empire of restaurants and hotels across Britain. But the country was still under rationing, the shadow of which was long and ominous. In spite of a decade of growth in the 1950s, some felt the country's food offering remained poor. Twelve years later, a satirist summed it up on television in one word: disgusting.

Released gradually from the privations of war, the experience of eating out for pleasure for the average Brit was a novel treat. No longer imprisoned by fear and worry, misery and danger, in the words of the late founder of the Tourism Society, Victor Middleton, 'even a long distance coach journey would be seen as a much anticipated source of magic and adventure'.

At a time when seeing a banana on display at the grocer's was exhilarating, a visit to a restaurant was a serious thrill. It's hard to imagine today the novelty of being able to eat out without having to manoeuvre past a sand bag to enter a restaurant or being able to sit at a table knowing the chance of having to retreat in haste to a bomb shelter was now remote.

But, casting an eye across the culinary scene of late 1940s and '50s, Britain, from the comfort, security and luxury of 2020, was drab, bleak and grim. Indeed, perusing it even in the early '60s, some contemporary writers were pretty unforgiving.

One such critical voice popped up on 22 December 1962. The *Radio Times* schedule for the BBC listed the last programme for that day, before 'Close Down' at 11.40 p.m., as *That Was the Week That Was* at 10.50 p.m. On this edition, the show – as ever, presented by David Frost – featured the writer Bernard Levin. His role that night, broadcast live from the 2-year-old BBC Television Centre studios in London's Shepherd's Bush, was to deliver a monologue on what he saw as the state of the country's culinary scene.

'If there's one word to describe the British hotel and restaurant industry – and there is – that word is disgusting,' he said. 'There are other words that might be pressed into service in emergency: lazy, inefficient, dishonest, dirty, complacent, exorbitant, but disgusting just about sums up.'

He recalled a recent stay at a hotel in Dartmouth, where he asked the proprietor if he could be served breakfast the following morning at 8.15. The man looked askance and uttered the immortal cry: 'You're not on the continent now, sir!'

Levin's experience was akin to the witty assertion made by the Hungarian-born British writer George Mikes, who, in his 1949 book *How to be an Alien*, commented: 'On the continent, people have good food; in England, they have good table manners.'

During the Second World War, Britain had willingly succumbed to rationing (a policy that continued until 1953, as food supplies slowly got back on their feet), due partly to a combination of patriotism and economic necessity. Far better to lower one's standards and expectations than to be perpetually miserable and disappointed by the food offerings of one's country.

Indeed, Britain's capacity to merrily cope with the meagre ration prevented riots. The bureaucracy was so efficient in providing the ration, week in, week out, that the government's pledge to provide each adult with the likes of just 4oz of bacon and butter and 12 of sugar was always fulfilled. (Even if, behind the scenes, there were many cliff-edge moments, as merchant ships carrying food across the Atlantic, for example, were sunk, along with tonnes of meat, wheat and sugar.)

Government-run canteens, called 'British Restaurants' by an optimistic Winston Churchill, served simple, tummy-filling fare. One such establishment in Colwyn Bay, where the Ministry of Food was secretly located, dished up a shilling lunch consisting of soup, roast meat and veg, a pudding and a cup of coffee.

The development of these British Restaurants, or Community Feeding Centres, signified one of the vast social changes forged in the war years: the normalisation of eating away from the home.

The number of people who regularly ate out more than doubled during the war and, in December 1944, some 170 million meals were eaten out of the home.

In the words of John Burnett, author of *England Eats Out*: 'Eating in public, before the war mainly restricted to a privileged minority, had been familiarised and democratised by British Restaurants, factory canteens and not least by the communal feedings of millions of servicemen and women.'

While the quality of the food was not an issue, its functionality did not go unnoticed by everyone. The writer Frances Partridge visited one such café in Swindon during the war, and wrote that it was

> *a huge elephant house, where thousands of human beings were eating, as we did, an enormous all-beige meal, starting with beige soup thickened to the consistency of paste, followed by beige mince full of lumps and garnished with beige beans and a few beige potatoes, thin beige apple stew and a sort of skilly [thin porridge]. Very satisfying and crushing, and calling up a vision of our future Planned World, all beige also.*

Since Britain emerged from the Second World War victorious, as well as healthier than ever, thanks to the meagre but nutritious rationing and the fact that Britons moved rather more than they do now, there was no national urge to fill the land with great restaurants. Nor was there the resource of supply or capital to do so.

While people seemed to have generally slimmed down their food expectations mentally, it was also physical. Stomachs had literally shrunk. The founder of Quo Vadis, Peppino Leoni, re-opened his establishment – one that continues to thrive today – after the war, and drew a menu with just three courses. 'War and rationing had considerably shrunk the English stomach,' he later told his biographer. Nobody wanted a five- or six-course dinner, he added: 'What people wanted was well-cooked food, attractively presented in relatively small portions.' Similarly, Mario Gallati, who opened Le Caprice in 1947, commented in 1960 that 'our stomachs must have shrunk ... people today don't have anything like the appetites they had before the war'.

Elizabeth David may have brought a dose of romanticism to the nation with her 1950 *A Book of Mediterranean Food*, but, for most, it was no more real than a quixotic novel. While she spoke of French country cottages with wooden beams hung with fragrant herbs, markets where boxes swelled with ripe tomatoes, families who gathered around tables to devour rich cassoulets and vibrant salads, in Britain, even those with money struggled to cook her recipes.

Supermarkets did not offer such riches: olive oil – as has often been written – came in small bottles at the chemist; avocados were not even a pipe dream.

And, even if entrepreneurs did see a gap in the postwar market to open restaurants that tallied more with the romance of Elizabeth David, they were held back by certain wartime laws that were still in place. Price constraints that came into operation in May 1942 restricted to just 5 shillings (25 pence today) how much a hotel or restaurant could charge for a meal. The same law also limited the number of courses that could be served at three, and all restaurants had to be closed by midnight.

The legislation was intended to prevent the rich from flouting the ration by gorging themselves at hotels, but there was a concerted effort by the wealthy to preserve their lifestyle in spite of the war, known as Ritzkrieg. British journalist Sherelle Jacobs recorded: 'As the Soviet army captured Summa, The Buttery at the Berkeley Hotel was serving new-season caviar, lobster, quail richelieu and jalousie Parisiennes. Guests enswathed in furs and pearls were knocking back Monkey Gland cocktails with grenadine, and Old Etonians with almond liqueur.' While British troops were fighting the French for Palmyra, and Stalin was putting his 'scorched-earth policy' into play in the summer of '42, a wealthy Londoner was recounting a dinner he had recently enjoyed at the Savoy in his diary: 'Under the aegis of three waiters and sommeliers, we did dine on Pimm's, consommé frappe, salmon in white-wine sauce with new potatoes and asparagus tips, praline ices and coffee.'

Many wealthy people managed to get around the three-course/5-shilling restriction by bringing their own estate-culled produce to restaurants – in particular, those at smart London hotels. Establishments such as The Ritz and The Savoy in London were also allowed to add a further surcharge of 8 shillings and sixpence, enabling the chefs to add more dishes to courses, if not actual courses!

The three-course and 5-shilling law was repealed in 1950 by the Labour government before that year's general election, which they won by a slim majority. But caterers faced continued restrictions, and rationing wasn't completely phased out until 1954.

The war years had limited both experience and imagination. As a pronouncement in the late Leonard Lickorish's book *British Tourism* puts it: 'Britain in the late 1940s was virtually bankrupt, having exhausted its reserves on the war effort.' There was little or no international travel; holidays were very seasonal, domestic occasions. Only 50 per cent of the population could afford to stay away from home, about once a year in July or August. Rationing also continued on petrol until 1950, and car ownership was a privilege. Indeed, many

Rebuilding amid the rubble of postwar London – a city of bomb sites, hollow shells of buildings and dilapidated warehouses.

of the cars people did have were unreliable and built prewar, and they were only used in the summer. Motorways were not built until the 1950s.

London – and other major cities and towns – in the 1950s was still badly scarred by war. It was a scene of bomb sites, hollow shells of buildings and dilapidated warehouses. This was a time when the idea of exciting entertainment included driving to Heathrow, sitting on a chair provided, and watching the landing and take-off of planes over a picket fence.

As for food: cheese was a narrowly defined concept that meant industrialised cheddar; ales, while never rationed, were watered down and didn't get back up to strength until 1950. Dishes thought of as delicacies in places like Simpson's in the Strand in London included 'creamed spam casserole', and Prunier's in St James's featured 'sardine with potatoes land girls' (less intriguing than it sounds, being simply mashed potatoes with dried egg powder).

A Gallup poll in 1947 asked a cross-section of the population what they would consider to be the 'perfect meal'. The consensus was as follows, and in this order: a glass of sherry; tomato soup; sole; roast chicken with roast potatoes, peas and sprouts; trifle with cream; cheese and biscuits; wine with the meal; and coffee to finish.

The menus in restaurants or hotels that aspired to be smart were still mainly in French. And this was by no means just an English habit. The restaurant menu in the Russell Hotel in Dublin (which opened in the 1880s and closed in the 1970s) was almost entirely in French, from the *potages* to the *poissons* and *grillades*. One can only imagine the expressions on the faces of those who saved up for a special dinner as they wondered at the dishes – be they entrées of *noisettes d'agneau bouquetière* or *ris de veau braisés clamart*, legumes of *velouté d'espinard* or *endives meunière*, or a dessert of *coupe Monte Cristo*. Perhaps embarrassed to show their lack of French, they would plump for the only English words on the menu: under the *grillades*, there was a 'lamb chop'; the *buffet froid* featured 'roast beef'; and a section of 'savouries' offered 'Scotch woodcock' and 'Welsh rarebit' (doubtless to the disappointment of the French chef).

There was a minor revolt, a skirmish, when, in 1952, the Imperial Hotel in Torquay re-opened, and re-launched its restaurant, as 'The English Hotel in the Mediterranean Manner'. The announcement made it clear that, in future, all menus would be in English. The no-choice menu for the opening night was heralded as something dramatically new. It was as follows: melon cocktail in port wine; West Indian turtle soup with golden cheese straws; filet of sole St Christopher; breast of chicken 'Imperial Torquay'; salad of the English Riviera; strawberry ice cake 'Elizabeth'; Devonshire dainty delights; empire coffee.

The British tradition of writing menus in French has all but gone today, although Buckingham Palace still resorts to the custom. President Trump would doubtless have sympathised with those Dublin diners as he perused the menu at the 2019 state banquet at Buckingham Palace. It heralded such things as *mousseline de cresson velouté au cerfeuil*, *selle d'agneau de Windsor Farcie Marigny* and *tarte sablée aux fraises*. Perhaps Her Majesty reassured Trump that the menu was simply halibut, followed by lamb, and then strawberries and cream.

Some London restaurants, though, were a little more accessible. Leoni's Quo Vadis on Dean Street in Soho featured recipes for some of its classic dishes and sauces on the back of its menu. A note also read: 'Should you find any difficulty in preparing these dishes, Leoni would be pleased for his chef to give you a demonstration. Leoni would be honoured for his clients to visit his kitchens at any time.'

Peppino Leoni, of London's Quo Vadis, printed recipes on the back of menus and invited guests to visit the kitchen.

Eating out for many families was mainly experienced during summer holidays at fully catered guesthouses and small hotels by the sea. Coastal resorts opened again for business quite soon after the war in 1946, but amid the sandcastles and rock pools were still very visible accoutrements of war: barbed wire, gun emplacements and concrete tank traps. Given that so many beaches were mined during the war in case of invasion, it's hardly surprising that, postwar, some people felt nervous about visiting and letting children build sandcastles, regardless of assurances from the authorities that every bomb had been located and removed.

Meanwhile, in hotels and guesthouses, ensuite bathrooms were rare, hot water and new mattresses came at a premium, a midnight call of nature was delivered in a chamber pot under the bed and, wrote Middleton, 'visitors were expected to bathe before they came away'.

Government campaigns during the war had encouraged people not to travel. A famous poster of a soldier standing in front of a railway ticket booth declaring 'Is your journey really necessary?' was intended to make people feel guilty about the idea of travelling for pleasure. One version of the poster shows a wealthy couple and small dog contemplating the idea of buying a ticket. The man wears a smart blue coat, chalk-striped suit and shiny spats shoes. The woman is in a fur coat and smart red hat with a feather. The message is clear: even the wealthy and privileged question the idea of social travel.

Ingrained during the war, it was hard for many to shake off the guilt. Eating out had the same connotations as holiday travel. If you didn't need to do it, you shouldn't.

Of course, not everyone was of this view. Many demob-happy wartime survivors, freed from the shackles of restrictions, sought enjoyment whenever and wherever, as long as they could afford it. This meant they did not discriminate and were easily pleased. Many restaurants weren't any good (viewed with the benefit of hindsight from the luxury of the early twenty-first century) because they didn't need to be.

It can be argued that victory in war was achieved partly through a unified country, patriotic to the point of being inward-looking. As Middleton put it: '1950 Britain was still primarily the collectivist, conformist, mono-cultural society that it had been in the prewar era. Immigration was unknown in most places. It was by modern standards a repressed, authoritarian society.'

The politician and diarist Sir Harold Nicolson, husband of the writer Vita Sackville-West, grumbled in his diary in 1953 that, after visiting an inn in Newbury, he had endured

> *a poor luncheon ... They gave us what they call* tartelettes de fruit *– a crumbly piece of shortbread with two cherries and artificial cream. I despair of English cooking. It is no good training the producer; it is the consumer who must be taught to notice when food is lazily cooked.*

It was this lack of discerning customers that prompted the writer Raymond Postgate to publish the first *Good Food Guide* in 1951. This was less a guide of good food for experts and more the sharing of positive experiences from British people who ate out – and who, more often than not, found themselves disappointed. Postgate wanted the British to improve their expectations of restaurants in the hope that restaurant owners would, in turn, up their game.

Postgate, born in 1896, was a lifelong socialist and conscientious objector. He even went to prison briefly for his pacifist activities while he was at Oxford University, during the period of the First World War. Disinherited by his

Conservative-supporting father, a Cambridge professor of Latin, for marrying the daughter of a socialist MP, he was a prolific columnist and contributor to magazines. One might assume that, as a committed member of the awkward squad and a founding member of the British Communist Party, he wouldn't aspire to fine dining. Yet he had a constant bugbear about poor food and service.

In the magazine *Lilliput*, whose contributors included Sir Sacheverell Sitwell (grandfather of the author of this book), Constant Lambert and H. E. Bates, Postgate's column highlighted, with considerable wit, what he saw as the poor state of British gastronomy. He invited readers to share their worst experiences, and collected them under the imagined auspices of the 'Society for the Prevention of Cruelty to Food'. This he then turned into a more positive vessel, with the better reviews appearing in the first 1951 edition of *The Good Food Guide*.

In the guide, he beseeched diners to take a proactive approach to improving restaurant food and service. If, for example, one noticed that the knives and forks or glasses were less than shiny:

> *On sitting down at the table, polish the cutlery and glasses with your napkin. Don't do this ostentatiously or with an annoyed expression, do it casually. You wish to give the impression not that you are angry with this particular restaurant, but that you are suspicious after a lifetime of suffering.*

Postgate's first guide listed 484 restaurants, hotels and pubs. It is indicative of the closed experience of the British diner in those early postwar years that only eleven establishments served what could be described as foreign food, all of which were European, with only one Chinese restaurant.

Postgate created an informal army of critics. He gave validity to the views of the average restaurant-goer. He democratised eating out – for those who could afford it. And now there really was a reason for chefs and restaurateurs to up their game. In giving a voice to the dining public, Postgate anticipated the food bloggers of the twenty-first century.

The guide's publication, encouraging consumers and chefs to have a more positive outlook, coincided with a national campaign of positivity: the Festival of Britain, organised to promote the feeling of British recovery after the war and celebrate progress and innovation in arts, science and industry. Those who flocked to the main festival venue on the South Bank needed feeding. And the man who had won the contract to do the major catering was an entrepreneur called Charles Forte.

Forte, by the '50s, saw the increasing business prospects that postwar freedom offered. But he was driven by numbers rather than quality. Born in Italy in 1908, but raised in Scotland from the age of five, his father ran a large Italian café in the Central Lowlands, where his customers enjoyed soda from a US fountain, coffee from an Italian machine, and authentic Italian ice cream.

In his late teens, Forte found himself working for a cousin in Weston-super-Mare, in the south-west English county of Somerset. The business, co-owned by his father, was a café and ice cream parlour, and Forte worked long hours. His father then moved from Scotland, seeing an opportunity to grow the café business in various towns along the south coast, and Forte went with him. Some ten years later, he branched off on his own, starting Forte and Company in 1935 at the age of twenty-seven, having spotted a story in the *Evening Standard* diary column about an Australian – one Hon. Hugh D. McIntosh – who had opened a milk bar. 'I took a day off and went up to London to look at it,' he later reflected. The décor was simple and the drinks menu brief, but 'the service was quick, and the turnover fast'.

He returned to Brighton full of excitement and shared the idea with his father, who was less enthused: 'You can't make any money just with milk,' he told his son.

But, undeterred, Forte began stalking London's streets until he found an empty shop on Upper Regent Street. For several days, he sat outside measuring the footfall of passers-by; people queuing at the bus stop, students and teachers coming in and out of a local polytechnic. Then he worked out the space he would need and the staff numbers to make a profit, taking into account the large figure of £1,000 that he would have to pay annually in rent.

With money raised from friends, relatives and a very reluctant father, he opened the Meadow Milk Bar.

But Forte had got his sums wrong. He had too many staff and not enough customers. So he took the risk of letting the space next door, in order to accommodate more people, but cut the number of staff. This worked. By 1938, he had five West End milk bars. In the words of one obituary, written after his death at the age of ninety-eight in March 2007: 'The combination of calculation and ruthlessness did the trick, as it did repeatedly for most of the next sixty years.'

Business was going well. By the end of the '30s, the trend for bars selling shakes had taken a foothold in London, as well as in towns in Yorkshire and Lancashire, much to the surprise of commentators at the time. A report in

Charles Forte, who opened Meadow Milk Bar, was one of many Italians in London interned on the Isle of Man in 1940.

News Review, the London-based news magazine, in February 1937, commented: 'People laughed at the idea of selling milk in Fleet Street. By the end of the first week, they were gasping. The bar was packed out. Reporters who had never before been heard to call for anything weaker than Burton were passing their tankards up for strawberry shakes.'

Forte was one of several to cash in on the new fashion for milk-based drinks, and the same *News Review* story stated that, across the country, there were 299 standalone milk bars, as well as 117 department stores and thirteen cinemas with their own milk counters.

But the onset of war brought the idea to an abrupt halt. Milk was, of course, rationed, and Forte himself, still an Italian national, was arrested. In July 1940, as Mussolini joined forces with Hitler, in the words of Forte, 'the fate I dreaded came knocking at the door'. Along with other Italian hotel owners and restaurateurs, Forte was interned at the Mooragh Camp at Ramsey on the Isle of Man.

However, he was soon released and returned to London, where he continued his, now rather curtailed, business. His contribution was considered valuable enough to ensure him a place on a Ministry of Food rationing committee, and, after the war, in 1947, he opened his first of several large London cafés at the old Lyons tearoom at Rainbow Corner on Shaftesbury Avenue.

Rainbow Corner was originally a club for American servicemen, and it continued to be popular with GIs who felt they could have a taste of home at this 'American-style' milk bar. Forte used the US history of the building for a publicity stunt in February 1948, unveiling a plaque that was 'a tribute to all ranks of the United States services who knew the original "Rainbow Corner"'. He managed to persuade both the mayor of Westminster and a former US brigadier, who served under General Eisenhower, to draw back the curtains of the plaque in front of an assembled crowd.

Forte's property dealings were inspired by a cockney property developer called Joe Levy, who once said: 'If you can't make a damned good living within 3 square miles of Piccadilly Circus, don't try this profession. And never go into a back street.' Forte leased the site and took a £35,000 loan from Prudential Assurance, which also covered refurbishment costs.

His tactic for success, on the advice of Levy, was a leaseback arrangement. The annual cost for the whole building was £12,000, so Forte leased the ground floor and basement to himself for £4,000 a year, and the upper part of the building to the Ontario government for £8,000.

Forte's premises were clean and modern. But there was another aspect to them. As the *Methodist Recorder* journal noted in August 1948: 'What distinguishes Forte's establishments from those of its competitors? Throughout the organisation, there is a clear anxiety to "serve" the customer in the fullest sense.

As Postgate was putting the finishing touches to his discerning guide in 1950, Forte then leased and re-opened the opulent Criterion restaurant on Piccadilly Circus (originally opened in 1873). Again, while his lease of the building was £12,000 a year (he used much of it as a restaurant, serving the likes of Maryland chicken and iced gateaux), he sublet other parts of the building, bringing him additional and guaranteed income.

His talent for economics saw him win that major food contract at the Festival of Britain. In 1851, the Great Exhibition had brought people to London to celebrate the achievement of the Victorian era. Chef Alexis Soyer had hoped visitors would see the displays and then flock to his restaurant in Kensington (Chapter 9). But the idea had failed.

One hundred years on, one of the great restaurateurs of the day decided not to dally at the edges, but rather get an actual catering contract at the 27-acre venue on the South Bank. Forte's deal included running a 'Dairy Bar' (naturally) in the 'Country Pavilion', funded by the Milk Marketing Board, where you could buy milk in very modern half-pint cartons.

But his main task was designing a vast cafeteria where he could serve snack meals to thirty-two people every minute.

With sponsorship from suppliers, Forte calculated that many of the tens of thousands of visitors would consume everything from a glass of lemonade to a

snack. It was a huge venture, but, recalled Forte, 'no gamble ... We knew from the start that we stood only to make a great profit.'

He and his co-directors were on site every day – unlike, he later noted, his competitors, ABC caterers, whose attitude was 'setting things up and leaving the staff to get on with it'. Forte's mantra on the business of catering was defined by his Festival of Britain operation, and it is one that any aspiring restaurateur should heed:

> *You cannot get results simply by sitting back and giving orders. You have to get down to the nitty-gritty of the business. The people who work with you must be aware of the fact that you know the ins and outs of the business as well as they do, that you are prepared to work with them at all times, and that you are not the last to come or the first to go.*

Hugh Gaitskell, the leader of the Labour Party, whose idea it had been to create the Festival of Britain (Winston Churchill had dismissed it all as socialist propaganda), later praised Forte, calling him '*the* greatest caterer in the country'.

A plan of the Festival of Britain, for which Forte secured the contract to run a vast cafeteria that could serve thirty-two people every minute.

Forte built on this success by getting contracts to cater at the new service stations that were popping up along British roads, as car ownership increased into the 1950s, and becoming the first caterer at Heathrow Airport. He would go on to buy other major restaurants, such as the Café Royal, as well as a vast number of hotels. By the end of the 1950s, his company, Forte Holdings, was one of the largest privately owned companies in Britain.

An obituary in *The Guardian* after his death noted: 'Forte had catering in his blood, despite the calculated naffness and mediocrity of most of his businesses.' The unnamed writer talked of how Forte's talent was to make money from what others might have seen as a distinctly unpromising environment. His success was built on, what *The Guardian* called, 'the uniform blandness of the mass-market part of his empire'.

Indeed, when 34-year-old Bernard Levin, symbol of the intellectually rebellious youth, keen to outrageously cock a snook at the establishment on *That Was the Week That Was*, made his remarks in the early 1960s, there was a man in the studio who was forced to listen to his rant. Charles Forte was a special guest that night. 'Mr Forte heads a vast chain of restaurants and hotels, which cover the country; a good man then to speak up for British food and British beds,' said presenter David Frost. 'As a travelling man, Mr Levin has had a fairly nightmarish experience of both.' On the show, explained Frost, Levin would be 'confining his attention to one man: Mr Charles Forte'.

Forte sat there while Levin ripped apart his apparent achievements. And it was his business skills that Levin particularly lacerated. Looking squarely at Forte, sat mere inches from him, Levin argued that the 'attitude of the average British hotelier is that it is a business; that the rules of business operate as they would in any other business and it doesn't make the slightest bit of difference to him whether he's running a hotel or restaurant, manufacturing bootlaces or selling insurance'.

The audience laughed, and Levin turned to them to lap it up. He paused for breath, before turning back to Forte. 'He has no pride in his great craft, he has no feelings for service and he has no genuine wish to house the traveller or feed the hungry.'

Levin also castigated Forte and his ilk for turning away families with children and dogs, and attacked the lack of homemade and fresh food in so many restaurants. Chefs, said Levin, 'could make mayonnaise with egg yolks and olive oil, rather than providing bottles of salad cream, which tastes, and is probably made of, little but boot polish'. He then declared:

> *The reputation Britain has abroad as providing the worst public food in the world is almost entirely justified. Why is it that the great traditional hospitality of mein host, with his pride in good food, is almost entirely dead? Why is it that, in a city in size and importance as Manchester, say, there is not a single hotel I could recommend to a foreigner without blushing? Why is restaurant food in Glasgow so cold? The notion of good service is almost entirely dead.*

And 'why', he asked, in another direct assault on Forte's Heathrow business, 'is the catering at London Airport a major national disgrace?'

Forte defended his industry by saying that 'British catering is on a par with any other catering in the world,' but the audience spluttered with laughter.

'We increase our business consistently, so some customers must be very satisfied,' Forte said, and then argued that comparing British food to the experience in Europe was ill judged. 'If we changed the system of catering in this country to continental catering, you would be the first to complain. Life here is different. Our system of life is different.' He also suggested that Levin was simply 'travelling third class around everywhere', to which the writer responded: 'Why should [people] not have, at their price level, food that is warm and promptly and efficiently and friendlily served in decent clean surroundings?'

Levin concluded: 'I ate your bacon and eggs at lunch today. The bacon tasted of nothing but salt and I had to ask three times for a glass of wine, and the plate was cracked.' His critique clearly stung Forte. It was a rare outburst of public criticism for the nation's food and hospitality offering. *The Good Food Guide* aside, Postgate's negative musings were confined to a small-circulation magazine. Most people did not complain, though some have since suggested that Forte's business success depended partly on the low expectations of the British.

At the close of the Levin/Forte debate, the great caterer then made a prediction: 'In a few years' time, I think we shall find that people will be coming to Britain for cooks instead of British people going to the continent to find them.' Levin was aghast. The audience laughed. Surely that could *never* happen.

13

The Invention of the Sushi Conveyor Belt

Frustrated by the lack of space and staff at his sushi restaurant in the Japanese town of Higashiōsaka, Yoshiaki Shiraishi invented a conveyor belt to move his food around the restaurant. Gradually, sushi spread across the world, and the appeal of fish, especially raw, saw huge growth, being seen as healthy, clean and fashionable. But then environmental catastrophe loomed.

When Yoshiaki Shiraishi opened his first sushi restaurant in the mid-1950s, his town of Osaka could still, just, be referred to as the Venice of Japan. Osaka is situated at the mouth of the Yodo River, which runs into Osaka Bay. Tributaries were built across the town, and those canals soon formed a great watercourse across the city. The people travelled along the canals and under and over small bridges. But Osaka always had an eye on the future. Water failed to move people quickly enough, and railways soon took precedence over canals. Streets were then widened, so trams and buses ferried the population about. Soon, factory chimneys appeared on the skyline, growing quickly from hundreds to thousands. The population also grew, the town advanced to becoming an industrial metropolis by the end of the early 1960s, and the city's traditional oriental character was largely lost. Any similarity to a Venetian lagoon of the Adriatic seemed but a long-gone figment of romantic imagination.

The development had been unstoppable, almost feverish. The Japanese surrender in 1945, which helped end the Second World War, had disarmed the country, dissolved its empire and moved the nation to democracy. The national resolve to rebuild the country – literal, through reconstruction, and economical, with a great focus on education – was acute in Osaka. As in other metropoles, the administration was a driving force, but, of course, it also took individuals to maintain the momentum.

One cog in that unstoppable development was restaurateur Shiraishi, whose sushi shop was in the eastern part of the city. His first business, having left the army, was a tempura shop, which he opened in 1947. In the early 1950s, he decided to sell sushi rather than tempura.

Sushi had emerged as a way of preserving fish in south-east Asia in the seventh century, when it was pickled and fermented. It developed in time to being vinegarised, before the raw was introduced in the early nineteenth century, when it was prepared and sold from stalls in towns and cities. In the mid-twentieth century, when refrigeration made the storing of fresh fish more viable and widespread, sushi became more widely available. Then, as cities like Tokyo modernised and became cleaner postwar, the idea of eating on the move, or standing up, became less acceptable, and counter shops emerged. Raw sushi epitomises the Japanese philosophy of minimal intervention, of avoiding artificial processes and letting the natural tastes pervade. The extraordinary innovation of Shiraishi would respect this, but also enable another facet of Japanese culture – the eager embracing of modernity – while not interfering with the essential offering of sushi.

By the time Shiraishi was trading, the essential offering was *nigiri* sushi (hand-moulded) and *maki* sushi (a roll of sushi wrapped with seaweed).

His game-changing idea grew from a frustration about the lack of space in his shop. There was no shortage of customers, most of whom were workers in local factories, but he needed to find a way to increase business without expanding the premises. Even if he could afford to pay for some more staff, there was barely room for them to manoeuvre between the tables.

What he did next would go on to change the business of sushi in Japan, and eventually around the world. In fact, it would help take Japanese culture on a global journey. Because Shiraishi's idea brought together two things that diners, wherever they are in the world, can't resist: taste and innovation – the latter, providing it is functional.

In 1953, he was invited to tour the Asahi brewery as a favoured customer. There he was fascinated by the conveyor belts that moved the bottles of beer around the floor. Back at his shop, he sketched out a plan of how such conveyor belts could carry the sushi from the kitchen and into the restaurant, around the counters and then back to where the chefs worked.

He made some investigations and found the firm that made the belts for Asahi. He convinced them to make a smaller contraption for his shop. 'I need a

The conveyor belt at Genroku Sushi was designed to travel at precisely 8 centimetres per second.

small conveyor belt, which can move round in quite a tight circle and I need it to travel quite slowly,' he said, as he made his enquiry.

It was a slow process, but, finally, in 1958, he invited journalists to his sushi shop, now renamed Genroku Sushi. Having summoned the local press to his re-opening, he announced: 'My plates of sushi circle the room like satellites in the sky.' Shiraishi used the language of the space age as he ushered journalists and customers into his establishment that day. 'You sit at the counter and just pick whatever dish takes your fancy,' he said.

The machine was switched on and the chefs placed their freshly made sashimi and sushi onto the belt. 'The belt travels at precisely 8 centimetres per second, which – I think you will agree – is just the right speed. It is just the right tempo for you to see and contemplate which dish you would like – a slower speed would be frustrating and a faster one too frantic.'

But then a sceptical reporter, sitting on a stool with other journalists, watching the encircling dishes of sashimi, piped up with a question: 'But how will you know what to charge us when all there will be when we've finished is empty plates?'

His question was met with nods and a smattering of laughter from the assembled press throng, all squeezed into the small establishment.

'Look at each plate that comes out of the kitchen,' Yoshiaki replied. 'Each one has a different colour or pattern. To work out your bill, we simply look at the empty plates you have eaten from and charge accordingly.'

The journalists were impressed, and *kaiten* sushi was born. This literally translates as 'turnover' or 'rotary' sushi, and it refers both to the rotating wheels of the conveyor belt and to how Shiraishi could merrily turn tables in his restaurant. The shop normally could manage just ten customers at a time, but now, with his speedy new technology, meals were delivered quickly and customers were only too happy to participate in the innovation and – in the spirit of the shop – not linger. The footfall duly doubled within days.

The economics was a revelation. The chefs prepared the items without waiting for orders, and no serving staff were needed (just those to clear up, reset places and sort the bill). Shiraishi also got around the issue of how customers could have tea if there was no one to serve it. He simply fitted hot taps at each station. So, alongside the essential ephemera for sushi (chopsticks, ginger, wasabi and soy sauce) were little cups and tea leaves. The savings he made on staff meant that Shiraishi could sell his sushi at a lower price than his competitors.

In 1962, while Shiraishi grew his business and opened more branches, he managed to register a patent. But his registration of a 'conveyor swivel meal table' was not effective enough to stop others copying his idea. And there were critics, too. Some saw the focus on speed as detracting from quality. Years later, Japanese cuisine expert Katarzyna Cwiertka reflected: 'The quality of the fish did not match the high standards of the specialist (traditional) sushiya.' Aficionados urged people to avoid *kaiten* sushi. Before the conveyor belt emerged, according to author Gillian Crowther, sushi was 'made for wealthy patrons by intimidating chefs'; it was upscale and formal. It was for the middle classes, for corporate people, for those who had saved up to visit such a shop, with its wooden counters where a single chef might prepare fish for under ten customers.

So perhaps it was the inferior quality that held the business back from expanding beyond Osaka. At the Osaka expo of 1970, Shiraishi built a stand to demonstrate his now decade-old innovation. But most visitors to the exhibition assumed it was a brand new invention.

'Shiraishi's system was a revelation,' wrote sushi historian Sasha Issenberg. Other exhibitors at Expo '70 – the mantra for which was 'Progress and Harmony for Mankind' – were a US business called Kentucky Fried Chicken and McDonald's. Amid the futuristic buildings and sculptures, the towers and time capsules (sealed for 5,000 years), was a stand devoted to America's growing franchise fast-food business (Chapter 11).

Shiraishi spent some time chatting with those manning the McDonald's stand, and then spent the ensuing years rolling out his business using the same franchise/owner model, until he had opened 240 branches.

Expo '70, incidentally, heralded McDonald's arrival in Japan. Until that year, the Japanese government had not allowed foreign capital ventures to operate in the country (in spite of American culture becoming part of the country's landscape as the US went from enemy to ally after the war). But 1971 saw the first McDonald's open in Ginza, a shopping district of Tokyo. This was followed by further joy: Mister Donut and Pizza Hut were not far behind.

And, despite Shiraishi's patent, *kaiten* sushi bars spread across Japan in the thirty years that followed. By the end of the twentieth century, there were thousands. Today, there is at least one *kaiten* sushi bar in every neighbourhood in Japan – some 3,500 establishments.

Then, in 1994, *kaiten* sushi finally reached London, when Caroline Bennett opened Moshi Moshi by Liverpool Street station. Having lived in Japan for a year, she returned with a craving for Japanese food, but no experience of the restaurant industry.

So, while her day job was at an investment firm, she raised funds from City friends and a government loan scheme to sate her craving for what she described as 'the sushi iodine freshness of the sea plus the hit of soy and umami comfort of miso soup'.

She would rave to friends about her love of Japan – a country that, as she put it, was 'modern and sophisticated, yet so utterly different'.

She opened her restaurant, but then, having not quit her day job, was seconded to Tokyo for several months. Somehow, she managed to work overseas and oversee her new business.

Moshi Moshi was certainly novel. 'People thought that I was mad, that conveyor-belt sushi was a gimmick that would never catch on, and that the idea of the British public acquiring a taste for raw fish was inconceivable.' But the idea was a success and appealed to the workers in the City of London.

But she never turned the idea into a chain. *Kaiten* sushi would remain in that City bubble for a few more years, until January 1997, when the first of the YO! Sushi chain opened in Soho.

Caroline Bennett, who opened the first kaiten *sushi bar in London in 1994, took bluefin tuna off the menu three years later. They were 'too delicious for their own good'.*

The individual responsible was Simon Woodroffe. Unlike Bennett, he had no knowledge of Japan, its culture or food. Divorced, unemployed, running out of money and depressed, he at least owned a small mortgage-free flat. Opening YO! Sushi was, in part, a reaction to his very real mid-life crisis. He was, after a career in TV and music, simply scouting around for new ideas.

'I couldn't really be employed,' he once said, 'I was actually going to do indoor rock-climbing walls and that fell apart.' He had dinner with a Japanese businessman, who was one of many people he sought advice from as he pondered entrepreneurial options. 'I said, "What about sushi?" [Woodroffe had come across sushi bars in California.] He said, "What you should do, Simon, is a conveyor-belt sushi bar with girls in black PVC mini skirts." I'd never heard those four words [conveyor-belt sushi bar] in a row.' Woodroffe later recalled a voice in his head saying that, if this were a good idea, surely someone who knew a great deal more about restaurants than he did would have done it a long time ago.

Woodroffe used the only asset he had to fund the fit-out of a site in Soho: he took out a loan against his flat. And, with start-up costs of £650,000, he also procured two £50,000 loans from friends, and a further £100,000 from the same government loan guarantee scheme used by Caroline Bennett.

After 'two very full years' of researching, planning and arranging the building lease, fit-out and staffing hire, YO! Sushi opened. 'The first week, nobody turned up,' he later said:

And the second week wasn't very good either. And then the second Saturday, we had a queue down the block, and then we had a queue for two years after that. It was like having a hit record. [At first,] people were simply scared to come in. They would just stop and watch the conveyor belt going round. You have to remember that there were hardly any sushi restaurants at all in London at the time. Then it all took off, and it was all due to word of mouth. If people hadn't turned up, I would have lost everything. The relief was absolutely amazing, and, within a year, we had a million quid in the bank.

Writing after attending a press preview the night before the official opening, Peter Popham, in *The Independent*, said that YO! Sushi reflected 'the Japanese genius for linking industrial technology and sensual pleasure':

Because sushi is eaten cold, it can truck along on the conveyor belt for some time without deteriorating. Each serving is roughly the same size, so fits on a uniformly sized plate on the belt; and the special advantage of the belt system is that it allows customers to be impulsive, to grab on a whim. The direct relationship with the master is replaced by typically modern impersonality. The quality of the food is only a fraction of that found in a traditional sushi restaurant – but then, so is the price.

Today, YO! Sushi has 100 sites worldwide (including France, Greece and the Middle East) and, having made acquisitions in retail, with the purchase of Canadian chain Bento and UK supplier Taiko foods, which supplies pre-packed sushi to supermarkets, it then merged in 2019 with the US operator of 700 sushi kiosks, Snowfox.

Simon Woodroffe, founder of YO! Sushi, made £1 million in the first year of business.

Woodroffe's idea worked. And he'd never needed to put in a chunky order for PVC.

Yet Britain was quite late to the sushi party. In Australia, Brazil, western and southern North America and along the Pacific Rim, sushi emerged as surely as Japanese immigrant communities did. And they spread across the rest of North America in the 1960s.

There had been significant immigration from Japan to America during the early part of the twentieth century, but it ceased during the hiatus of two world wars. Immigration was made legal again in 1952 and, as well as new families arriving, established individuals became eligible for naturalisation.

The security that this brought encouraged Japanese Americans to establish more firmly cultural roots, and, in due course, these citizens sought and achieved success in everything from politics and academia to arts, business, technology farming and food. Many restaurants opened to serve these communities. Japanese businessmen travelling to the States also sought home comforts in sushi bars, and Americans planning trips to Japan got a taste of the culture and customs of the country in advance by visiting Japanese restaurants.

As Crowther wrote: 'An appreciation of all things Japanese brought a prestigious status to Japanese dining.' The staff were usually Japanese, front of house and in the kitchen, which made the experience authentic, and the food was aesthetically pleasing, artfully simple and healthy-looking.

Another facet in the spread of sushi to the US is that it represents a challenge to the notion that all globalisation is either American or westernised. For, while the emergence of US burger chains across Japan or China is described as having 'Americanised' those cultures, when Californians revel in their regular consumption of sushi, no one says that they've been 'Japanised'.

And, of course, just as tacos were bastardised (Chapter 11), so was sushi. Though it was actually Japanese chefs based in Los Angeles (a city that saw its first Japanese restaurant open in 1955 in the new Little Tokyo district) who invented the California roll, substituting avocado for tuna, Japanese sushi connoisseurs would not recognise sushi if it didn't contain fish. But it helped to hook the Americans to real sushi; it has often been said that the California roll was the gateway to the hard stuff. One can only imagine the aficionados' pain as America embraced sushi and then mixed apple, avocado and salmon for a New York roll, cream cheese and salmon for a Philadelphia roll, and (purists must look away now) beef and cucumber for a Texan roll.

The *New York Times* heralded the first sushi restaurant in the city on its front page in 1972 – a sushi bar in the elite, members-only Harvard Club. Between 1988 and 1998, the number of sushi restaurants in the US quadrupled. The Zagat restaurant survey of 2006 showed the remarkable statistic that, in virtually every American city, sushi restaurants were the most popular. Today, there are over 5,000 across the country.

Britain and Europe's lag owed much to the lack of Japanese immigration. Restaurants that did open were directed at Japanese businesspeople, diplomats and tourists, rather than locals.

While the yuppies of 1980s Thatcherite Britain were attracted by the rarity and price of London's few exclusive sushiya (there was a popular sushi counter in the food hall of department store Harrods), it was the novelty of *kaiten* sushi and its cheaper bill that spread its popularity in the late 1990s.

'*Kaiten* sushi was the innovation that transformed sushi from an exquisite, intimate, expensive experience to a snack food with the convenience and mass appeal of hamburgers and noodles,' wrote Popham. Where once the sandwich reigned, sushi was the new lunchtime snack of choice.

In due course, fortunes were made across the world as turnover sushi chains were rolled out, each seemingly with its own exclusive patent – though, once again, this didn't appear to stop anyone else building a conveyor belt.

But the global spread of sushi exemplifies one of the largest dilemmas in the story of food, one that constantly rears its awkward head and for which there appears to be no feasible solution.

When Yoshiaki Shiraishi opened his sushi restaurant, he did it for entrepreneurial reasons. Retired from the army, he needed a business that would provide for him and his family. When faced with issues about how to expand his enterprise, he was resourceful, innovative and took risks. Those risks paid off, and his success spread an idea across Japan that, after several decades, crossed oceans and became embedded in other cultures.

One of the key components of his success was that he made what was formerly a domain of the rich few accessible to the many. He democratised sushi. He made it cheaper. Across the world, workers at lunchtime could sit at counters and dab sushi and sashimi with a crunch of pickled ginger; they could enjoy a little wasabi, possibly nestled between a slice of raw tuna, eel, shrimp or salmon and rice; they could dip the mixture in a little saucer of soy. This touch of ceremony was so much more exotic than a simple sandwich or pie or taco; the moulding of tradition and technology brought a little dash of joy to the daily grind. It was healthy, too – and not just the fish. There was a supporting cast of wasabi (rich in antibacterial properties) and seaweed (high in calcium, magnesium, phosphorous, iron...). Not to mention the pure and environmentally positive wooden chopsticks.

And, while Shiraishi may have provided a poorer quality sushi, people didn't complain. Instead, they voted with the feet and their wallets.

Others also saw the opportunities in the business and launched replica models in territories where it would be novel. And, of course, many people and businesses benefited as a result. Landlords leased properties, building contractors renovated, interior designers suggested wall colours and furnishings, waiters and waitresses got jobs, fisherman sold fish.

Big business then got involved in fishing. In Japan, Mitsubishi, otherwise known as a motor vehicle maker, got in heavily. Today, its subsidiary business Cermaq is one of the world's largest fish producers and the second largest Atlantic salmon farmer, casting its net – literally – around the world, and currently planning to build salmon farms, hatcheries and processing plants in the Canadian province of Nova Scotia.

Every year in Tokyo's fish market, new records are set for the price of fish. In 2012, a 269kg tuna fish sold for $736,000; the following year, a 222kg tuna went for $1.7 million. At the relocated fish market in Ginza in 2019, a 278kg bluefin tuna sold for £3.1 million. The purchaser was a corporation running the Sushizanmai chain of restaurants across Japan, bringing a publicity triumph of awe and wonder to their branches.

The Japanese alone consume a third of the world's fished tuna – some 600,000 tons a year. It's hardly surprising that environmentalists calculate that the world's stocks of tuna have declined by 90 per cent over the past thirty-five years.

In 2004, the British journalist Charles Clover wrote that eating fish 'has become a kind of dietary talisman for western consumers. Nutritionists tell us that fish is good for us ... studies even indicate that consuming fish slows down the ageing process. Skinny models ... don't need to smoke to stay skinny. All they have to do is eat fish.' His book and ensuing documentary, *The End of the Line*, shocked many with its statistics and colour about modern-day fishing. 'Our love affair with fish is unsustainable,' he wrote. His book was a warning, a passionate aim to reveal 'what industrial techniques, unchecked market forces and lack of conscience are doing to the sea'.

His analysis was devastating: 'As a method of mass destruction, fishing with modern technology is the most destructive activity on earth.' His work would 'show the true price of fish that wasn't written on the menu'. A journalist in the *Financial Times* echoed many people's sentiments, writing: 'This book made me feel sick. It also, quite effectively, made me feel ashamed, despondent and anxious ... and, above all, guilty.'

So innovators spread the concept of a delicious food culture and consumers queue up to enjoy it, and then, having had their taste buds tickled, their cultural horizons widened and their conversations enriched, they get clobbered for having participated in an act of selfish global destruction.

The reality of large-scale fishing. Two decades after Woodroffe said 'YO! Sushi', campaigners were yelling 'NO! Sushi'.

It's a familiar story. Populations grow, globalisation flourishes, and middle classes swell. Consumer aspirations increase and entrepreneurs do everything they can to supply the demand. From coffee to beef, water to wheat, no sooner have these products been packed, dispatched, packaged, purchased and consumed than news emerges of their detrimental effects. There are the labour forces, who are employed on low wages and for long hours to farm and harvest the goods; there's the land used for growing, which is abused by pesticides and too rapid consecutive seeding-and-harvesting cycles; there is the carbon used in their transport, the plastic in their packaging, the energy for their refrigeration...

The demand for foods like fish has led to unnatural habitats being created by ingenious scientists, and others, in their ambitions to mimic nature and cut costs.

Hatched in laboratories, farmed salmon live in pens out at sea, in which thousands – fed to grow fast, and rich in glowing pink flesh – are then hoovered out of the water onto a conveyor belt, where they are either dispatched with a blow to the head or have their gills cut so they bleed to death. These are the intensive chicken farms of the ocean. Their knock-on effect – for example, when farmed fish mix with wild salmon – is not yet fully known.

And those who were told that eating sushi – and lots of it – is good for you (all those omega-3 fatty acids doing wonders for your brain) then discover that, in fact, they are consuming dangerously high levels of mercury, which can lead to neurological problems. There are also high levels of salt in seaweed and soy sauce – the over-consumption of which can heighten your blood pressure, strain a number of your vital organs and arteries, and give you a heart attack or dementia. Two decades after Simon Woodroffe said 'YO! Sushi', campaigners began firmly yelling 'NO! Sushi'.

Not long after Clover's book was published, the journal *Science* delivered the results of a four-year survey carried out by ecologists and economists. It calculated that, if humans continued to kill and eat fish at the rate they were, by 2048, the world would run out of seafood. 'There are too many boats chasing falling numbers of fish, with whizzy technology such as satellite hunting equipment and nets that are the size of Wembley stadium,' wrote author Hattie Ellis, in her book *What to Eat*. She also pointed out how wasteful industrial fishing is: 'In profligate Europe, around half the fish caught in the North Sea are thrown over the side of the boat, dead, because they are illegal to land or not valuable enough to sell.'

If the consumer cares about any of this, and one has to assume that many fish-eaters don't, then there is a considerable dilemma. Should you simply abandon eating moderate amounts of fish despite the health benefits and considerable pleasure? In the UK, the Marine Conservation Society offers advice on what fish to eat, and profiles 144 different species, rating them for their sustainability credentials. But what quickly becomes clear is that there are no hard and fast rules. Tuna can be eaten, depending on both the type and method of fishing. Other fish, such as pouting, are sustainable, but only if they have grown to over 20 centimetres.

Getting MCS labelling and approval for the species you sell in your fish and chip shop costs money, and there are examples of very worthy fish and chip shops that source their fish with great care, but can't afford the certification.

And, while some high-end London restaurants sell fish that the MSC would not approve of, as Charles Clover once pointed out, McDonald's Filet-O-Fish is sustainably sourced.

Caroline Bennett of Moshi Moshi became aware of issues of sustainability when orders of bluefin tuna didn't arrive. She contacted the World Wildlife Fund and then Greenpeace, before having a conversation with a man called Carl Safina, founder of the Blue Ocean Institute, a non-profit conservation organisation. 'The bluefin tuna is endangered and is similar to eating a rhinoceros,' he told her in a telephone call. These were words, she later reflected, 'that would change me for ever'.

In 1997, just as YO! Sushi was opening, Bennett took bluefin tuna off the menu. 'The poor little fish were far too delicious for their own good,' she reflected. In 2012, she conceived an initiative of linking fish restaurants to small-scale sustainable fisheries. But, as despondent environmentalists will admit, a small country like the United Kingdom upping its game won't make a dent in the problem while the rest of the world continues to catch the fish and sushi bug. As Ellis commented, finding solutions to the problems of the sea 'will require the efforts of people who can span all the different aspects: fisherman, consumers, regulators and retailers'. She provided a six-point plan for the consumer, whose freedom to choose wields considerable power: broaden your tastes; be aware of the catching method; enjoy shellfish; go 'oily'; think about farmed fish; and cherish the local. Moreover, unless it's farmed, she urged one to remember that fish are essentially wild.

Clover's documentary did, however, have considerable impact. Some 4.7 million people watched or became aware of it. A newspaper campaign named and shamed London restaurants that served endangered fish. The celebrity hangout Nobu was exposed for selling bluefin tuna. The restaurant then added an asterisk describing bluefin tuna as 'environmentally challenged', leaving the onus on the customer as to whether to eat it. Campaigners were not impressed.

Some British supermarkets responded by removing endangered fish from their shelves. Today, many fish restaurants market themselves on the basis of their sustainable menus, although perhaps the most ethical thing a fish restaurant could do would be not to open.

Ultimately, governments must be bold and ban and tax out of existence bad practice. Pity the poor consumer, gazing in wonder at the encircling dishes of sushi as they travel through the sushi bar, wanting nothing except fishy pleasure, but left scratching their head, wreathed in guilt, instead.

14

Le Gavroche Opens in London

Albert and Michel Roux opened Le Gavroche in London and then the Waterside Inn in Bray, Berkshire, sparking a restaurant revolution in the UK and spawning a new generation of British cooks.

The excitement that the two French brothers felt was palpable. It was 1964, and 23-year-old private chef Michel Roux was visiting his brother, Albert, aged twenty-nine, and also a private chef. While Michel was employed by the Rothschild family, working mainly in Paris and at their summer retreat on the Côte d'Azur, Albert was in Kent, the southern county of England. His employers were a family called Cazalet.

Albert lived with his wife, Monique, and Michel had brought over his wife, Françoise. The four of them were back at Albert's Kent home, after spending the evening in London. This was the third of such forays that week. Albert had made a list of restaurants that the two couples should visit together. It included The Empress, Le Coq d'Or, La Belle Meunière and Prunier. These establishments represented the finest that Britain had to offer.

Monique and Françoise – like their husbands, sticklers for classic French dining – couldn't believe how poor the experience had been that night. The gang had trooped to Charlotte Street to dine at La Belle Meunière, a French institution from the 1950s. The *escalope maison* was tough enough to use as a weapon to deal a mugger an ugly blow. The *crêpe suzette*, to their astonishment, had clearly not been made to order, but removed from the fridge so that its cloying texture seemed an abrupt collision with the violent cheap brandy sloshed on top. And, among the disappointingly brief list of French wines, bottled beers of English Bass and Worthington ales had equal billing.

The depressed nonchalance of the one French waiter seemed to sum up the night. So the wives were somewhat bemused that their husbands appeared to be absolutely delighted by the discovery of yet another terrible so-called 'fine dining' restaurant in the British capital.

But the brothers had been fairly certain that this was what they would find on their visits to London. 'They confirmed our prejudices,' Michel would later reflect. And, as they explained to the girls, the worse the restaurant, the better the opportunity. 'The food was poor and the service worse,' said Michel, 'all of which strengthened our resolve to set up in Britain.'

As private chefs to wealthy upper-class families, the Roux brothers were perfectionists when it came to French food; obsessive about ingredients, cooking methods, order and cleanliness in their kitchen, and about correct and courteous service.

At the time, Michel was being trained for life – even if he didn't know it then – by Cécile de Rothschild, the grande dame of the family. She made, in his words, 'everyday life ... the melodrama of an operetta'. There were constant changes in timings of meals and numbers of guests, but she had high standards and impeccable taste. 'I learned to be a gourmet, an essential quality for a chef,' he wrote.

He also learned from her extraordinary exactitude when it came to ingredients. Pheasant meat must only be from the hen, entrecôte steaks from a 3-year-old heifer, legs of lamb from a ewe. How else would one get the right tenderness, succulence and delicacy?

Tomatoes were not to be served in Paris. Only in Provence could they be picked, ripened from the sun, and used immediately, the warmth of the rays still prevalent in their flesh.

Her precision extended from cooking methods to serving, from wine to the state of the kitchen; she often inspected the latter late at night to ensure the room was clean and items put away correctly.

But the appearance of food was never for its own sake. 'Remember,' she once advised the young Michel, 'a dish must be good to look at, but it is better for it to look less good if, that way, it tastes better.'

She was, said Michel, 'an encyclopaedia of taste and knowledge about food'. She imparted to Michel both management skills and how one's taste should not be affected by whether a dish was elaborate or simple. It was nothing less than an education. 'For me, the Rothschild school was the school of perfection,' he said.

Albert was similarly learning from aristocracy. His first British employer, when he was only eighteen, was the then elderly Lady Nancy, Viscountess Astor, the American-born one-time British member of parliament and controversial figure, who lived at Cliveden in Berkshire. His bosses' tastes were less obsessive than the Rothschilds', but their style and grandeur were considerable.

These two young private chefs were part of a heritage that could be traced straight back to the private chefs of the aristocracy of late eighteenth-century France (Chapter 6). But, whereas their professional forebears escaped France to avoid the calamities of a revolution, the Roux brothers went to England having spied opportunity. And it was an opportunity that would turn out to be a revolution – but of an extremely tasty kind.

The food landscape of Britain that the Roux brothers surveyed had been in the doldrums since at least the Second World War (Chapter 12). It was one that the first editor of *The Good Food Guide*, Raymond Postgate, wished to improve. But there was another guide that Hungarian writer Egon Ronay hoped would assist Britain in releasing herself from her partly self-inflicted purgatory. His guide was first published in 1957 – selling 30,000 copies – and he went on to

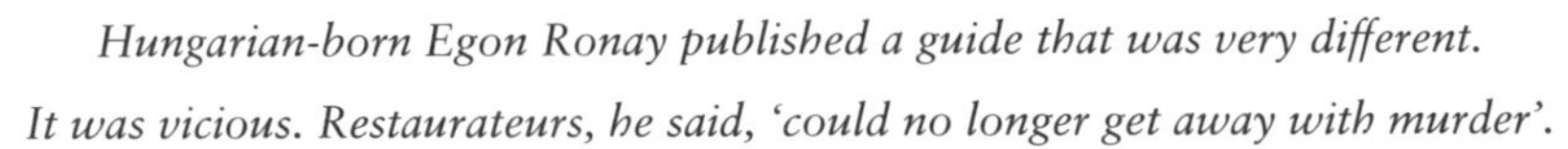

Hungarian-born Egon Ronay published a guide that was very different. It was vicious. Restaurateurs, he said, 'could no longer get away with murder'.

recruit inspectors, whose full-time jobs were to, anonymously, eat some eleven meals each week, never accepting even a free glass of brandy. Their jobs saw them driving, taking the train and eventually flying hundreds of miles, month in, month out.

'It's a great life,' Ronay once said, 'or at least a fortnight. After that, it gets to be hell.'

Ronay's guide had a vicious streak not seen in Postgate's tome. He lashed out at railway cafés, provincial hotels and motorway service stations – the very establishments that had so inflamed Bernard Levin when he attacked Lord Forte one night on television in the early 1960s (Chapter 12).

His guides had the effect, said Ronay, 'of telling people that they could no longer get away with murder – because I would expose them'. He didn't mince his words. The food provided at one motorway service station was described as 'pigswill'.

At the time Ronay's first guide came out, if an establishment wasn't French or Italian by design, it was essentially whacky. El Cubano, on Brompton Road in London's Kensington, was heralded on a Pathé news film as offering 'foods that reflect the modern demand for variety and modernisation'. Waitresses dressed like Spanish gypsies; male staff from Trinidad walked about with parrots on their shoulders. Black coffee was served with a slice of orange peel; one particular open sandwich contained a mixture of fresh fruit, walnuts and cream cheese.

There were some notable exceptions, though. Restaurateur George Perry-Smith had opened the Hole in the Wall in Bath in 1952. At the centre of his restaurant was a table spread with charcuterie, potted fish and paté, which customers helped themselves to as their first course. As well as taking the pressure off the kitchen, who did not have to cook starters, it was an appealing sight for everyone as they entered the restaurant.

Another provincial oasis was Restaurant Elizabeth in Oxford, opened in the late 1950s and run by Kenneth Bell. The leaded windows of his place looked out to Christ Church college, and, on a winter's night, eager and greedy dons and wealthier undergraduates would repair there for a richly flavoured dish of oxtail, slow-cooked in wine. His wine list was rated as one of the finest in the country.

Both Bell and Perry-Smith's mantra was real food, cooked without shortcuts, with the best ingredients sought, whatever the cost.

By the 1960s, the British restaurant picture was little more than a gentle evolution of the previous decade. The French and Italian institutions survived,

El Cubano restaurant, Brompton Road, London, was the epitome of modern: waiters had parrots on their shoulders; there were sandwiches of fresh fruit, walnuts and cream cheese.

and there was a new concept in the British bistro. It was, in the words of British food editor and writer Caroline Stacey, 'a blend of diluted French, trattoria and school dinners [that] represented the trickle-down effect of the best, more faithful continental cooking'.

Competing with this were the 'Britalian' joints. Cheaper than the more upmarket Italian restaurants, they were comforting for the British palate as there was nothing too exotic on the menu – spaghetti Bolognaise (still a dish of controversy, as no one in Bologna has ever heard of it) served with chips. Such restaurants weren't thought of as authentic unless they had Chianti bottles hanging from the ceiling, reassuringly clad in their tight little 'fiasco' straw baskets.

In cafés and mid-scale restaurants, regardless of their ethnicity (a ripple of Chinese and Indian restaurants were spreading to the provinces, see Chapter 16), steaks were 'sirloin', chicken Kievs ran rampant, as did prawn cocktails, and, if you were lucky, you might get an avocado pear for starter, the unripe flesh hollowed out and filled with 'French dressing'.

Two restaurants, opened in the '50s by the designer and retailer Terence Conran (Chapter 16), born in 1931, had also survived: Soup Kitchen and Orrery. But they were both in fashionable, swinging Chelsea, the preserve of the rich and fabulous.

What no one was doing was French, the way the Rouxs knew it to be: fine dining, and every bit as good as the food they cooked privately.

After their first joint visit to London in 1964, Michel and Albert would spend a few days with each other both summers of the next two years. They continued to eat out. They continued to be joyfully disappointed.

In between meetings, they would write to one another describing the dishes they were cooking for their bosses, and then drafting menus for their jointly owned imagined restaurant.

Then Albert put some flesh on the bones of the idea by visiting markets and auction houses at the weekend and purchasing silverware and crockery. He stored it in his garage, ready to be viewed by an excited Michel on his next visit. He also began visiting restaurants in London that were up for sale. Michel looked forward to each letter that would arrive in Paris. He would reply by return. If Albert didn't receive a letter within a few days, he would telephone Michel to ensure his ideas had not gone astray.

When they met again in the summer of 1966, they decided the time had come to found a company, Roux Restaurants Ltd. Albert put in his savings, as well as an investment from his supporting employers, the Cazalet family, and some of their friends, sitting as sterling in his bank account. 'It cost me £1,500 to set up ... and we had only £500,' Albert said years later. 'The Cazalets gave me £500 as a leaving present and they raised the other £500 that we needed from their friends.'

Michel then did his best to match Albert's investment. His money was in French francs. 'I transferred my savings of 50,000 francs at the highly unfavourable rate of 13.60 to the pound as my contribution to the capital [around £3,600].'

They had a restaurant company with no restaurant. But they had one hell of an idea. It was a considerable achievement for two boys born in the small French town of Charolles, in a house above the family charcuterie shop. Both brothers had decided to become pâtissiers. Albert, a few steps ahead, had then become a sous-chef at the British Embassy kitchens in Paris, and had helped to get his younger brother a job there as pastry chef. Their careers were interrupted by compulsory military service, after which they went their separate ways into the world of private cheffing, using contacts they had made at the embassy.

Over the winter of 1966, Albert narrowed down a choice of venues he had seen, and then, as the new year dawned, he telephoned Michel to describe a site on Lower Sloane Street. An Italian restaurant called Canova was closing, and Albert had managed to secure the lease. Michel trusted his brother's enthusiasm and judgement, and resigned to Cécile de Rothschild, but only after being made to wait two weeks for her to agree to a meeting, doubtless fearing her protégé was about to flee the nest.

'She heard me out, twisting a strand of her hair, just as she had done the day she took me on,' he recalled. He agreed to work his three months' notice and then, on 3 April 1967, he landed at Dover.

He arrived to be greeted by grey skies and perpetual rain. England looked miserable compared to those summer days in Kent. He spoke no English and the worries of family and friends weighed heavily on him. 'Nobody understood my decision,' he said. They all talked of the huge set-up costs in London compared to Paris, of the vast issues he would face, from finding supplies to additional bank funds.

But he tried to stay positive as he chugged up the road from Dover to London in an overloaded Renault 4 with Françoise by his side (their two young daughters would join them once they were settled). The boot was filled with additional crockery and cutlery, chefs' jackets and trousers. On top of this pile was a painting he had spotted at a market stall in Montmartre: an oil of a typical Parisian urchin, known in French as a *gavroche*. Françoise had rolled her eyes as he'd finished stuffing the car and placed the painting on top of their load.

Up in London, Albert had been working hard on the refit and had also employed the services of Antonio Battistella, who had managed Canova. Battistella hired five other Italian waiters, Albert found a cook and Michel engaged the services of an old colleague from the Rothschild kitchen in Paris.

In the frantic few weeks before the restaurant's launch, the brothers worked with builders and other tradesman, Albert translating for his brother: 'I began to understand how dependent I would be on him to begin with,' Michel said. He could at least lay claim to a major initiative: the name. 'It was my idea,' said

Michel. 'That famous street urchin had no money and, while I wasn't penniless, I certainly had very little. I admired the determination of that plucky little boy.' While they had confidence in the idea of 'Roux Brothers', or using their names some way in the title, that boy in the portrait Michel had bought in Montmartre cemented Michel's inspiration.

A few days before they opened, he found a space to hang the picture. He stepped back, and Albert, walking past, paused. Together they took in the painting, reflecting perhaps on the boldness of their own initiative. 'It was to become our symbol,' Michel later reflected. Indeed, in years to come, a new set of crockery would be designed featuring the image of the little boy on every plate. And the humble boy was in good company. The Cazalets had lent a number of paintings for Le Gavroche. The proud urchin sat beside a Chagal, a Miró and a Dali. The art would help convince the first guests that these Roux boys really knew what they were doing. It wouldn't occur to them that, while the brothers had serious culinary skills, they had absolutely no experience of running a restaurant.

Although the first night would be a buffet-style party from a guest list drawn up by the Cazalets, the Rouxs spent hours drafting the menu proper for day two. It had thirty dishes and was in French. There were soups, hors d'oeuvres, fish, shellfish, vegetables, meat and poultry, but it was about half the size of the menus they had seen in other London French restaurants like Prunier. And there was another stark difference: there was no smoked salmon, no potted shrimp and no prawn cocktail.

Michel and Albert were offering genuine French gastronomy, whether London liked it or not. And there were complaints. 'The portions were too small,' was a frequent grumble, uttered by couples whose dress was considerably more shabby than that of the clientele in Parisian restaurants.

'This is French gastronomy,' Michel told one such couple, with his finest charming smile, a few days after the launch, impressing himself that he had managed to string together four words in English.

'We [had to] be prepared to accept criticism even insults, since we were introducing a culture shock to a London dominated by mediocre Italian restaurants and Lyons Corner Houses,' he later reflected. 'I realised I was going to need great strength to rise above the mediocrity around me.'

But, while there was the odd grumble, there were enough Londoners to keep the restaurant busy and full from day one. By March 1968, Le Gavroche was famous.

The Roux brothers, Albert and Michel (in 1988), who founded Le Gavroche. London in the 1960s was a culinary desert that provided a golden opportunity.

As for their suppliers: 'We could get beautiful lamb and beef, and I persuaded fishermen to send me the whole of their catch, whatever they'd caught, so that I could serve it really fresh in the restaurant,' said Albert. But, for poultry and other items, England couldn't deliver. The brothers needed French produce. Albert conceived an ingenious plan: 'Monique used to drive to Paris every week with a car full of the finest beef and lamb we could get to swap for good chicken, foie gras, mushrooms and charcuterie.' She gave her best smile to customs officials at the docks, but occasionally they checked the contents of her boot and sent her packing. Determined not to let her husband down, she simply drove to another port and attempted the voyage again. 'It was illegal and risky, but the results were worth it and she never failed to make the crossing,' he added. It greatly amused Albert on the various occasions in 1967 when he served plate after plate of French delicacies to Fred Peart, the then minister of agriculture, fisheries and food: 'I was at a loss to know where on earth he thought these foods were coming from!'

Forty years later, in May 2007, writer Margaret Clancy reflected in *The Caterer* on quite what an achievement is was that the brothers managed to write a menu and deliver it in London in the late '60s: 'The logistical problems of running a high-class restaurant forty years ago are almost unimaginable today. England had seen the end of rationing only relatively recently [thirteen years previously, see Chapter 12], and the idea of specialist growers or top-end ingredients on our own shores was unheard of.'

By 1970, the brothers had opened two further restaurants in the City, and, by 1972, according to Michel, 'I was exhausted ... but I was also a little bored.'

So the brothers employed their hitherto successful policy of finding culinary deserts. Now they would ponder on somewhere out of London; a place where there appeared to be wealth, but nowhere decent to eat.

And thus, on a spring day in 1972, the 31-year-old Michel was poking about in a shabby old pub in the village of Bray in England's Berkshire countryside. The building was by the river; it was a bright day, and the glimmering water was the only thing that sparkled near the grotty premises.

The estate agent – operating for the pub's owners, the giant brewing firm Whitbread – looked despondent. Why would a Frenchman, a chef, indeed, buy a rundown pub in the middle of nowhere? But, just as the brothers had explored London, so, too, had they driven around the Berkshire countryside, spotting the large houses with expensive cars parked outside, in towns like Marlow and Henley.

Outside the tired Waterside Inn, the paving stones were cracked, slippery and miserable-looking. Inside, it was filthy.

'I remember walking across a damp room that looked out to the river,' recalled Michel. 'Except you couldn't see the river. You needed a razor blade to scrape the filth off the windows. It was just a grotty, dirty, smelly pub. It seriously stank.'

Michel told the estate agent he needed to go and find a telephone box to call his brother. When Michel returned, the estate agent was prepared to conclude another unsuccessful viewing. Michel stuck out his hand for a shake. 'We'll take it,' he said. 'It's perfect.'

'Even I had to work hard to persuade myself that we really could transform the place,' reflected Michel, decades later. 'But there was this beautiful willow tree by the river whose leaves danced in the afternoon light. And it made me hopeful.'

In four months' time, as the builders began to pack up and leave, Michel sat down in the considerably spruced-up dining room, with the River Thames casting its dappled light through the clearest glass windowpanes, and planned the menu. With him was his first head chef, Pierre Koffmann. A few days later, in early September, just five years after the opening of Le Gavroche, the Waterside Inn opened.

Koffmann, who had come to England to watch a rugby match and never left, had previously worked at Le Gavroche. Showing serious promise, he had been promoted to sous-chef after just two months. Koffmann was twenty-four years old and excited to be head chef at the Waterside Inn, because he felt that the food at Le Gavroche, in his words, 'wasn't bad, but it was miles and miles away from French food'. Yet it still compared very favourably to the contemporary scene: 'The food was very poor at the time.'

At the Waterside Inn, he said, 'I was able to do the food I wanted. They never interfered with me and I really enjoyed it.' Plus, he claimed, the Roux brothers 'were very rarely there, so it was like running my own place'.

Unlike Le Gavroche, business did not boom from day one. 'The first two or three years were not easy,' reflected Michel. 'Weekdays were as dead as a dodo – we had just ten to twenty covers for lunch and dinner. But weekends were packed. We only had a skeleton staff, and it was myself and Pierre cooking side by side,' he said.

Fortunately, the success of the other restaurants in the business – Le Poulbot in Cheapside and Brasserie Benoit by the Old Bailey, as well as Le Gavroche – supported the struggling new Roux establishment.

But then, in 1973, along came Egon Ronay, whose articles in the *Daily Telegraph* were by now preyed on by those looking for advice on where to eat. 'One day,' wrote the Hungarian-born critic, 'the Waterside Inn will be the best restaurant in Britain.' Ronay's article made a very positive impact on the business. 'It brought us clients from far away,' explained Michel. 'We started to break even. Life was starting to smile on us.'

The following year, Michelin (Chapter 17) helped the restaurant on that journey to greatness by awarding it a star. By then, the establishment was well known for its location – a perfect place for a drink on the terrace by the river before dinner – and its impeccable service by a team of smartly dressed waiters. As for the food, it was a menu that combined the classic French cooking of Michel Roux with the south-west France roots of Koffmann.

The menu was divided into soup, starters, crustaceans, fish, main courses, vegetables, cheese and dessert. Except, of course, it was all written in French. Of the soups, there was *potage Parisien*, for example, or *consommé royale*. As Michel reflected in his memoirs: 'At the Waterside Inn, there is not a day without soup on the menu at lunchtime. This is because I like soup, and I only offer customers what I like.' Some soups included a light and airy velouté, made with sorrel from the garden, a pea soup, a consommé of lobster or crayfish, and a delicate broth with a little homemade ravioli floating in it. Then there was the famous *velouté de coquillages aux huitres*, made with an abundance of shellfish, whose juices were retained for the soup and added to fish stock, herbs and cream. Finally, an oyster was placed in the broth, the heat of which gently poached it, keeping it just raw in the middle.

The hors d'oeuvre offering in the early days saw the likes of Bayonne ham and various pâtés, not to mention a variety of egg dishes. Fish included turbot or sole, grilled and served with béarnaise sauce.

The main courses (*entrées*) were all meat dishes, and among the beef and lamb was a gutsy *cassoulet Toulousain*. Desserts, or rather *entremets*, included *tarte au citron* and a fruit sorbet. The cheeses were all French. As at Le Gavroche, the menu was French, it was written in French and virtually all the ingredients were from France. And, as well as Michel and chef Koffmann, all the other cooks were French. But, as word spread about the Roux brothers' business and their novel passion for wanting to properly train their chefs, that singular nationality was diluted. Many believe that it is this aspect that really defines the impact Michel and Albert had on the British restaurant scene.

Marco Pierre White, in 1986, was a brooding, long-haired rock star, with a cigarette always perched on his lips. 'Discipline', he said, 'is born out of fear.'

Also pondering on forty years of Le Gavroche's existence in 2007 was *Observer* restaurant critic Jay Rayner. 'Le Gavroche matters because of the people who have worked there,' he wrote. 'Without the restaurant and the patronage of brothers Michel and Albert Roux, the thriving British restaurant scene as we know it would look completely different.'

Indeed, the names of those who worked in the various Roux kitchens, and would go on to create some of the greatest British restaurants of the 1980s, '90s and beyond, include Marco Pierre White, Rowley Leigh, Gordon Ramsay and Marcus Wareing.

By the time Marco Pierre White knocked on the door of the office of Albert Roux in 1981, Le Gavroche had won two stars from the Michelin Guide in 1974 and 1977. It had also just relocated to a building in London's prestigious Mayfair district. Diners entered through a door on Upper Brook Street and descended to the dining room in the basement. With little natural light and certainly no views, all the focus would be on the food and service.

Twenty-year-old White had made the journey from West Yorkshire and had just £7.36 left in his pocket, a small box of books and a bag of clothes. Albert took one glance at him and said: 'Report here on Tuesday.' He began as a junior chef's assistant: a commis. Albert looked at this young man with his long raggedy hair, piercing blue eyes and almost obsessive ambition, and referred to him, with just a little irony, as 'my little bunny'.

It was at Le Gavroche where the little bunny said that he learned that a kitchen could not be run without discipline. 'Discipline is born out of fear,' he wrote in his autobiography:

> *The set-up of the finest [is] something akin to the mafia. Albert was definitely the godfather, the boss of bosses. He would be played by Marlon Brando ... in an apron. He was a father figure with a very dominant presence and could philosophise in that godfather style. While you worked for him, you felt you had his protection. You knew you were with the don.*

In 1982, Le Gavroche won a third Michelin star. White went on to work under Pierre Koffmann, who had left the Waterside Inn to pursue his own interests. In 1987, White opened his own restaurant on London's Wandsworth Common: Harveys. He built a reputation as a fiery cook. Chefs were dispatched as often as the menu changed, and there was White: the brooding, long-haired, moody rock star. Most portraits featured him with a cigarette perched on his lips; he slung out miscreant customers; there were tales of a brutal regime in the kitchen, of imperfect cheese trolleys flung against the wall, of chefs complaining of the heat and finding White slashing holes in their chefs' whites for some economic air conditioning.

In January 1995, at the age of thirty-three, he became the first and youngest British chef to win a third Michelin star. The plates of food he delivered – roast scallops with calamari and sauce nero (blackened by squid ink), oysters with Champagne sabayon, velouté of celery with poached egg, pig's trotter – were classics of French gastronomy, refined and perfected by White. Yet he had never even set foot in France.

In turn, White, as the Roux brothers had done, set another generation of chefs on the road to success, each of them later merrily recounting tales of how they had survived his kitchen.

Today, the British food landscape is shaped by some of the men who learned under his unique style of mentoring: chefs such as Gordon Ramsay, Phil Howard, Bryn Williams and Jason Atherton.

However, when asked once what the best restaurant in Britain was, White replied: 'Le Gavroche or Waterside Inn. They have that old-fashioned charm and romance. Do they serve the best food? No, but they offer the best package.' And that package included service, another aspect of the restaurant trade that the Rouxs help to transform.

In 1974, Italian Silvano Giraldin became general manager at Le Gavroche, having started as a waiter in 1971. Another Italian, Diego Masciaga, joined Le Gavroche in 1983, and became general manager of the Waterside Inn. Giraldin gave thirty-seven years of service to Le Gavroche; Masciaga, thirty to the Waterside Inn. The two of them set a new standard for service; they made it a career to aspire to. Young men and women from around the UK and overseas beat a path to their door to learn the trade of great service.

'I helped them to understand that they're not just here to do a job, they're here to do a very important profession,' Masciaga once said, in between training young men and women in the art of customer service, pouring a glass of wine or carving a duck at the table. 'At the end of the day, it doesn't just bring you happiness,' he continued, 'but also wealth, as the guests will always come back to you.'

Masciaga and Giraldin gave interviews on the subject of service, they wrote books, they were heralded in the pages of magazines, they were paid to address seminars on the subject, and they lectured at catering colleges. A young Bernard Levin (Chapter 12) would scarcely have believed his eyes.

By the mid-1980s, the brotherly partnership of Albert and Michel had begun to break down. Michel had been happy for his elder brother to take the lead in the early days, because he spoke English. But, some twenty years later, he did not appreciate this embedded bias. There were constant niggles. Albert got carried away on trips to the market and, according to Michel, he 'could not keep to the agreed buying list. He swamped our restaurants with an exaggerated quantity of lamb or salmon ... This annoyed our chefs, who did not want to waste anything.' Worse, 'Albert was cutting me out of decision-making,' he later wrote. 'After more than ten years of almost idyllic cooperation, relations between the two of us had become very tense.' As plans intensified for their move from Chelsea to Mayfair, 'I found I was not consulted on the new site for the restaurant, its decoration or on the specific planning of the kitchen.'

In 1982, when Le Gavroche became Britain's first three-star Michelin restaurant, Michel raged that 'my brother claimed the credit'. 'Until then, we had always shared everything.'

A couple of years later, when their mother, Germaine, joined the brothers for the filming of a BBC programme, she scolded them: 'You spend more time quarrelling than cooking. I am ashamed of you.'

It was time for them to end most of their joint enterprises. Michel took the Waterside Inn; Albert, Le Gavroche. The rupture endured in the ensuing decades. 'He should stay in the mountains of Switzerland,' Albert once said of Michel, who had bought a house in the Alpine town of Crans-Montana. Would he entertain his brother at his own establishment? he was asked. 'I wouldn't let him in,' said Albert.

But, back in the '80s, Michel made Bray his home. And he had a new wife, his beloved Robyn, who would go on to oversee the interior design of the Waterside Inn – his devotion to his business having helped to wreck his first marriage. Albert, too, would divorce Monique, and then his second wife, Cheryl, in due course also.

It is a familiar theme in the restaurant story. As the British restaurateur Keith Floyd, born in 1943, who lit up food for the British public via the medium of television in the 1980s, once said: 'Don't ever go into the restaurant business. It kills marriages, it kills relationships, and it kills life. It kills everything. And I, the man with four ex-wives, should know.'

But the Roux dynasty lived on through the children of Michel and Albert, and today Michel's son Alain is chef-patron of the Waterside Inn, and his cousin, Michel Jr, son of Albert, similarly owns and runs Le Gavroche.

The Roux brothers spawned an empire and a culture. Some of their descendants practiced the art of gastronomy through fire and fury; others, such as Rowley Leigh, ran more therapeutic kitchens. The latter, though originally Roux-trained, became part of a new breed of English cooks who perhaps owed more to the roots of George Perry-Smith and Elizabeth David: Simon Hopkinson (Chapter 16), Sally Clarke and Alastair Little. And they, in turn, would seek and cherish influence from the creator of a very calm revolution, which would unfold some 5,000 miles away, in the gentle suburbs of San Francisco.

15

Chez Panisse Opens in the US

Gently, quietly, sometimes even at a whisper, Alice Waters created a food revolution; a connection between chefs and farmers. In due course, she passionately argued for free school meals and relentlessly urged other cooks, chefs and writers to rise up against the mighty beasts of US fast food.

In the late 1960s, in the city of Berkeley, east of San Francisco, a car ride over the Bay Bridge from that hilly Californian metropolis, a 27-year-old woman opened a small restaurant. 'I was disillusioned with politics and needed a way to make money,' she later wrote.

The political aspect cannot be underestimated. Indeed, those who knew could deduce it from what appeared on the plate at Chez Panisse – the vegetables, salads and herbs unfamiliar to many Americans at the time.

Waters was also driven by a passion and yearning for food, inspired by youthful experiences of France, but her political motivations mark her out from other restaurateurs of history.

There is nothing to suggest that Primus fed Pompeiians for any other reason than they desired feeding (Chapter 1); the private chefs of aristocracy opened restaurants in Paris in the late eighteenth and early nineteenth centuries because they needed work, and cooking and serving was what they knew (Chapter 6). The Kohinoor family started their café in Bombay in the early 1920s because the British colonialists needed some non-spicy food (Chapter 10) – the place may have united people of differing class and politics, but that was not the patrons' motivation. The Roux brothers spread gastronomy around London in the late '60s and early '70s because there was none at the time (Chapter 14).

The very ingredients used in the Chez Panisse kitchen, and the method in which they were sourced, were an embodiment of a set of values, a demonstration

The roots of Alice Waters' restaurant Chez Panisse drew nourishment from the social unrest of early '60s America.

to modern, industrial, big-business America that things could – and should – be done differently. It was an exquisite and palate-pleasing opening salvo in a cultural, political and social war. But, while its effectiveness can be called into question, of its motivation, there is no doubt.

Chez Panisse (named after a character in a French film) opened in 1971. But the roots of its philosophy drew nourishment from the febrile time of social unrest of early '60s America.

When Alice Waters began studying at UC Berkeley in 1964, she couldn't have picked a time when the campuses of America were more agitated. That summer, President Lyndon B. Johnson had ordered the bombing of targets in North Vietnam, a retaliatory measure after Vietnamese torpedo boats attacked two US destroyers in the Gulf of Tonkin. By the time the bombings became more regular, the following February, critics were questioning the US government's assertion that it was simply engaged in a battle of democracy to liberate the people of South Vietnam from communist aggression.

Three years later, with more than 15,000 US troops killed and over 100,000 injured, anti-war demonstrators were drawn from a wide demographic. But the protests' origins bubbled among students and teachers in places like UC Berkeley.

In fact, at Waters' own campus, the university establishment chose to put itself at odds with the community it managed. Implementing his own mini regime of totalitarianism, the then dean, Peter Van Houten, banned political activity and related fundraising. And he wasn't some crusty 65-year-old academic from another era; he was only thirty.

'If a student stood up on campus to speak out about Vietnam, they'd be dragged off by the campus police,' recalled Waters. But this was the perfect way to motivate a generation of students to embrace the politics of protest. And their lecturers were similarly stimulated. In order to teach, they were forced to sign an oath of loyalty.

In choosing a subject to major in, Waters went for French cultural history, 1750–1850. 'The French Revolution, of course,' she once chuckled.

Then, with a friend, she manufactured a year in France for her studies. The trip would open her mind quite extraordinarily to the possibilities of food. It had never before been a feature of her life. Born in New Jersey and moving to California when her father relocated the family there for work, she had always been a fussy eater, reflecting, 'I was very skinny and didn't like to eat much.' School food 'smelled bad and all looked brown', and, until she discovered Paris and the south of France, it had never occurred to her that enjoying food could be a thing. Her love of France was 'insatiable'.

She recalled the sublime simplicity of a vegetable soup at the first hotel she stayed at in Paris: 'Tiny cubed vegetables floating in a clear amber broth.' The simplest of discoveries overjoyed her: varieties of lettuce she had never seen; learning that most French people served salad as a refreshing course before dessert; the sourdough baked in Paris by Lionel Poilâne. And, in Brittany, she experienced a no-choice menu. Three courses: ham and melon; trout with almonds in browned butter; raspberry tart.

She then came across the young salad leaves known as mesclun. She brought seeds back with her to the US and grew from them. They became a staple on the menu of Chez Panisse, and demand from other restaurants saw farmers planting and harvesting them, too. 'I think if there's one thing I'm responsible for in this country,' she reflected in her memoir, *Coming to My Senses*, 'it's the propagation of real salad in the United States.'

Back in the States, Waters tried to cook the way they did France. But she had to work hard to find the produce. The supermarkets of the late '60s were, she said, 'all about frozen foods and canned goods ... the exact opposite of the French markets'.

In between working as a waitress and teaching young children, she got a reputation for the frequent dinners she cooked for her friends with the narrow assortment of ingredients she bought in bulk from co-ops and the few speciality stores that existed. She also had a newspaper column, 'Alice's Restaurant', in radical political newspaper the *San Francisco Express Times*, in which the recipes presented were served in her fantasy establishment.

She seemed to be cooking so often for her large circle of friends that it made sense for her to widen the offering. If it was good enough for them, there would surely be a market beyond...

She started looking for sites to open a restaurant – a small venue, with a maximum of forty covers. These searches took place around her political activities; marches, meetings, debates...

Her friendships and relationships were fuelled and driven by politics; it consumed her. When people she thought should get elected – and for whom she had canvassed – failed to get to congress, she was 'profoundly depressed ... I mean I really lost hope', she wrote.

From music to food, everything was political. When she found the site for Chez Panisse, at 517 Shattock Avenue, it felt right partly because it was close to a cheese shop run as a worker collective and there was also a Peet's Coffee around the corner, which sold hand-roasted beans in small batches. (Peet's Coffee would go on to spawn a monster – the founder, Alfred Peet, mentored and shared his business practice and supplier details with three men, who then started a company called Starbucks.)

Waters bought the lease with an option-to-buy three years later for $28,000. On the opening night of 28 August 1971, the restaurant, refitted from a plumbers' store, was a French-like bistro scene of second-hand chairs and furniture, the tables covered with checked cloths, mismatched dishes and old glassware bought from flea markets, and fresh flowers. There were three wines on the list: a red and a white from the Mondavi winery in nearby Napa Valley, and a Sauternes dessert wine. And on her no-choice menu: pâté en croute, served on a plate with parsley, pickles and mustard; roasted duck with olives; and plum tart.

Waters, worried about being understaffed, had hired a team of fifty-five to serve fifty guests. There was chaos in the kitchen and an hour's wait between the starter and main course.

'It was mayhem,' she recalled. 'We were ... making it up as we went along. It was totally insane.' A friend described it as 'a clown show'. But the guests were all fed – somehow – and, later, as she would often do in future, Waters 'opened a bottle of fumé blanc and toasted getting through the night'.

As for what was put on the plate that night and on future nights: 'Food is the most political thing in all our lives. Eating is an everyday experience, and the decisions we make about what we eat have daily consequences. And those daily consequences can change the world.' Waters, her friends and associates, saw the restaurant as an embodiment of the anti-establishment culture of the period: the counterculture. Its diminutive size was a two-fingered salute to the big institutions of the day; the no-choice menu was unheard of in any city in California or beyond.

The US was still enjoying its postwar freedom by eating as much beef as possible in the ever-expanding burger chains. Big was beautiful – from supermarkets to restaurants. The modern America of 1970 was chasing a new dream of speed and instant gratification. For a great many people, the best, greatest, most exciting cheese came out of an aerosol can.

US author Elissa Altman described Waters' approach as a 'single-minded commitment to a clear moral issue: that good food – honestly grown, picked at the height of its season, prepared simply, served beautifully, eaten slowly and convivially – should be available to everyone'.

'Our place didn't look like other places,' said Waters, 'we had a different set of values.' It was rare for a woman to own a restaurant, and very rare for women to be found cooking in the kitchen. Plus, most of the staff had no previous experience.

The restaurant felt different – so different from the McDonald's, the Pizza Huts, the Kentucky Fried Chickens and the Taco Bells (Chapter 11) that were consuming the minds of most hungry Americans of the era. When Waters talked to customers on the frequent occasions she waited tables, she discussed her food, and its source.

In the months that followed, she visited farmers and producers and asked if specific plants could be grown for her. She hired a full-time forager, whose job was to find produce and small producers, from fishermen to ranchers. She paid what she felt was a fair price, and she talked about it with her customers. 'Some of the ingredients we use are expensive. But that's because it's right to pay the farmworker,' she would say, proud at how the farmer's name was on the menu. 'The food that's on your plate is social justice in action.'

Founder of Chez Panisse, Alice Waters. It was rare for a woman to own a restaurant, rarer still to find a woman cooking in the kitchen.

Her customers lapped it up. Many were at the forefront of counterculture themselves: film-makers, journalists, photographers and writers. Waters' connections with farmers created the mantra of 'farm to fork'. As she secured supplies in the early days, months, then years of Chez Panisse, a whole network of farms and ranches developed in the Bay area. Forty-two years on from launching the restaurant, Alice Waters mulled over those early days of the business, as she sipped a green tea under a vast and ancient redwood, a little bowl of fresh apricots placed on the white, metal garden table. 'I love and treasure the farmer,' she said. Farmers 'are the stewards of the land'.

When Chez Panisse began, it was thought that there just wouldn't be enough farmers to support such an endeavour and that she wouldn't get the consistency of ingredients that is so vital for a restaurant to succeed. But, she explained:

> *If you pay farmers the right amount and encourage those who are doing the right thing, then you find that more come out of the woodwork. We started buying from farmers and paying them a real price, and they started flocking. Now we depend on them and they depend on us. It's something really beautiful.*

The food served on the plate at Chez Panisse was a demonstration that there was a better way to do things.

But, while the food and the chat and the spirit of the age was all about politics, it was a certain kind of politics: left-wing politics. The anti-establishment counterculture was on display in all its glory at Woodstock, the 1969 music festival of legend. It may have been just 'three days of peace and music', but the legend perpetuates. And the Woodstock spark of beauty, mud and love was fully at home at Chez Panisse. Alice Waters has freely admitted her unbuttoned attitude to sex: 'We were all free and easy,' she wrote in *Coming to My Senses* (subtitled *The Makings of a Counterculture Cook*). In a 2019 US podcast with NPR host Guy Raz, she acknowledged: 'There was a free-speech movement, the sexual revolution, drugs – I mean all these things, right? ... It really was [an exciting time].'

According to one of Waters' lovers, Jerry Budrick, on the night of Chez Panisse's one-year anniversary, 'Alice seduced me, right there in the restaurant'. And a friend, Barbara Carlitz, even said that 'one reason the story of Chez Panisse is so complex is that Alice was involved with so many of the men'.

Moreover, if Waters wasn't smoking dope (though she did admit to taking acid on one occasion), there were many tales of the staff doing so – stories of waiters exhaling dope smoke as they brought dishes to the table. Indeed, while her parents had helped with funds for the restaurant, according to author Jesse Jarnow, in her book *Heads: A Biography of Psychedelic America*, many of the original investors were drug dealers. 'They were the only people who had money,' Waters is quoted as saying. 'The only sort of counterculture people who had money. We couldn't get it from a bank. God knows.'

James Villas, the food and wine editor of US magazine *Town & Country*, once described Chez Panisse as 'a hippie, drug-ridden explosion in a playpen'. Thomas McNamee's biography of Waters (*Alice Waters and Chez Panisse: The Romantic, Impractical, Often Eccentric, Ultimately Brilliant Making of a Food Revolution*) also talks of the kitchen drama and of service interweaved with lots of drugs and sex. One chef, Willy Bishop, said McNamee 'liked to make brunch on a mild dose of LSD'. Then there were the accounts of mounds of cocaine snorted on the top of the chest freezer.

And, of the mild-mannered and quiet Waters, US chef Anthony Bourdain once described her food agenda as 'very Khmer Rouge' (a reference to the communist rulers of 1970s Cambodia, whose stock-in-trade was execution and forced labour), and US blogger Todd Kliman, casting an eye over her forty-year career, talked of her 'inflexible brand of gastronomical correctness ... Cooking, after all, is not about doing good; it's about tasting good.' Even the *New York Times* referenced her as the 'self-dramatizing Joan of Arc of American cuisine', and *Vanity Fair*'s David Camp once wrote that 'the magnitude of Chez Panisse's achievements is tempered by a certain cloying self-aggrandizement. This is a restaurant that never lacked a sense of its own importance and was celebrating its birthday with commemorative limited-edition posters as early as 1973.'

As to the finances, they were better considered in a haze of cannabis smoke. The early $4.50 set menu cost $6 per head to produce. Debts mounted quickly, and Waters owed some $40,000 within weeks. Her backers tried to rein her in, but, in the words of British food writer Elfreda Pownall, 'something as trivial as money was not going to stop her'.

Critics of Waters also raised their eyebrows at the debts of Chez Panisse. Her philosophy was to pay farmers a fair price, but, in those early days, as the debts mounted, she evidently wasn't paying quite a number of them anything.

The restaurant continued to be loss-making for some eight years. But it soldiered on, in the words of Seattle-based journalist David Laskin, 'by some convergence of karma and zeitgeist'. Chez Panisse settled firmly into its niche and got the attention of diners in California and across the US. It also captured the imagination of another very vital group of people: cooks. Just as Le Gavroche and the Waterside Inn (Chapter 14) trained a generation of chefs who would go on to spread great food around the UK, the list of those who worked at Chez Panisse and would go on to be the culinary stars of America is extraordinarily significant.

The roll call includes: Judy Rodgers (famous for San Francisco's Zuni Café, whose book of Zuni recipes is often heralded as the best cookbook written by an American chef); the influential *New York Times* columnist David Tanis; the celebrity chef and restaurateur Mark Miller; Jonathan Waxman, the Manhattan-based chef-patron of a number of restaurants in New York, Atlanta and Nashville; Los Angeles-based Suzanne Goin (celebrated for the fine-dining restaurants she runs in LA); and acclaimed baker Steven Sullivan.

And there was also Jeremiah Tower. Tower would go on to have a lifelong feud with Waters. If she was the mother of the American food revolution, then he believed he was the father.

American journalist Dana Goodyear wrote in the *New Yorker* in 2017 that Tower worked with Waters to transform Chez Panisse 'from a place where friends gathered to eat food that reminded Waters of meals she'd had in Brittany into a world-class restaurant'. Indeed, the acclaimed US wine writer Robert Finegan also said of Chez Panisse that it was a 'beef-stew-and-fruit-tart bistro for students and junior faculty. That's all it was. The presence of Jeremiah is what changed everything. Jeremiah really made the restaurant.'

In 1975, *Gourmet* magazine ran a review of the restaurant in which Tower was hailed for 'joyously exploring *la vraie cuisine française* in all its vigor, freshness, and variety, and ignoring those French dishes that turn up elsewhere with such monotonous regularity'. Tower later accused Waters of writing him out of the history of the restaurant. He recalled her showing him the first Chez Panisse cookbook, and was flabbergasted to see that 'she had taken all the dinners I dreamt up, written the menus for and cooked, and said that she did it'. Indeed, while the cookbook makes mention of almost thirty individuals who worked and collaborated with Waters, no mention is made of Jeremiah Tower.

The feud simmered for decades. Twenty-eight years after he joined Chez Panisse, Tower would begin an interview with the *New York Times* by declaring his self-imposed moratorium on discussing Chez Panisse. He wouldn't be drawn to the subject of Alice. Except that he couldn't help himself. 'She never knew a little vegetable from a rotten vegetable,' he muttered towards the end.

Similarly, in agreeing to a documentary film made by Anthony Bourdain in 2016, Tower stipulated that there must be no Waters-bashing. Within the first few seconds of the trailer for *Jeremy Tower: The Last Magnificent*, he attacked Waters for claiming his work as hers.

It seems he couldn't resist. But then their relationship was complicated, very complicated.

Tower, a self-taught cooking enthusiast with no serious experience, arrived at Chez Panisse in the winter of 1973. Born in 1942, with a degree from Harvard and an English accent gained from a boarding-school education in the county of Surrey, he had seen an advert in a newspaper. 'Immediate opening in a small innovative French restaurant for an inspired energetic chef who will plan and cook menus weekly for a single entree five course dinner à la Elizabeth David and Fernand Point.' The wording was as breathless as it was free of grammar.

He badly needed the money, and carried samples of menus under his arm. The interview was scheduled for 6 p.m., which surprised Tower, as he assumed that this would be the restaurant's busiest time, pre-service.

Indeed, having steeled himself to enter the place, he was told that chef Alice was busy and asked if he could return the next day. He may have come from a prosperous family, but, at that moment, he had almost nothing. The cost of the trip to the restaurant had used the last of the cash in his pockets.

Having walked down the restaurant steps, he decided to have another go, this time via the kitchen. He found the entrance, walked in gingerly, announced himself again, only to find himself face to face with the diminutive Waters. She took one look at him and said, 'Do something to that soup, will you?', before striding off to the dining room.

Bubbling on the stove was a vast aluminium pot of purée. He stuck a finger in, tasted it, and resolved that it needed salt, but then, looking around him, he found some white wine and cream, which he also added.

Alice returned, tasted the soup, and said, 'You're hired,' and then walked off to see to something else. Other chefs at the time dispute this version of events, claiming that a number of chefs came for interview, along with Tower, and they 'auditioned' for the role in the ensuing days.

But Tower got the job and worked at Chez Panisse for five years. He was gay and Waters was in a relationship. But the pair had an affair anyway. Tower says he also took Waters' boyfriend on holiday to Hawaii...

If there was tension in the kitchen, it was productive. Amid the fights and flirtations emerged a serious, game-changing restaurant – Waters' idealism combined with Tower's passion for nostalgia.

Tower brought order to the chaotic, culinary counterculture of the kitchen. In the words of Goodyear, he produced 'exquisite prix-fixe menus, scholarly treatises on the great cooks of France, and, eventually, manifestos for the future of food'.

Tower created divine dishes from the growing list of ingredients culled from the budding number of local producers. He worked with beefsteak tomatoes from Sonoma and fresh Californian goat's cheese. He defied the law of Elizabeth David that *bouillabaisse*

England's Elizabeth David inspired Alice Waters, who, in turn, was an inspiration for the British chef Sally Clarke.

could only be made in the Mediterranean; his combination of local clams, prawns, squid, lobster, crab, onions, saffron, garlic and fennel was breathtaking. And he claimed that it was he who first name-checked producers on the menu. A menu that survives from the latter part of his tenure includes 'Monterey Bay prawns' and 'California-grown geese'.

And, while Waters, the diligent companion at his side, service after service, as ever the immaculate figure, a bandana around her head, would walk the room quietly towards the end of service, he was a more flamboyant character. He didn't mind if people felt he owned the room. And he could also be pretty lively in the kitchen.

On the restaurant's third birthday, in 1974, the chef was notably sagging. 'Everyone was buying me Champagne, which slowed me down even more,' Tower later recalled. The word went out that the chef needed a boost and, a few minutes later, he was ushered over to the waist-height chest freezer, where a waiter then chopped and readied several lines of cocaine and handed Tower a rolled-up $20 note.

'In an instant, I was back at the stoves,' said Tower. Then a conga line formed at the back of the kitchen. 'The night was a huge success,' he said. It was, he said, 'the drug that made all the long hours possible, then impossible, in the kitchen'.

After five years, in 1978, Tower left Chez Panisse, possibly to Waters' relief. Of his era, Waters was diplomatic, calling it:

> *A period of time when I was very much on the foraging side and Jeremiah was very much on the cooking side, so we fit that together. I had always intended Chez Panisse to be a simple little place. Never wanted anything more, and I still don't want anything more. When Jeremiah came, he had a whole other vision of the food. It was just the kind of food that I ... wasn't cooking. And I was fascinated by it at the time.*

Eight years later, after a period of teaching and cooking in a variety of places, Tower opened Stars. It became one of the most successful restaurants in the Bay area. And, uninhibited by political correctness or a mission to save the planet, Tower delivered his flamboyance both on the menu and in the dining room. It was at Stars, according to fellow chefs like Bourdain, where Tower elevated the status of the chef.

'Jeremiah changed the world of restaurants and restaurant cooking,' explained Bourdain:

Having left Chez Panisse, chef Jeremiah Tower opened restaurants with flamboyance both on the menu and in the dining room, where the chef became the star.

> *Prior to Jeremiah, the chef was the backstairs help. The dining public didn't particularly care what the chef's opinion was or what the chef thought they should eat. The chef was there to serve them. People showed up at Jeremiah Tower-run restaurants to see Jeremiah, because they wanted to be in his orbit.*

At Stars, Bourdain continued, Tower 'had an open kitchen, a restaurant where one walked in wanting to see the chef. Before that, the last person you wanted to see, much less hear the opinion from, was the chef. At Stars, people insisted on it.'

According to the US chef and food writer Ruth Reichl, 'Jeremiah at Stars defined what a modern American restaurant could be.' When he was done with service, Tower didn't just work the room, he made it a party. He then opened Stars restaurants in other US cities, before taking the brand overseas, to Manila, Singapore, as well as opening the Peak Café in Hong Kong.

Tower was one of the first chefs to spread a high-end restaurant brand across the world. But, at the end of the '90s, he sold the business, and then, as the millennium approached, Tower quit the restaurant scene altogether and moved to Mexico for a quieter life. Today, he is softly spoken, elegant, witty, a great conversationalist and a very fine dining companion. Indeed, in his manner and tone, he is not unlike Alice Waters. But, while Tower is happy to enjoy a mellow retirement and eat the fruits of his protégés, Alice Waters never stopped campaigning.

She never opened a second restaurant, but her passion for farmers' markets and then organic produce encouraged a phenomenon to unfold across the country. 'In every city in America and far beyond, farmers' markets abound; organics are widely available; small organic vegetable gardens thrive from inner cities to suburban front lawns to the White House,' wrote Elissa Altman.

Waters' other mission was to capture the minds of children, to make them appreciate food and even aspire to become farmers. 'We have to get to the children first,' she once said, under the shadow of that giant redwood:

> *We can teach them about affordability and stewardship. We need to introduce food in kindergarten; they should be taught to count with fruit, to draw pictures of food, to cook in dramatic arts classes. Food is fundamental to life, fundamental to the life of the planet, and there is nothing more important than to teach that.*

Her 1995 initiative, the Edible Schoolyard, which, in Waters' words, was founded 'to create and sustain an organic garden and landscape that is wholly integrated into the school's curriculum, culture, and food program', was running in thirty-three countries by 2019. And her mission to disparage and shame the big businesses that continually perpetuate fast food showed little sign of abating as she reached her mid-seventies. 'It's tough because the fast-food industry has a pile of money,' she said, 'and they're lobbying in an outrageous way, they are influencing congressmen and senators, and it's really frightening.' When she had various opportunities to meet President Obama, she used to whisper three words in his ear: 'Free. School. Lunches.'

In the Trump era, with a president proud of his consumption of fast food, Waters' lobbying became even more challenging. Indeed, many might question whether she really made a difference, when even the schools in her Berkeley neighbourhood still don't serve food that is up to her standard.

In 2020, the US fast-food industry is forecast to be worth more than $223 billion. The number of franchised fast-food restaurants has increased by 28,000 in the past ten years.

Yet her passionate message that food should be seasonal, local, simple and communal resonates across the world. In 2014, *Time* magazine heralded her as one of the most influential people in the world. 'Chez Panisse is undoubtedly the most influential restaurant of its time, but Alice's legacy extends far beyond that,' the magazine declared. 'She proved the power of a chef, showing an entire generation that one passionate person can reshape the eating habits of a nation.'

One protégée of Waters was a British chef who never worked in the kitchen of Chez Panisse, but got a job in Malibu in 1979, after studying Le Cordon Bleu in Paris. Sally Clarke knew of Chez Panisse, so, a week or two after settling in, she booked a table, flew to Oakland Airport, and headed for the restaurant.

'The moment I put my hand on the door handle, I was spellbound,' she said:

> *What was happening there was exactly what I had dreamt of doing since I was twelve or thirteen years old. The only way I thought you should run a restaurant was to do it as one does at home: you pick from the garden or the market, you choose what's best, and that's how you create a menu.*

As she took her seat in the dining room, the light from the sun setting across the bay bleeding into the room, she was handed a piece of paper that changed her life. It was a menu with no choice. 'I saw that this idea really could work and I thought, *Why can't I try this in London?*'

Over the following months, every free weekend Clarke had, she took a flight to Oakland Airport and headed straight for Chez Panisse.

'I ate lunch and dinner, then lunch and dinner. I just ate,' she recalled. 'I never worked there, I just sat there like a sponge. I took everyone I knew there. It was the only place I wanted to be.'

In 1984, Sally Clarke opened Clarke's in London's Notting Hill. Her restaurant, along with a number of young English chefs, would create another revolution, but this time it would be a very British one. There was Clarke and Rowley Leigh and Alastair Little and a young man called Simon Hopkinson. After years of French dominance in an era commanded by the Roux brothers and their fine dining (Chapter 14), London was about to get a taste of something very different.

16

Bibendum Opens in London

Chef Simon Hopkinson teamed up with designer and restaurateur Terence Conran and opened Bibendum in London. The food in the kitchen was mainly French, but the dining room was very different to other Gallic places. It was casual, unstuffy and boisterous. Hopkinson was a new kind of cook, catering in an era of peak Thatcherite meritocracy. Dining became a serious hobby in Britain and helped to spawn another new phenomenon: restaurant PR.

Thirty-three-year-old chef Simon Hopkinson was in the kitchen of Hilaire, in west London, when a note arrived that would change his life.

It was a letter from Terence Conran. Hopkinson was winding down after lunchtime service at the small Old Brompton Road establishment, and he unfolded the note to see that it was just a little sketch with three words beneath it.

The pencil drawing was of Monsieur Bibendum, the Michelin Man, his body made up of rolls like a stack of tyres. The words read: 'I've got it.'

Hopkinson realised that things were about to get exciting. A few months later, Bibendum opened.

Conran made Hopkinson a shareholder, and the restaurant was housed in the redeveloped Michelin Building in South Kensington. Conran had been vying for it for some time. Opened in 1911 as the UK headquarters of the tyre company, as well as a depot for tyres, it was a decorative building made of the then novel substance concrete.

By 1985, it no longer suited the company and, once up for sale, had gained interest from a number of individuals interested in a space that was now in a very fashionable district of London. Conran fought for it, as did a man called Paul Hamlyn, a publisher. The two men were friends, but, due to the secrecy of their ambitions, did not at first realise they were bidding against each other. Once they

Hopkinson and Conran's Bibendum served gutsy French bourgeois food to Britain's new meritocracy. It quickly became the most fashionable restaurant in London.

discovered this, they decided to merge their ideas and partnered to beat off other bidders, purchasing it for £8 million. The redevelopment would house Hamlyn's publishing business, as well as Conran's plan for a shop, bar and restaurant.

Conran had met Hopkinson at Hilaire. He became a firm fan, dined there every week and made good friends with the chef.

One evening, as they chatted, Hopkinson said to Conran: 'I want to have my own restaurant. Would you back me?' For Conran, looking to open a new restaurant, it was a no-brainer.

Hopkinson had been a shy boy. He had a beautiful singing voice (and was a choral scholar at St John's College School, Oxford) and he was one of two boys born to a dentist father and schoolteacher mother in Bury, Lancashire. He had worked at a local French restaurant in Birtle in the school holidays, and, by the age of twenty, had opened The Shed, a five-table restaurant near Fishguard, on the Welsh Pembrokeshire coast. Having caught the eye of Egon Ronay (Chapter 14) and won one of his stars, he later moved to London, where, in due course, he was installed at Hilaire.

He had an obsession with doing things correctly and had grown in confidence. Some inspiration had come from Jeremiah Tower (Chapter 15), whose restaurant, Stars, he had visited in San Francisco. 'I was fascinated by him,' recalled Hopkinson, over thirty years later. 'He loved traditional French food, he was flamboyant and glamourous, a bit of a star, and I knew he was gay.'

The first recipe in Hopkinson's acclaimed book *Roast Chicken and Other Stories* (first published in 1994 and co-authored with the cook Lindsey Bareham) is 'Jeremiah Tower's Montpelier Butter'. It was included partly as an homage to Tower, and partly because it's just very good.

However, a cursory glance at Hopkinson's menu at Bibendum, when it opened in November 1987, might have made an habitué of the London restaurant scene sigh. It was a long list of dishes, and most of them were written in French. There was *soup de poisson*, *endives au gratin*, *escargots de Bourgogne*, *oeufs en meurette*, *poulet de Bresse rôti*, and *sauté de veau aux morilles*.

Was London still slavishly kowtowing to the French? Even in this brand-spanking-new restaurant opened by one of the great designers of the age?

But, while the menu may have been mainly in French (though there were a few English dishes there: 'crab mayonnaise', 'cream of celery soup', 'grilled lobster in garlic butter'), the food was very different. It was definitely not haute cuisine.

Conran and Hopkinson had had many conversations about how the food should be at Bibendum, but they had also travelled to France on field trips. One restaurant they visited was a three-star Michelin establishment that served a large number of dishes, all with delicate, pretty garnishes. 'I can't bear this hunker-munker food,' declared Conran. Bibendum would be very different. It would be robust, but it would also be authentic; it was, said Hopkinson, 'gutsy French bourgeois brasserie cooking'.

The room in which it was served was bathed in light. With a tall ceiling and vast windows, it was, said Hopkinson, a place of 'bustle and noise and convivial, but not stiff in any way'.

To cement this spirit, Hopkinson headhunted a man called John Davey for the role of maître d'. So the moment a customer entered, they were met not by a bowing, scraping, flattering, obsequious Frenchman or Italian, but by a friendly and gregarious Englishman.

'He was casually smart,' said Hopkinson; Davey's presence softened the grandeur of the room. But there was still luxury and comfort, and, for a generation of newly moneyed Londoners, it quickly became a social haunt – a restaurant that brought together people in fashion, design, television and politics. The likes of David Frost – the TV presenter – would have their regular tables, and part of the joy of the restaurant was the walk from front desk to table. As Davey led his guests through the room, he would have to pause as they greeted friends on virtually every table they passed.

Bibendum was very different to the sorts of places the Roux brothers (Chapter 14) had opened. The atmosphere at Le Gavroche or the Waterside Inn was more refined and quieter. The food on the plate much prettier and seemingly more sophisticated. But Hopkinson still relied on the brothers, if only for supplies.

A great number of the ingredients that Hopkinson needed could only be acquired through the supply company that the Roux family had set up. From poultry and puff pastry to ceps (the British penny bun or the Italian porcini) and certain vegetables, Bibendum, and a great many other restaurants of the day, relied on the Rouxs.

When it came to dessert, Hopkinson also did something different; he revelled in what the English did best: puddings. So there on the menu was Queen of Puddings and a steamed ginger pudding. There were French dishes, too, like *tarte fine aux pommes* (a classic French apple tart) and chocolate pithiviers. (Hopkinson first ate the latter at chef Michel Guérard's restaurant at Eugénie-les-Bains in south-west France, where the chef was, Hopkinson once wrote, 'conveniently lost for words when it came to giving me the recipe'. Back in London, Hopkinson worked it out himself, and later concluded that, 'in the end, mine was better'.)

This confidence to mix genres – the best of brasserie French and old-fashioned English, presented in a grand room with a casual atmosphere – was very, very different. And London loved it.

Conran looked around the establishment at his co-creation and revelled at how he was feeding the meritocracy of Britain. This was just a few months after Margaret Thatcher's third consecutive election victory, her second landslide triumph.

Bibendum had quickly become the most fashionable west London restaurant. Celebrities were there not to be seen, but because they wanted to be there. Hopkinson recalled a booking for a table for three that saw Alec Guinness, Lauren Bacall and Alan Bennett dining together. Conran later reflected:

> *The tastes of Londoners were changing and there was a great opportunity to do something special. Our vision was to create something entirely new, placed somewhere between the relaxed atmosphere of a Parisian brasserie and the precise, elegant formality of somewhere like the Connaught [a high-end Mayfair hotel]. It was a watershed moment for me, too, and my first serious step on the gastronomic ladder.*

Bibendum's consequent success gave Conran the confidence to go on to open a number of other restaurants across the capital.

The critics raved. And many were impressed that Hopkinson had resuscitated and restored the reputation of the word 'continental'. The postwar years had seen nothing but dismal offerings under that label. Hopkinson described the food as 'very, very continental', but his fare was far from previous incarnations of 'continental', which had included atrocities like spaghetti and chips (Chapter 14) or the then exotic avocado pear and French dressing.

His menu featured *tête de veau* (calf's head), tripe (stomach from cattle or sheep), rabbit in mustard sauce and *boudin blanc* (a white pork sausage). There was also fish and chips, and, on Sundays, roast beef. The *Guardian* critic Paul Levy revelled at the time at what he called Bibendum's 'gastro-retro, reactionary chic French bistro food: herrings, braised endives, pink roasted veal, chocolate pithiviers, mmmm'.

Meanwhile, in the kitchen, there was a young crew of British chefs. They included: brothers Henry and Matthew Harris; Phil Howard; and Bruce Poole – all of whom would go on to light beacons of the new British food revolution in their own establishments.

Chef Alastair Little, along with Rowley Leigh and Hopkinson, formed a holy trinity of British culinary stars.

At last, a British cook was at the helm of a fashionable restaurant in London. And he wasn't the only one.

Another Brit making similar waves was Alastair Little. His self-named restaurant opened in Soho in 1985. A Cambridge graduate, he was also smitten with Elizabeth David's recipes. He offered no tablecloths, the napkins were paper, and his light, fresh, simple food saw him badged with the label 'godfather of modern British cooking'.

Then there was Rowley Leigh, who had been trained by the Roux brothers and was another admirer of Elizabeth David. He opened Kensington Place in London's Notting Hill in the same year Bibendum started. Like Bibendum, Kensington Place was big and airy, with an entire wall of windows down one side looking onto the upper end of Kensington Church Street.

Leigh had joined forces with two other men: Nick Smallwood and Simon Slater. Having started at Le Gavroche, Leigh was made head chef of the Roux brothers' City of London restaurant, Le Poulbot, and, as he looked around at the capital's dining scene, all he could see was fine dining or cheap-and-cheerful. 'There wasn't anywhere in London with any ambition that wasn't fine dining,' he said.

Leigh's menu saw a simple omelette (cooked to Elizabeth David's recipe), his ingenious 'chicken and goat's cheese mousse', a whole fresh and griddled foie gras served on a pancake of sweetcorn, and sausage and mash. It was innovative, crowd-pleasing and exciting. The restaurant was noisy beyond belief, and it had a similar mix of customers to Bibendum, except, because of its location (Kensington Palace was within walking distance), Diana, Princess of Wales, might sometimes be dining at one end, while journalists from the nearby *Daily Mail* building dined at the other.

According to the BBC radio producer and food writer Dan Saladino, Kensington Place had 'one of the most talked-about dining rooms in British restaurant history'. As for the restaurant's menu, it was, said British chef Cath Gradwell, who worked in the kitchen in the late '80s, very simply, 'brave'. She added: 'No one else could have put chips on the menu and got away with it. It was a revolution and definitely the moment when things changed.'

But opposite Leigh's Notting Hill establishment was another restaurant, one that had opened in 1984: Clarke's. There Sally Clarke, inspired by her endless lunches and dinners at Chez Panisse (Chapter 15), replicated Alice Waters' Berkeley restaurant with her no-choice menu. 'Vegetables, herbs and salads are my inspiration,' she once said. 'So, when I arrive here between 7.30 and 8 a.m., I see what there is and set my mind to the balance of the menu.'

Like Waters, her restaurant never spawned a sibling, let alone a chain. Chez Panisse was the constant inspiration. 'That restaurant is the best in the world,' she once declared. 'The ethos, the team, the support, the mutual love. I just aspire to that every day of my life. I've always got Alice on my shoulder; I ask myself with each dish if she'd like it.' In fact, in celebration of thirty years of trading in October 2014, Alice Waters travelled to London and, for a week, acted as maître d' at Clarke's.

Back in the late '80s, there was a major difference between Kensington Place, Alastair Little, Clarke's and Bibendum: the price. 'Bibendum', conceded Hopkinson, 'was very expensive.' Indeed, the writer and restaurateur Nicholas Lander once wrote: 'I was informed, with horror at the time, dinner for two cost over £100.'

Hopkinson defended the pricing as the result of the cost rates. They employed a very large number of staff – some ninety people – and, of course, didn't stint on ingredients. But, if some were astonished that such costs could be levied by a restaurant that wasn't offering fine dining, it didn't seem to harm the business. This was, after all, the year that Harry Enfield's character Loadsamoney was gracing UK screens...

Henry Harris, whose brother remained at Bibendum for many years while he founded the Knightsbridge bistro Racine, described Hopkinson, Leigh and Little as 'a kind of holy trinity'. They were also gentle cooks. Although Hopkinson has admitted that his kitchen 'was a bit shouty in the beginning', it was nothing like the brutality being meted out on the young cooks by a very different kind of chef, Marco Pierre White, across town and over the river on Wandsworth Common, where he was running Harveys, which also opened the same year (Chapter 14).

One of White's protégés, Gordon Ramsay, went on to build his own restaurant empire, turning kitchen brutality into an art form. His swearing persona spawned TV shows, and he capitalised on the ensuing fame by opening restaurants – the principle (not always successful) being that fame helped bring in customers.

Hopkinson's modus operandi was to talk to his chefs about authenticity, flavour and the importance of getting things right. He told them to read recipe books by his guiding mentors Elizabeth David and the French cookery writer Richard Olney.

While Marco Pierre White was slashing the shirts and aprons off the backs of any chefs who complained about the temperature, Harris said of Hopkinson: 'I remember him sitting me down and getting me to read a paragraph by Richard Olney on how to make stock.'

'When I got the hang of somebody,' said Hopkinson, 'and I could see that they were intelligent, I would leave them to think of things and come up with ideas; that could make me happy and very excited.'

Rowley Leigh, meanwhile, has described his approach to cooking as 'therapy'. But he, too, was a stickler for accuracy and good behaviour. And his admonishments were not always confined to his staff. He wasn't afraid of asking

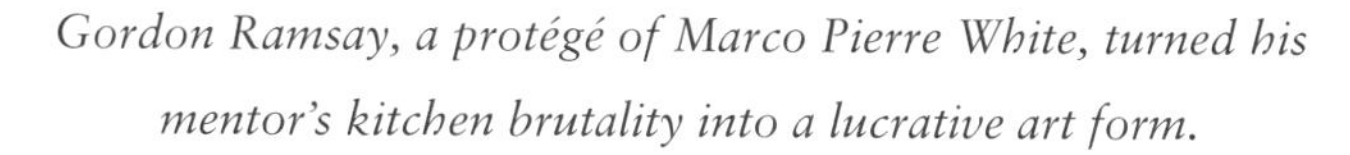

Gordon Ramsay, a protégé of Marco Pierre White, turned his mentor's kitchen brutality into a lucrative art form.

a boisterous customer to come and see him the day after a rowdy evening in the restaurant, ordering them into his small office above the kitchen, and giving them a stern dressing-down for their bad behaviour. And then there was Alastair Little, who came across as more amiable schoolmaster than chef, with his beard, glasses and quizzical look.

But, if Hopkinson couldn't have been more opposite in style, temperament and education to Marco Pierre White, they did have one thing in common: a man called Alan Crompton-Batt, who would single-handedly propel chefs from stove slaves to stars.

Hopkinson, at the end of the '70s, had been an inspector for the Egon Ronay guide, before enjoying a stint as a private chef. A fellow inspector was Alan Crompton-Batt, a man with a mop of yellow hair flopping over his eyes, who often looked bedraggled, even while in a jacket and tie.

Crompton-Batt almost fizzed when he talked about food and drink. It's hardly surprising that the pair became friends and, for a time, shared a flat.

Having tried a music business career in the 1970s managing punk bands, including one called the Psychedelic Furs, he then decided to pursue a greater love: food. His taste buds had been awakened when he was sent to an English boarding school in Penang, as his family followed his RAF father to Singapore.

He passed the Ronay practical exam and, merrily in his mid-twenties, found himself travelling the country, eating for a living. He learned what made a good restaurant and how the best ones were run. A few years later, exhausted from the grind of eating twice a day and – as a gregarious character – finding lone dining unbearable, he found a job at a restaurant business called Kennedy Brooks, first as a restaurant manager and then as marketing director. There he began to carve out his own niche, courting journalists and taking them to dine at some of the group's restaurants.

He would entertain them at the company's expense and talk up the people in the kitchen. Crompton-Batt liked to take some credit for the rise of Simon Hopkinson, because he had suggested Hopkinson leave his employ as a private chef and work at Hilaire, which is where he was spotted by Terence Conran, possibly at the suggestion of Crompton-Batt.

Soon, Crompton-Batt decided to start his own business. Alan Crompton-Batt Public Relations set out to take the quiet checked-trousered artists of the kitchens and get them into the pages of the country's glossy magazines. Today, hundreds of PR firms vie to promote London and the UK's restaurants and their chefs to the media. From the mid-1980s to the end of that decade, ACBPR had the field more or less all to itself.

With Crompton-Batt was an endless supply of pretty young assistants, whom his wife and erstwhile business partner, Elizabeth, coped with – until they divorced in 1995. They were the Battettes. Most of them were blonde, and Alan, also fair-haired, decided to dye his hair even blonder. It was the '80s, so, to match his New Romantic long locks and suits, he bought a white BMW. 'He drove it from appointment to appointment, sometimes in a wobbly line,' recalled the British restaurant critic Fay Maschler after his untimely death in 2004 at the age of fifty.

Journalists willingly accepted his invitations to lunch, which would be very long, very liquid and, of course, free. They, in turn, were only too happy to help Crompton-Batt make stars of his clients in the pages of their newspaper supplements and gossip columns. One of those stars was Marco Pierre White. White had first met Crompton-Batt while he was working at Le Gavroche, and later recollected: 'I used to walk home every night down the Kings Road and stop at Kennedy's, a brasserie where Alan was the manager. We used to chat and he would tell me stories about Le Gavroche and Albert and the restaurant business in general. We became great friends.' White was struck by Crompton-Batt's knowledge and passion for food. 'Alan was obsessed with food,' he said, 'and he had a photographic memory of every dish he'd eaten and where he'd eaten it.'

When Crompton-Batt set up his new business with Elizabeth, White was one of the first to hear the news. 'He was one of the kindest people I've ever met,' said White. 'And, when I opened Harveys, he did the PR for nothing. He never, ever gave me a bill.' Crompton-Batt, White reflected, 'believed in me when I was nineteen and fresh out of Yorkshire. He told me I would be the first British chef to get three stars.'

ACBPR's other clients included the notoriously difficult Nico Ladenis. The Greek-born restaurateur was known for kicking customers out of his restaurant if they committed a crime such as asking for salt. He disliked people slouching when they ate his food, and once kicked the chair leg of a diner who was looking a little too relaxed, barking: 'Sit properly in my restaurant!'

Given that White had worked for Ladenis, he had doubtless learnt from the master. White's favourite stunt was called the 'whoosh'. If a customer refused to leave at the behest of the chef, the waiters would descend on the table, remove all the crockery and cutlery, and then the maître d' would 'whoosh' away the tablecloth in a final flourish.

White stopped carrying out whooshes when, following large amounts of press coverage, he noticed a certain kind of wide-boy banker and his inebriated friends doing their best to see if they could also get thrown out.

Crompton-Batt didn't stop such stories from appearing in the papers. According to an obituary for Crompton-Batt in the *Telegraph*:

> *If a journalist asked him to confirm a story about a client, Crompton-Batt might reply: 'Yes, totally true. And this is what he's going to say.' He would then launch into a faultless impersonation of the client, giving a line with all the appropriate phraseology and histrionic effects; he fondly believed that the client would not remember whether or not he had spoken to the press.*

Crompton-Batt elevated the status of the chef and made stars of the country's culinary talent. And, in the case of White, he was helped by the images taken by the photographer Bob Carlos Clarke. 'Alan invented restaurant PR and, with Bob, they created the cult of the chef,' said White. Crompton-Batt may have lunched himself to an early grave, but, White added, 'he had the greatest palate of anyone I ever knew. He was like a great chef, except he couldn't cook.'

The '80s was his heyday, but, in due course, other PR firms launched – some spawned by girls who had once been Battettes, whose staff then went on to spawn other firms, and so on – and, nowadays, almost every restaurant in the UK worth its salt has a publicist.

Levy wrote: 'Alan Crompton-Batt was in the vanguard of the British restaurant revolution. He was one of the people accountable for those strange features of modern life where going out to restaurants is a recreational activity and cooking is a hobby rather than daily drudgery.'

But, as fashions changed and the electric blue suits and gold jewellery of ACBPR went out of fashion, so, too, did the glitz of the '80s dim. The 1990s saw a chill economic wind that meant chefs and restaurateurs were reluctant to grant their publicists vast lunch budgets. There were also fewer journalists able to spend an entire afternoon carousing. ACBPR began to run out of steam. 'Everyone had run out of money and I ran out of options,' Crompton-Batt once said. 'It was not a good time to ring someone and say, "We're doing terribly interesting things with a duck down in Harrow." In a way, we deserved it – we created a bubble and it burst.'

But, while Crompton-Batt's personal bubble may have burst, the '90s continued to see huge growth in the opening of restaurants, particularly in

London. The year 1994 saw the opening of Fergus Henderson's St John; Heston Blumenthal started the Fat Duck in Bray in 1995; and 1998 saw Gordon Ramsay setting up on his own place in Chelsea. There was even a high-end magazine, *Food Illustrated*, launched in 1998, which would chronicle the new era of budding British restaurants, their chefs, and the blooming number of small producers who supplied them.

Although smart magazines and newspaper supplements focused on the new wave of British cooks, and attempted to define 'modern British food' during the 1980s and '90s, there was another part of the restaurant sector that food writers and critics ignored: the phenomenon that was the Indian restaurant. Food writers, critics and restaurant inspectors may have mocked such establishments for their wallpaper and traduced an entire musical genre as 'curry house music', but there were many more independent Taste of Indias than there were Bibendums.

Indeed, the fastest growth in the story of the Indian restaurant was between 1980 and 2000, when the total number grew from 3,000 to 8,000.

There was much drudgery in the UK restaurant scene after the Second World War, but there was a serious success story when it came to the curry house. The immigration of Bangladeshi and Pakistani families across the country meant that a great many towns didn't just have one Indian restaurant, but often several. As the historian Lizzie Collingham wrote in her book *Curry: A Tale of Cooks and Conquerors*, 'curry houses are not the first things which spring to mind when Leamington Spa is mentioned', but, in 1975, a visitor to that town counted five there. It was a genre that had quite a head start.

Thanks to the East India Company (Chapter 10), Indian dishes began to appear in London in the early 1800s. In fact, in 1811, an advertisement in *The Times* heralded the newly opened Hindoostane Coffee House, which offered retired officials of the East India Company 'Indian dishes in the highest perfection'. This was a glorious irony because, to soothe the tender palates of the British toiling for the British Raj, a number of very English clubs had opened across India (Chapter 9). But, once back in Blighty, they missed this more exotic cuisine. The décor, the bamboo-cane chairs, the hookah pipes and, of course, the curries could take these 'nabobs' back to the good old days. Curries were increasingly included in nineteenth-century recipe books, and more and more shops opened selling spices, chutneys and curry pastes.

But the seeds of the modern Indian restaurant were sewn in the 1940s, when a number of cafés grew in the capital in the likes of Brick Lane and Commercial Road

The seeds of Indian restaurants in Britain were sowed in the 1940s when cafés opened in east London to cater for the community of seaman that had come over from the Sylhet district of Bangladesh.

to support a community of seamen from the Sylhet district of Bangladesh. Many of them, having survived a hideous journey from Calcutta, had jumped ship at Southampton or Cardiff and made their way to the East End of London.

There were smarter Indian restaurants, too, such as Veeraswamy, which opened in 1926 on Regent Street. Like the Indian coffee house of the early 1800s, such restaurants catered for those retired from service in India – ex-army or civil servants – and were usually staffed by the Sylhetis and their families. Indeed, it was their entrepreneurial endeavours that saw these immigrants buying up a large number of the bombed and derelict cafés that were scattered across London after the Second World War – an opportunity that was also not missed by a number of Chinese and Greek-Cypriot immigrants.

The '50s and '60s saw Indian restaurants spread across towns and cities in the UK, and they were a favourite economical option for students. The Sylhetis, who eventually became known simply as Bangladeshis, catered for the tastes of those retired Anglo-Indians, but also found their food popular with those who were tasting it for the first time. There were creamy kormas sprinkled with almonds, hot Madras curries with a squeeze of lemon juice, and pilau rice flecked with colour. The British palate was challenged, but not overly, and, wrote Collingham, 'the restaurants appealed to their customers as inexpensive places where the food was served promptly'. Beer was then integrated into the offering, poppadoms and chutneys became starters, the Balti emerged; none of these things would have been recognised in India.

There was further excitement when Gaylord in London installed a tandoor oven – 'a proper mud oven', as the 1968 *Good Food Guide* described it – and then, as Collingham noted, 'the food in Indian restaurants took on a life of its own, independent from the food of the Indian subcontinent'.

The British came to see Indian curry as theirs, as much of a culinary staple as roast beef. And, as the pendulum swung across history, the lack of authenticity of British curry would give a new generation of Indian chefs the opportunity to shun this bastardised food and create a wave of new restaurants that reflected the regions of India and the real dishes of that country.

So successful was one chef, Atul Kochhar, that he became the first Indian to win a Michelin star, at Mayfair restaurant Tamarind in 2001. He was still at it in 2019, opening Kanishka, which specifically served the food of north-east India – the regions of Arunachal Pradesh, Assam, Meghalaya, Manipur, Mizoram, Nagaland or Tripura. It may have meant little to the London diner, but no one ever complained about having a new Indian restaurant pop up on the landscape.

The growth of Indian restaurants was mirrored by the exhausting spread in the 2000s of a plethora of new dining experiences that brought food from almost every corner of the globe to the UK. Meanwhile, some of the protagonists of the British food revolution of the '80s were hanging up their aprons.

After years of cooking, Alastair Little gave up the restaurant business and opened a shop called Tavola on London's Westbourne Grove. 'I liked the prep and dealing with producers,' he said, but 'service was long, hard and tedious ... you fill the plates and send the food out.' And, as British food writer Caroline Stacey wrote in *The Independent* in 2003, Little's 'equally literate contemporaries, such as Simon Hopkinson and Rowley Leigh, don't rattle the pots and pans every night [any more]'.

Hopkinson found the relentless pressure of service too much. Seven years after Bibendum opened, he quit the restaurant kitchen for good. 'It just all got too much,' he later reflected. 'I broke down. It was terrible, awful. And that was it for me. I couldn't do it now. I'd be terrified. I'd chop my fingers off or something.'

Leigh, meanwhile, went on to open Café Anglais in Bayswater, where he created a dish as historic as his chicken and goat's cheese mousse: parmesan custard with anchovy toast.

Hopkinson, Leigh, Little and Clarke changed the British dining scene for ever. They won plaudits from critics and were celebrated for their writings. But there was one thing that eluded them, whether they cared or not: a Michelin star...

17

The Death of Bernard Loiseau

The suicide of celebrated chef Bernard Loiseau sent shock waves across the restaurants of France and around the world. Questions were asked about the pressure placed on chefs and, in particular, the influence of guides such as the Michelin Red Guide and the power of restaurant critics. In turn, their power was challenged – by a phenomenon called blogging...

It was around 4 p.m. on Tuesday, 25 February 2003, in a smart restaurant in Saulieu, a small town in the heart of Burgundy. A young woman sat in the corner of the dining room, surrounded by people listening intently, writing her words into their notepads. Stéphanie Gaitey dabbed her red eyes, breathed in deeply and said simply: 'We don't know why he did it.'

It was the afternoon after the most traumatic day in the restaurant's history, and, with lunchtime service over, the press were allowed in to speak to a few select members of staff.

Gaitey was the now former assistant to Bernard Loiseau, one of the country's most celebrated chefs. Many young cooks had flocked to train in his kitchen. Customers came from all over the world to dine and stay in his beautifully furnished rooms with their own log fires.

One day before, Loiseau folded his chef's apron and retreated to the bedroom he used at the Hôtel de la Côte d'Or – the hotel that housed his establishment – for his ritual undisturbed daily nap. Except, on that particular day, a siesta was not on his mind. He shut and locked the door, walked around to a chair, sat down, and manoeuvred a shotgun into position, so that the barrels were pointing straight at him. Then he squeezed the trigger.

It was his wife, Dominique, who found him. Returning to the hotel and restaurant at around quarter past five, she came to retrieve a document she had

Hôtel de la Côte d'Or, where chef Bernard Loiseau had his three-Michelin-starred restaurant. His obsession with perfection ended in tragedy.

left in the room. The door wouldn't budge, so she went around and tried another, which she knew would open as the lock hadn't worked in years. But there was something blocking the door, so she gave it a shove and stumbled into a scene that she would struggle to erase from her mind. It was fortunate, she said, that it was she who had found him, and not her children. The weapon he had used had been a gift from her.

That night, dinner at the three-Michelin-starred restaurant went ahead as normal. 'We still served our customers,' recalled Loiseau's head chef, Patrick Bertrand, some ten years later. 'Most of them didn't know until the next day.

We continued serving because it's a bit like a theatre. The show must go on and the cooking must go on.'

For Loiseau's widow, there would be no question of turning people away, many of whom would have booked tables months previously and travelled a considerable distance to be there. 'Of course we served dinner that night,' she said, adding: 'We sell happiness.'

Lunch service went ahead, similarly, the next day, although the news had broken on every French TV network that morning.

Before evening service on Tuesday, the press queuing outside the restaurant were invited in. Loiseau's assistant had little to add. She just shook her head with tears in her eyes.

But, if Gaitey wasn't offering a reason that the chef, who had retained three Michelin stars for twelve years, had taken his own life, some 200 miles away, in the town of Lyons, a fellow chef and friend of Loiseau had no doubts.

Paul Bocuse, who operated a chain of brasseries, in addition to his famous three-Michelin-starred L'Auberge du Pont de Collonges, didn't mince his words when a call was put through to his kitchen office from the French daily newspaper *Le Parisien*.

'Bravo, Gault Millau,' he said, 'you have won.'

Bocuse had last spoken to his friend on Sunday, and recalled that Loiseau had been distraught. The Gault Millau guide (founded in 1965 by two restaurant critics, Henri Gault and Christian Millau) – while not as high-profile as the

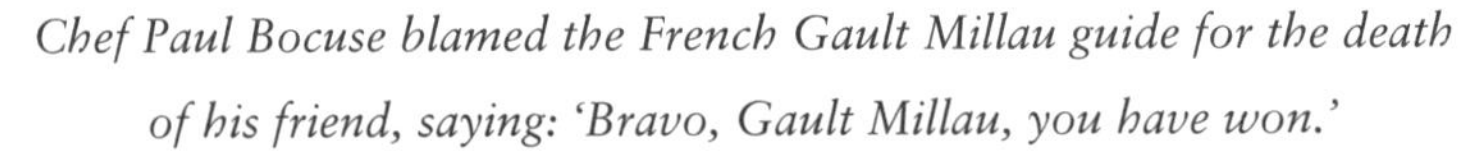

Chef Paul Bocuse blamed the French Gault Millau guide for the death of his friend, saying: 'Bravo, Gault Millau, you have won.'

Michelin Guide, it still had considerable influence – had informed Loiseau that he would be docked two points in their forthcoming book for 2003. His score would go from 19/20 to 17/20.

This followed some mumblings among a few of the country's restaurant critics that Loiseau's sauces were not quite as they had once been.

Loiseau had also heard rumours that Michelin was considering docking one of his stars. He had even had a meeting with a senior figure at the organisation who had told him: '*Il n'y a pas de feu au lac*' (there is no fire in the lake). That conversation seemed to break the great man's confidence. 'I'm finished, I'm no damn good, I'm nul,' a colleague heard him mutter in the kitchen.

Bernard Fabre, the company's finance director, also encountered a defeatist Loiseau. 'I'm going to lose my third star ... That's going to make me lose money and drive me into bankruptcy, and they'll take my hotel away from me,' Loiseau told him.

Days later, the world heard the news of the demise of one of the great practitioners of French gastronomy. Loiseau's cooking wasn't just classic; he had further refined some of the nation's greatest dishes. His frogs' legs with garlic and a parsley sauce, for example, was as miraculously tasty as it was simple. The legs were fried in butter, the garlic brought to the boil and cooled some seven times to remove its astringency, the parsley simply made into a purée. The legs were then fanned around the circle of green purée, and a smaller circle of now smooth and rich garlic sauce sat in the middle. Diners could just pick up the legs with their fingers, dip them in the sauces and enjoy this dreamy concoction.

Loiseau, with his team and his wife by his side, was, for years, fulfilling a dream. He told his wife that, as a 15-year-old, he had decided that he would become a chef who, in time, would get three stars. 'As a young man, every day when I put my socks on, I would pull up each one saying, "I will get three stars, I will get three stars."'

He had risen to become one of the greatest cooks of perhaps the world's finest cuisine. And he had a beautiful restaurant and hotel, set in the prettiest of gardens at the gateway to one of the world's finest grape-growing regions, Burgundy.

In 1991, he had been telephoned by a Monsieur Naegellen of the Michelin Guide. 'Monsieur Loiseau, I'm calling to tell you that your establishment will have three stars in our next guide,' he told him.

After the call, he had taken Dominique in his arms and said: 'This is the greatest day of my life.'

But success had come at a price. In the words of Loiseau's maître d', Hubert Couilloud: 'Ever since he won the third star, he had been haunted by the idea of losing it.'

A psychiatrist, Dr Ladislas Kiss, commented that Loiseau 'couldn't understand that you can have a life of just plain excellence. He was caught in a trap of his own perfectionism.' Naturally, he was a workaholic. 'His life was here [at the restaurant], not at home,' said Dominique, and he never took a day off:

> *We never closed. He didn't want a hobby, he didn't want to spend too much time with the children [aged thirteen, eleven and six at the time of Loiseau's death], so we didn't often have meals together. It was deeply hard, but I never showed it to my husband because it was his life, it was his job, and, when you marry somebody, you can't change who they are.*

Loiseau was not, of course, the first chef to become obsessed with perfection, nor would he be the last. The great chefs of the nineteenth century, such as France's Marie-Antoine Carême (Chapter 8) or London's Alexis Soyer (Chapter 9), were devoted to their craft, to delivering faultless precision. And their devotion helped to elevate dining from a necessity to an extravagant recreation.

British chef and TV presenter Keith Floyd said of the restaurant business: 'It kills marriages, it kills relationships, and it kills life' (Chapter 14). But, while Loiseau had also demonstrated that he was prone to depression ('He could be the best chef one day and the worst the next,' commented Dominique), his death cast a light on those whose métiers were to examine, criticise and sometimes mercilessly savage a chef, more for entertainment than information. Although no one suggested this was the case with the Michelin Guide, many did raise questions about the power it wielded and the effect that it could have on chefs.

The Michelin Guide, by the time Loiseau was becoming dangerously anxious about its pronouncements, was pre-eminent among restaurant guides. Its reach and power was global. The little red books pronounced on, and guided diners towards, restaurants and hotels, from Singapore to the Middle East, Africa to Asia, the United States to Europe. In many countries, rival guides were launched, but none was able to topple Michelin from its perch. Whatever alternative ratings systems were posited, be they Italian Gambero Rosso forks, American Automobile Association diamonds or British AA rosettes, nothing had quite the meaning of a Michelin star – or, indeed, three.

As UK chef Marcus Wareing, a protégé of Gordon Ramsay and, in 2019, a holder of one star for his London restaurant Marcus, once put it: 'Those little macaroons, those little stars, in that book, with that history – it's something so small, but it has so much clout.'

The Michelin Guide was originally designed by founders of the tyre company, André and Edouard Michelin, as a marketing vehicle for its products. Today, while it may not feel like it, the essential raison d'être remains. Although the guide is a considerable business in itself, the countries it launches into are countries in which Michelin also wants to sell tyres.

In the early days of motoring, precarious roads meant tyres were often damaged, so the first French guide gave details on garages for tyre repairs and doctors, too, in case anyone in the car had been injured by an unfortunate meeting with a pothole.

In 1908, the guide developed into a handbook that offered information for tourists about areas and places to visit. Perhaps the more adventurous the guide made people, the more likely they were to burst a tyre and bring business to Michelin.

In 1926, the guide began to rate restaurants with stars, which became a formalised system in 1933. The system, recognising the best places, remains unchanged. One star is 'a very good restaurant in its category'; two stars denote the famous phrase – and with elegant understatement – 'excellent cooking, worth a detour'; and three stars represent 'exceptional cuisine, worth a special journey'.

The inspectors have always visited anonymously in the first instance, and, in modern times, after a few inspections of places that merit stars or hold them, a visit will be made known, usually after the meal. At which point, the inspectors often ask to see the kitchen.

The guide spread its tentacles across Europe in the 1960s, with the first *Michelin Guide: Great Britain & Ireland* being published in 1974. The first guide to the US came in 2005, and the guide reached Tokyo in 2007. There are now twenty-three countries vying for stars in the guide, and, as the guide has grown, so, too, has controversy associated with it.

There is venom from some that the guide favours a classical French style of cuisine. Indeed, when a former inspector, Pascal Remy, wrote a book about his experiences working for the business, he alleged that two French chefs, Paul Bocuse and Alain Ducasse, were, in his words, 'untouchable'. But then, when the guide in the UK started giving stars to pubs, critics called it erratic.

Marco Pierre White, the youngest ever chef to receive three stars in the UK (Chapters 14 and 16), admitted that he used to worship the guide: 'As a boy, to gain a Michelin star was like winning an Oscar.' But, as it tried to get to grips with an increasingly diverse restaurant scene in individual countries across the world, it became 'inconsistent'. 'Today they dish out stars like confetti,' he said. 'It's as if they are trying to win favour from the chefs to promote and sell their guide. I don't think Michelin understands what it's doing itself. It's unhinged.'

In 1999, five years after he was awarded three stars, White announced that he was handing back his stars. He had fulfilled his dream and, for five years, had maintained the consistency. But White had other things to do. Like fishing. 'I didn't want to live a lie,' he said. So, as he was no longer always at the stove, he no longer thought it right to be rated by the company.

Nine years later, opening a restaurant in Singapore, he said that, if he knew Michelin inspectors were coming, he would refuse them entry. 'I don't need Michelin and they don't need me,' he said. 'They sell tyres and I sell food.'

The late American chef Anthony Bourdain also disparaged one of the central tenets of the Michelin Guide: the idea that consistency is an unshakeable virtue. 'There's no other profession where it's all about consistency. It's one thing to do the greatest plate of the greatest piece of fish in New York, but that's not enough. You have to do it exactly the same, and do it for ever.' That, he maintained, was just not healthy.

Another British chef, Skye Gyngell, complained that being in the guide gave people a false idea of the sort of experience they would get at her restaurant. It was, she said, 'a curse'. 'People have certain expectations of a Michelin restaurant, but we don't have cloths on the tables and, here, service isn't very formal.'

When 72-year-old street vendor Jay Fai received a star for her Bangkok wok-cooked seafood, so many people came to her restaurant that they disrupted the quiet neighbourhood and she had to introduce something she had vowed never to have: a reservations system. And, while many restaurants have used winning a star to put their prices up, savvy landlords in Hong Kong went a step further. Several restaurants that were heralded by the Hong Kong edition of the guide in 2008 found their rents increased. Some couldn't cope and had to cease trading.

In 2017, chef Sébastien Bras asked Michelin to exclude his restaurant, Le Suquet (in the Massif Central town of Laguiole, France), from the next guide. He had three stars and wanted to shed the 'huge pressure' the stars conferred on him and his staff. But Michelin ignored him. In 2019, he was back in the guide, this time with two stars.

Some have argued that the pressure Michelin puts on chefs is damaging for the mental health and wellbeing of individuals who crave that kind of kudos.

And, while Marcus Wareing won a Michelin star within seven months of opening Petrus in London in 1999, was the glamour of such an accolade really worth the dedication needed? 'When I was training, I worked sixteen to eighteen hours a day for two years,' Wareing said. 'I never went to bed before 2.30 a.m., but you need that attitude to take you where you want to go.'

And what of the teams who work under such chefs striving to the reach their goals? Gordon Ramsay was famously brutal when it came to detail. 'I'll get furious with one of my staff because they haven't opened a £2.70 scallop properly, and I think to myself, *How much pain is a £2.70 scallop really worth?*' he once said. 'But the day I can accept that opening a scallop correctly doesn't matter is the day I have to get out of the business.'

Despite attaining considerable success in his early career, it wasn't until he received that elusive third Michelin star in 2001 for his Restaurant Gordon Ramsay that he felt able to say: 'For the first time in my life, I feel I've achieved something.'

Across the world, however, a number of chefs followed White's example and rejected the stars they were given, although Michelin's senior figures dismiss the idea that this can be done. 'It's not like an Oscar – it's not a physical thing,' the international director of the guide, Michael Ellis, has insisted. 'It's really an opinion. It's recognition.'

Yet it's clear that Michelin revels in the power it wields. It knows that so many young men and women, striving at catering college or in their first restaurant jobs, have two dreams: to own their own place and to get a star. And Jean-Luc Naret, a former director of the guide, has reflected on what it's like to deliver the news to a chef that their dreams have come true:

> *It's a beautiful call to make. When you go from two to three, you're making them the dream. You get an incredible, beautiful reaction. But when you have three, and you're calling them personally the night before you actually launch the guide, they know it's not because you've created just for them a fourth star. And that's a difficult call to make.*

A chef who was once on the receiving end of positive news was Atul Kochhar (Chapter 16). In January 2007, a journalist from the London *Evening Standard* put a call through to his Indian restaurant Benares, located on the eastern side of Mayfair's Berkeley Square. He needed a quote, if possible, from Kochhar. A girl on reception put him through to the kitchen. A young Indian chef answered the call. 'Is Atul Kochhar available?' the reporter asked.

'No, sir,' came the reply. 'May I help, sir?'

'I want to ask him how he feels about getting a Michelin star,' the journalist explained.

'We don't have a Michelin star,' the chef replied, and promptly hung up.

The journalist made a few more attempts that morning, and finally tracked down Kochhar.

'I thought it was a friend playing a trick,' he recalled years later. 'I had been cooking a rather more refined style of Indian cuisine, but I never thought that we would ever get on the Michelin radar.' Yet it was true, and the receipt of this star from the Michelin Guide changed the restaurant's fortunes and the career of Atul Kochhar.

There are similar stories across the world. Heston Blumenthal was about to close his experimental, but loss-making, Fat Duck restaurant in Bray, Berkshire, when a star gave his place a new lease of life and set him on the path to worldwide fame.

Yet, while a restaurant like the Waterside Inn (Chapter 14), which changed the way the UK dined at the end of the 1960s and '70s and trained generations of chefs, still retains three Michelin stars, those heralded as the vanguards of the new British food revolution in the 1980s – the likes of Simon Hopkinson, Rowley Leigh, Alastair Little and Sally Clarke (Chapter 16) – have never won stars. 'There are restaurants in this country that don't have Michelin stars and it confuses me,' remarked Marco Pierre White.

Jeremy King, one of the UK's most successful restaurateurs, along with his business partner, Chris Corbin, created some of the most iconic restaurants in the capital. Le Caprice, The Ivy, J. Sheekey and The Wolseley are some of the most famous names in modern restaurant history. Yet none has ever won a star. 'Michelin is so confused,' said King, 'I cannot pretend that I understand for a moment what the Michelin categories are.' Some of the restaurants to receive stars left him 'incredulous', and he asked: 'What are restaurants for? A restaurant is a catalyst for having a good time. When it comes to cooking, Michelin has been genuinely a really good arbiter, but, when it comes to restaurants you actually want to go to, it hasn't got a clue.'

But the Michelin Guide is not the only famous resource of opinion for diners seeking ideas for eating out. Because, of course, the restaurant spawned that other monster: the critic.

The game changing US restaurant critic Craig Claiborne made food a subject for the front page and held his post at the New York Times *for twenty-nine years.*

There have been verbose food writers penning their finest throughout the centuries. The Sicilian poet Archestratus, in 350 BC, complained of dining in the Greek city of Torone, where too often he found shark steaks with 'thick sauces poured over, cheese melted over, too much oil over'. And then one Mustafa Ali (Chapter 2) described the food he ate at a minaret in the 1500s: 'Their soup has turned into dishwater, their rice and puddings into vomited matter.'

John MacCulloch (Chapter 7) wrote with panache as he described the excuse for food he was served at a Scottish inn in the 1820s. But, as restaurants proliferated in the twentieth century and dining out flourished after the Second World War, so, too, did writing about restaurants develop into an art.

Before the digital revolution at the turn of the twenty-first century, the world of print was where the kings and queens of restaurant criticism ruled.

The game-changing critic in the US was Craig Claiborne. In 1957, at the age of thirty-seven, he joined the *New York Times* as food editor, after a stint at *Gourmet* magazine. For the next twenty-nine years, he would be the newspaper's restaurant critic.

According to US writer Thomas McNamee, the United States shared something with the United Kingdom in the years following the Second World War (Chapter 12): bleakness. It was a 'gastronomic wasteland'. From his new position at the *New York Times*, wrote McNamee, Claiborne looked 'out across the whole dreary landscape of American food [and] knew the challenge, and his great opportunity'. With his food writing, 'he could be a cultural critic on a par with the paper's critics of art, music, books, and the theatre. He could change the way Americans ate, the way they thought about food, the way they lived.'

Before he tackled the subject, restaurant write-ups felt like advertising. Indeed, more often than not, money changed hands in return for coverage.

If money didn't change hands, then you could be sure the editor and his family were at least able to dine at the restaurant as often as they liked for free. There were no negative reviews. Claiborne changed all that. 'There was no such thing as food criticism at the time [the 1950s],' said McNamee, 'and no such thing as a critic.'

Claiborne would visit a restaurant several times, always anonymously and never alone, and then give his verdict and a score out of four.

He had an eye for detail, and, having had culinary training himself, could focus also on the chef's technical ability. He once wrote of the evidence of a 'sad decline' in standards, having spotted a red pencil protruding from a restaurant manager's breast pocket.

In the late 1950s, an article he wrote on how 'elegant cuisine' was on the wane made the front page of the paper. The idea of a food story making page one was unheard of at the time.

'Two time-honored symbols of the good life – great cuisine in the French tradition and elegant service – are passing from the American scene,' wrote Claiborne. And he disparaged the advance of fast food across the US (Chapter 11): 'The quality of restaurant cuisine has declined because Americans seem always to be in a hurry. The public has not time to relax over courses.'

As James A. Beard – the famous food writer, who later had a series of awards created in his honour – told Claiborne: 'This nation is more interested in preserving the whooping crane and the buffalo than in perpetuating classic cookery and improving standards of table service. We live in an age that may some day – with all justification – be referred to as the decline and fall of the American palate.'

Claiborne's weekly columns consisted of capsule reviews, and then, in time, he began to focus on a single restaurant. As the columns grew in length, the language could be a little more languid. 'The décor is a conversation piece sufficient in itself to sustain a lively causerie through a leisurely lunch,' he wrote of the newly opened Four Seasons in October 1959. He also broke new ground by mentioning the chefs in his reviews. Just as Alan Crompton-Batt would do in the UK in the 1980s (Chapter 16), Claiborne planted a seed of the idea that a chef could be a personality.

By the 1960s, Claiborne had become powerful enough to merit a profile in *Time* magazine. 'When he says good, it is very, very good for the restaurant's business,' the magazine reported in October 1965. 'When he says bad, it can be horrid.'

More reviewers joined the fray, but, according to writer Nora Ephron, writing a piece for *New York Magazine* in September 1968, Claiborne 'does what he does better than anyone else'. He could bring down restaurants, and had 'become the most envied, admired and cursed man in the food world'.

But Claiborne did not revel in the power he had. In fact, he admitted to tossing and turning in bed at night, worried that a piece of mere writing could change the course of another's life, wondering 'whether I was justified in referring to a chef's mournay sauce as pure mucilage or whether that unaccustomed flavour in the hollandaise was actually basil or rosemary as I had judged it to be'.

Eventually, he wrote, he became 'bored with restaurant criticism':

> *At times, I didn't give a damn if all the restaurants in Manhattan were shoved into the East River and perished. Had they all served nightingale tongues on toast and heavenly manna and mead, there is just so much the tongue can savour, so much the human body (and spirit) can accept, and then it resists ... I found myself increasingly indulging in drink, the better to endure another evening of dining out.*

In January 1971, he quit. Claiborne was once asked what qualities were needed to make a good food critic. 'The ability to write, and a conversance with food,' he said, adding: 'I think you are born with a seed for making a sentence that reads well.'

His most famous successor at the *New York Times* was Frank Bruni. By the time Bruni's column appeared, between 2004 and 2009, such was the status of food that he wasn't just regarded as wielding power in restaurant circles; the UK *Observer* newspaper once described him as holding 'one of the most powerful jobs in the US media'. Bruni made the job of critic a complex role of almost interminable eating and organisation. His one weekly review consisted of multiple visits (at least three), and he employed countless fake identities when booking. But, since he couldn't keep track of whether he was Mr Webster, Mr Roget, Mr Fodor, Mr Frommer, Mr Wharton, Mr Eliot, Mr Didion or Mr Turow, he often struggled to get past the front desk.

'As a restaurant critic, I discovered I needed to be more than just a gourmand,' he once wrote. 'I had to become a concierge, a cruise director, a counsellor, a covert operations agent.' Some of his verdicts are the stuff of legend.

On Gordon Ramsay's arrival in New York, Bruni wrote: 'Seldom has a conquistador as bellicose as Mr Ramsay landed with such a whisper.' The potatoes he ate at Harry Cipriani 'had somehow acquired the texture of Brillo and could almost have been used to scrub whatever pan they had emerged from'.

And the restaurant Ago (part-owned by Robert de Niro), he claimed, 'isn't in the hospitality business':

> *It's in the attitude business, projecting an aloofness that permeated all of my meals there ... nights of wine and poses for swingers on the make, cougars on the prowl and anyone else who values a sort of facile fabulousness over competent service or a breaded veal Milanese with any discernible meat.*

In Britain, similarly, the restaurant critic became an envied artist. But the scene grew to be more crowded than in New York. No single reviewer ever held power and sway like Bruni.

From 1986, for fifteen years, it was arguably Jonathan Meades, as restaurant critic for *The Times*, who held the wittiest and most polymathic pen. Some years after he left *The Times*, he penned a piece in the *Telegraph* castigating the kind of dining experience Michelin had encouraged. It made those unfamiliar with Meades almost mournful they had missed his era, as he wrote:

> *The self-regarding, hermetic world of gastronomy has produced few constructions more likely to promote teeth-gnashing, mockery and despairing contempt than 'fine dining', which should be pronounced in a refrained accent – think Lynda Snell or Sir Elf Remsey or Morningsaide. It is a branch of restauration characterised by smarmily sycophantic service, grotesquely over-elaborate cooking, fussiness, pretension, absurdly high prices and moron chefs who appear to think they are philosophers.*

In 2019, the UK's longest-standing critic was Fay Maschler, who began her *Evening Standard* column in 1972. Her quiet, considered, orderly and wise prose have made her criticisms all the more savage. And there was a time when the opinions that most mattered to chefs and publicists were those of Maschler or A. A. Gill (the late critic for the *Sunday Times*). As the author and restaurant critic Charles Campion responded when asked by a young journalist how he might become a restaurant critic: 'Since there are more Formula 1 drivers than national newspaper restaurant critics, the answer is: with considerable difficulty.'

But that was before something called blogging happened. In 1999, a list compiled by a man called Jesse James Garrett noted twenty-three blogs on the internet. By 2006, there were 50 million. Quite a lot of them were about food.

The established restaurant critics, gathering at launches and parties, would look around them and wonder who these interlopers were. Most of them started writing their blogs as hobbies. Many later quit their day jobs to blog full time. The power of social media then saw these blogs transforming into Instagram posts, where a photograph taken on a phone apparently has more power than 1,000 carefully crafted words. The UK Instagrammer Clerkenwell Boy, for example, had some 200,000 followers in 2019. And websites such as TripAdvisor also muscled in on the act, citing the authority of its everyday users.

But, in a world of an unedited plethora of what became known as 'content', the opinion of a few critics, and, of course, Michelin, is still what many chefs care about – or fear.

No chef has yet stuffed his head in an oven because of what a blogger wrote. Although many have, usually regretfully, used their own social media platforms to fight back when criticised. After blogger James Isherwood described French chef Claude Bosi's then restaurant Hibiscus as 'average', Bosi responded on Twitter saying: 'I think your [*sic*] a c**t'.

It wasn't 1,000 clever words that tipped Loiseau over the edge. He grappled with a perfect storm of panic and despondency, fuelled, no doubt, by the fear of losing a Michelin star. But his restaurant didn't lose a star in the days that followed his death. In fact, in 2019, it still had three stars. Under the new regime of his widow, the restaurant no longer opens seven days a week, holidays are compulsory, and the frogs' legs are still some of the best in the world.

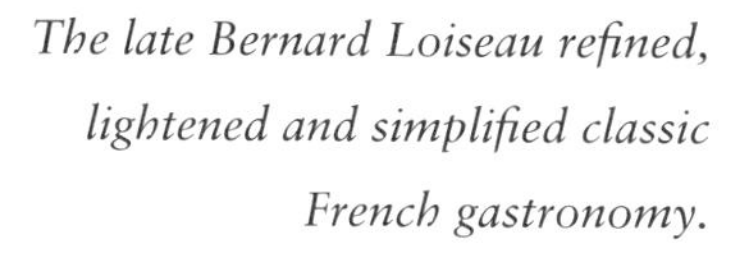

The late Bernard Loiseau refined, lightened and simplified classic French gastronomy.

18

The Future of Eating Out

When Ovnew opened in the Spanish city of Barcelona, the restaurant declared its food to be a new culinary art known as 'neurogastronomy': the study of people's perception of flavour, and how that affects cognition and memory. Customers didn't just reserve a table; instead, they were invited to 'book a trip'. The people who cooked were not chefs, but 'captains', taking diners on a 'multi-sensory' journey. The story of eating out has reached a point where food is provided not to sate a physical need, but to stimulate emotions.

For centuries, it had been quite reasonably supposed that people were enticed into restaurants because they were hungry. The Pompeiian Inn of Primus (Chapter 1) attracted the attentions of passers-by with the smell of food that wafted through the window of its takeaway section. There was the legendary sign above the door of Boulanger's 1760s Parisian establishment that declared: 'Come to me, those who are famished, and I will give you sustenance' (Chapter 6). And, in the 1940s, for just $1, a hungry punter could feast on the all-you-can-eat Buckaroo Buffet at El Rancho Vegas, a casino on the Las Vegas Strip.

Of course, people have sought out restaurants for other reasons, too: a place to meet, socialise, do business, romance a loved one, plot a coup. But being hungry is an assumed pre-requisite.

Ovnew, however, situated in a flying-saucer-like capsule, perched on top of a skyscraper off a highway not far from Barcelona Airport, didn't wish for its diners to arrive with massive appetites. Indeed, it was a preferred pre-requisite that they didn't. 'Try not to come after a long walk or exercise,' read one of the instructions on a list entitled 'Get Ready For Your Trip'. The restaurant declared on its website: 'To enjoy Ovnew, it is important that your body, mind and soul are in total harmony.' Thirst and hunger are distracting emotions.

And, if you did arrive parched or famished, the usual rules around perusing the menu and getting your taste buds excited went out of the window. A typical dish in one of the multi-tasting courses read: 'Sinestesia. Experimentation two-way operating mingling among them.' To which the response 'I'd like that medium rare' would get one nowhere.

In the second decade of the twenty-first century, in a city with a tapas bar on almost every street corner, the idea of opening a restaurant that just served food on a plate and drink in a glass in exchange for cash was never going to fly.

So captains Jon Giraldo and Jaime Lieberman decided to do something different. Writer Jessica Prupas described them as 'gastro-anarchists', delivering a 'seven-course space odyssey ... [in] a spaceship on the side of a motorway'. Columbian-born Giraldo described himself as a 'multidisciplinary professional, specialising in the world of cuisine, hospitality and modern art'; his partner Lieberman, from Mexico City, a 'culinary artist', who delivered 'holistic cognitive sensorial gastronomy'.

On the twenty-eighth floor, over 300ft up, diners were greeted by women with green faces, large furry cat ears and reflective boots. Each sitting was two hours precisely and started in the kitchen with some bite-sized nibbles, including a piece of grilled cheese topped with Vegemite (an Australian yeast-flavoured spread like Marmite) and vanilla ice cream.

Then, once seated in the dining room, its roof a vision of metal, glass, sculpture, twinkling lights and the stars of the night sky beyond, the seven-course 'Taste of the Five Continents' (for €160, without drinks) would begin. It started with 'Primeval Be', an idea of taste at the beginning of time, exampled by things like 'grilled whorl' and 'crunchy corn-moringa'. Then there was 'Mesopotamia: The Mystery of Arab Alchemy' – its embodiment on the plate included 'lamb neck in juice, creamy saffron, summac gel'. After the 'Sinestesia' course was 'Amazonia', featuring 'salsa chontaduro, açai and tucupí', and then came the 'Far East', with its 'squid and truffle dashi'. To close, 'Sweet Bigbang', a spread of six desserts, with the outrageously ordinary 'cocoa and pistachio ice cream'.

Confronted with a menu of some unfathomability, it was best not to ask any questions and merely go with the flow. After all, the restaurant itself advised diners: 'Keep your mind open to the experience. Things are perceived better if the mind is receptive.'

Prupas pronounced on the restaurant's 'intergalactic, multi-sensory experience', saying that it 'beats a petrol-station sandwich'. Ovnew (a combination of 'OVNI', which means UFO in Spanish, and 'new') posited itself as a futuristic mystery. Mocking such a place is not a struggle.

Yet it is only one of a great many restaurants to have posed the question of why people eat out if they can eat in very adequately and for very little money.

The latter part of the twentieth century saw haute cuisine – more complicated, more expensive fine dining – become more accessible to the masses. Mourad Mazouz, who opened the west London restaurant Sketch in 2003, defended his establishment from criticisms of the elaborate, garish, space-age rooms and menu (diners were directed to eat items on some plates, created by the French chef Pierre Gagnaire, in order of temperature) and from *The Guardian*'s claims that it was 'the most expensive restaurant in Great Britain', serving what critic Matthew Fort called 'a lot of bollocks'. 'Some people save up all year to watch a football match, some for the theatre,' said Mazouz. 'So it's reasonable to expect others to save up for a dinner at a place like Sketch.'

Other restaurants – like Le Gavroche (Chapter 14) under Michel Roux Jr (son of Albert) – were, by the early 2000s, creating set menus that included a glass of wine, coffee and service for £45, though many people still saved up for a lunch at Michel Roux Sr's Waterside Inn, or at another of the country's smart restaurants. People even planned holidays based not on the beaches, but on the food, and organised entire weekends around dinner at a famous restaurant, booked several months in advance.

And, while those visitors would doubtless go to the restaurant hungry, the desire and need for the experience was considerably more complicated than hunger alone. Why people choose to seek food as entertainment, rather than eat a simpler meal at home, 'takes us into a realm of social and psychological desires, in which physical needs are subordinate to mental and emotional satisfactions', wrote John Burnett in his social history of eating out.

The Ovnew captains chose Barcelona for a good reason. A hundred miles up the coast, near the Catalonian village of Roses, the restaurant El Bulli had opened in 1964. It began as a beach snack-bar, but, by the 1980s, had developed a reputation for creating food in the *nouvelle cuisine* style. This lighter method of cooking, with its emphasis on presentation, grew to become a pejorative term – its lightness a euphemism for minimalism: small items on small plates on small menus, but with a large bill that would leave diners out of pocket while still empty of stomach.

As the pendulum of food trends moved back to traditional and authentic, chefs and customers once again embraced the classics, but some essence of

Ferran Adrià of El Bulli (photographed here in 1995) influenced, for good or ill, a global array of young chefs, who were drawn to experiment with 'molecular gastronomy'.

nouvelle cuisine remained. Bernard Loiseau's frogs' legs with garlic and parsley sauce (Chapter 17) were a perfect example of this: a classic dish made lighter, without compromising its roots, integrity and flavour.

A 22-year-old chef, Ferran Adrià, had joined El Bulli when it was at peak *nouvelle cuisine*. He enrolled at the restaurant after doing military service, in which he was able to engage his more peaceful persuasions as an army cook. His diligence and creativity paid off and, eighteen months later, he was made head chef by the restaurant manager, Juli Soler.

In 1987, inspired by a conference in Nice that questioned the concept of creativity, Adrià's mind began to race. That winter, the restaurant had a prolonged closure – six whole months – which enabled Adrià to sit in his workshop and, casting aside every cookbook he had previously used as a reference, experiment and create what he saw as completely new and avant-garde dishes.

When the restaurant re-opened in 1988, it had a new identity and a very novel menu. There was cutlery designed for specific dishes, there was no bread and butter, and the menu was long – very long. In the ensuing years, it would get even longer.

The year 1990 saw Soler and Adrià form a partnership, purchase the restaurant and set it on a course that would see it become one of the most famous – and, more importantly, most influential – restaurants in the world. It gained a second Michelin star that year.

In 1995, it was given a 19/20 rating in the Gault Millau guide (Chapter 17), which was crucial, as it meant a French guide was placing the restaurant on the same level as the best restaurants in France. In 1997, Michelin awarded El Bulli a third star.

By the late 2000s, the pattern of El Bulli was firmly established. For €200, without drinks, each guest was served a tasting menu of between twenty-eight and thirty-five dishes. This comprised cocktails, snacks, tapas dishes, pre-desserts, desserts and 'morphings', which were Adrià's idea of petits-fours – often delicate, coral-like concoctions, crafted from chocolate and ingredients like raspberry.

His most acclaimed dishes included 'lobster gazpacho', 'savoury tomato water ice with fresh oregano and almond milk pudding', 'white bean espuma with sea urchins', 'textured vegetable panache', 'two ways of presenting chicken curry', 'caramelised quail's egg', 'pea soup 60°/4°', 'spherical melon caviar' and 'pistachio-LYO with black truffle jellied consommé and mandarin air'.

The dishes used techniques that were subsequently employed in kitchens across the world. Respectively: a garnish came to the table and the soup was poured over it in front of the guest; a savoury dish was presented frozen (challenging preconceived ideas and assumptions, and blurring boundaries between main courses and desserts); a foam was created out of white bean (lighter than mousse, but with more flavour); a single ingredient was used, but prepared and presented with different textures; two dishes were prepared using the same ingredients, but with radically different results; a liquid centre appeared miraculously after a crunchy bite; a hot and a cold liquid appeared in the same glass, next to each other, but without mixing; a flavoured liquid was jellified before spherification took place, presenting tiny little spheres that popped in the mouth; food was freeze-dried.

These few dishes alone showed the quite extraordinary creativity and vision of Adrià, along with delivering what every diner wants: flavour. The influence of El Bulli can still be seen across the world.

'I think my virtue was I never thought, *This is impossible*,' Adrià once said. In his workshop, he ensured that every dish was carefully catalogued. Each one went through a painstaking seven-point process, which always started with sketches, if done by Adrià, in a notebook, as he dragged on a Marlboro cigarette. Tests were carried out on the dish, it would be made to the standard required to serve in the dining room, feedback was taken from the guests, and then the dish would be further refined before reaching the official catalogue.

Over twenty-four years, El Bulli created and catalogued 1,846 dishes. Every dish was photographed and logged. The culinary discoveries, similarly, were painstakingly recorded and dated. Adrià also collaborated with scientists to understand what other things influenced taste – the things that he couldn't necessarily control in the kitchen.

Working with a professor of experimental psychology at Oxford University, Charles Spence, for example, he learned that a strawberry mousse was judged to be

10 per cent sweeter when served on a white, rather than black, plate. There were similar effects perceived when food entered the mouth on a different material, be it a stainless steel or a wooden spoon. Indeed, Spence also worked with the British chef Heston Blumenthal (Chapter 17) to see how sound affected the perception of food.

Adrià saw his work as having ramifications outside the realms of his own dining room. If Formula 1 car-racing informs the world far beyond racing circuits – from domestic car design to how factories can learn efficiencies from the way teams work in pit lanes – so, too, could his culinary work have a wider reach than dining for pleasure and entertainment. For him, cuisine and science could learn from each other.

'What is cuisine?' he once asked. 'You have got companies, institutions, a home kitchen, education, health, hospitality, industry, restaurant businesses, hospitals, airports, agriculture, fashion, new technologies. It's the most transversal discipline you can find.'

In 2008, Adrià published his methods in Phaidon's *A Day at elBulli*. It included his story, offered insights into his methodology and philosophy, and gave chapter and verse of some of his recipes. They were not for the faint-hearted.

He reprinted the menu, by then drawn into four 'acts', and published a map of how guests would move from the kitchen to the terrace (*salón*) to the dining room (*comedor*), and then through the kitchen again on leaving. He also presented his thoughts on how, in his words, 'contemporary fine dining has reached a stage when it can be compared with art as a means of expression'.

But his work was at the vanguard of this progression. 'The notion of creative cuisine as an art form is still in its infancy,' he wrote. He even assured the world that, however artful or technologically complicated the plates of food at El Bulli were, and however unlike conventional food they may have seemed, 'there is no suggestion that any dish should be appreciated purely aesthetically as a work of art'. He still wanted to feed people. And he also recognised that getting the opportunity to be fed by him was a challenge. So he explained how the booking system worked.

The issue of reservations was, he wrote, 'now the only unsatisfactory aspect of El Bulli'. He doubtless felt despondent when drawn to media coverage that focused more on the story of how difficult it was to get a table at the restaurant than what he was doing in the kitchen.

He had considered opening for lunch, or staying open for ten, rather than six, months per year, or expanding the restaurant. He could increase the number of meals served each year from 8,000 to 30,000. But that wouldn't be enough to alleviate the issue: 'The number of refusals would still be enormous ... and the service would definitely suffer.' So he rejected all such considerations. And he also refused to take advantage of the restaurant's popularity and increase prices. 'It is important that the restaurant does not become inaccessible due to its price,' he declared.

Yet getting a table continued to elude the majority. Every year, 2 million requests were made for 8,000 places. Journalists arrived in Barcelona to see if they could find a way to get a table. Features appeared in magazines suggesting where those who were bold enough to chance a last-minute cancellation could eat while hoping to get into El Bulli.

Adrià's story spread across the world. He was feted at literary festivals, culinary conventions and conferences. He thought he must have answered every question that could be posed about his work and his life. Although he never gave an interview in English, he wouldn't even bother to listen for the translation of a question to end. He knew exactly what every journalist wanted to ask, and he'd answered every question a hundred times.

In 2011, Adrià revealed his next step. He wouldn't build another dining room, extend the kitchen or reform the reservations system. In July of that year, he closed the restaurant. In its place would be built a 'creativity centre', managed by a private foundation. Its objective: to 'be a think-tank for creative cuisine and gastronomy'.

Not everyone mourned its passing. The British writer Richard Ehrlich eviscerated the idea that El Bulli had, in the words of its own rhetoric, 'changed the way we eat'.

'We are talking about a type of cooking that is available to perhaps 0.1 per cent of the world's restaurants,' he argued, adding: 'What I really hate about El Bulli is the slavering media hype that it has engendered.'

He also poured scorn on Copenhagen-based chef René Redzepi, who once said: 'Ferran and his team are culinary freedom fighters.'

'Freedom fighters are people who work to liberate the oppressed,' stormed Ehrlich. 'Chefs are people who cook dinner for strangers. Now that El Bulli's gone, maybe we can get comfortable with that idea once more.'

Another British writer, Fuchsia Dunlop, was scornful of the influence that Adrià had on other chefs. 'Ferran Adrià has fucked it all up,' she said, 'because now young people don't want to learn how to cook, they want to learn to be like him. And he may do what he does brilliantly, but few others can.' Friends of hers in Barcelona also complained that El Bulli 'had a catastrophic effect on the younger generation of chefs. They all wanted to become a gastro-magician, a celebrity, a superstar...'

The British chef Gordon Ramsay, who dined at El Bulli on several occasions and described Adrià as a culinary 'standard bearer', offered some sanguine advice to chefs, before they attempted to emulate Adrià's style of cooking:

> *Understand it properly, put in a minimum of five to eight years, and don't dare try it unless you understand it fully. There [have] been so many rip-offs, it's been embarrassing. I recently had a salad in New York from a chef who was air-spraying an aerosol can across the table, spraying the customer with an odour of basil and chocolate, and it was hideous.*

Those who weren't skilled enough found themselves more in the realms of the Italian futurist Filippo Tommaso Marinetti, whose 1932 *The Futurist Cookbook* included such recipes as 'drum roll of colonial fish', 'Tyrrhenian seaweed foam (with coral garnish)', 'tactile vegetable garden' and 'aerofood'. Instructions for eating the food encouraged you, while tackling 'aerofood', to stroke a sheet of sandpaper with your right hand, or, for the 'tactile vegetable garden', to be sprayed in the face with cologne by a waiter in between mouthfuls.

The difference between Marinetti and Adrià was that the Italian's dishes were a spoof and never intended to be cooked or consumed.

Yet they were not dissimilar in name to some of the offerings at Ovnew, whose chefs seemed to be the very target of Dunlop's ire. They sounded like the very people she was targeting when she complained of a young crop of chefs who just 'want to invent and play – but they no longer want to learn the basic skills of Catalan cuisine'.

Also not embracing the foundations of Spanish cooking was chef Paco Roncero, who, in 2014, opened Sublimotion in Ibiza, one of the Balearic islands of the Mediterranean.

Roncero described himself as a chef, confectioner, engineer, designer, composer and magician. His table at the Hard Rock Hotel was, he said, 'a stage', where he teamed up with filmmakers, set designers, musicians and special effects experts. Diners would eat little bits of fish from a cockleshell while sharks swam around them, or deconstructed shrimp scampi while riding the Orient Express, or a plate of vegetables on a hill in the countryside. Trolleys moved around the room pushed only by the legs of a waitress; one course required the donning of virtual reality headsets; chocolate desserts spun and levitated above the table.

Paco Roncero's Ibiza restaurant Sublimotion had one table – he called it a stage. The restaurant was a collaboration of filmmakers, set designers, musicians and special effects.

There was only one dining room, with seats for just twelve diners. And, on an island famous for its expensive prices, Roncero had no qualms about accessibility. The dinner charge was €1,500. Roncero was duly rewarded with the media tag of running 'the most expensive restaurant in the world'.

In a world of recession, food shortages, environmental concern and poverty, there would always be room at the top end. Indeed, the riskiest thing to do in the 2010s was to diligently work to create a chain of restaurants that appealed to the middle market. The British restaurateur and TV star Jamie Oliver learned this to his cost in 2019, when his restaurant group, launched in 2008, went into administration. His earnest endeavour, passion and hard work weren't enough; twenty-two out of his twenty-five restaurants closed and 1,000 jobs were lost. Many reasons were cited for the collapse of his restaurant chain, but it was part of a bursting bubble that saw reality bite for mid-tier restaurants that had overpaid when competing for sites, meaning revenue could never match capital cost. The introduction of the National Living Wage in 2016 also added hugely to costs, though the mid-market did find one solution for growth in 2019: collaborating with supermarkets and setting up concessions in stores. YO! Sushi (Chapter 13), for example, began opening sushi kiosks in Tesco. But many in the restaurant business sought solace at the high end.

Perhaps Oliver should have followed the example of Rancero. Or Sirocco restaurant in Bangkok, where a single dessert in 2019 cost £534. Or New York restaurant Serendipity 3, which sold an ice cream sundae for $1,000. Or Hubert Keller's burger, which retailed at his Las Vegas place, Fleur, for $5,000.

Those who attacked the vulgarity of such offerings were simply falling into the restaurants' PR trap. Adrià was no doubt only too happy to retreat to his bunker and avoid press questions as to whether he felt he bore any responsibility for the wilder food pairings or concoctions, if not their price tags.

Of course, there were other talented chefs whose whacky menus belied serious intent. Heston Blumenthal, at his Fat Duck restaurant in Berkshire, UK, may have made his name with 'snail porridge', 'egg and bacon ice cream' or 'mustard ice cream', but he argued that he was both challenging popular assumptions – for example, that vanilla is sweet or that you can't have snails with oats (it's like a risotto) – and delivering great flavour.

His collaboration with Charles Spence saw the creation of a dish entitled 'Sounds of the Sea', during which guests listened to waves crashing and seagulls flying overhead through earphones, presented in a conch shell, while eating what looked like the shore: seaweed, sashimi, foam for the froth of the waves, and edible tapioca 'sand'.

One of Blumenthal's interests was what he called 'contextual trigger'. The actual sound of the sea could take a diner back to a moment in their childhood or a holiday, which would trigger happy memories. That happiness, he explained, could improve the diner's enjoyment of the fish: 'If you can put somebody in a state of excitement, all of your senses are heightened.' His research also uncovered evidence that 'anxiety can lower your sense of sweet by 30 per cent and increase your sense of bitterness and acidity by 50 per cent'.

And Spence went further, saying: 'Sound is a forgotten flavour sense.' The evocation of the shoreline concentrated the minds of the diners on what was on their plate, rather than on the restaurant, its décor or the distraction of other diners. Like Adrià, he focused on cutlery, too. 'Cutlery hasn't evolved,' he once mused to an Australian journalist. 'What could cutlery be? What do you want to get out of it, as the interface between you and the food?'

For the hungry diner or cynical journalist, it was easy to raise an eyebrow at such pronouncements. And the more that 'molecular gastronomy' was attempted by chefs, the more defensive and irritated Blumenthal and Adrià became. Indeed, in 2006, the pair got together with food science writer Harold McGee and US chef Thomas Keller. The latter had pioneered another cooking technique that became ubiquitous at so-called 'fine-dining' restaurants – *sous-vide* (the French for 'under vacuum') – which is very precise, low-temperature cooking, whereby food is vacuum-packed and cooked in a water bath. The four men then issued a

The growth of vegan and plant-based establishments brought together a perfect mix of global concerns, bestowing a badge of of-the-moment principles.

statement that attempted to create space between them and their imitators. They wrote that the new approach to cooking they had embraced 'has been widely misunderstood. Certain aspects of it are overemphasized and sensationalized, while others are ignored.'

They set out the principles of their cooking as 'excellence, openness, and integrity'. This meant they had a 'commitment to excellence', held 'integrity' as 'paramount', and made sure their work was 'sincere', but did not 'follow the latest trend'. Their craft evolved from the finest traditions of cooking and, while they embraced innovation, they did not 'pursue novelty for its own sake. We may use modern thickeners, sugar substitutes, enzymes, liquid nitrogen, *sous-vide*, dehydration, and other nontraditional means, but these do not define our cooking.' And they cast off the label of 'molecular gastronomy': 'It does not describe our cooking.'

Finally, they declared that they believed in the spirit of collaboration and 'a readiness to share ideas', though added, with almost a hint of menace, that it had to go 'together with full acknowledgment of those who invent new techniques and dishes'. Indeed, they were fed up with chefs pinching their ideas and fed up of being labelled as the godfathers of every annoying froth, smear, foam or flabby piece of salmon that came out of a water bath before being singed with a blowtorch. They even instructed their PR people to quash any utterances by journalists that mentioned their names in the same sentence as the words 'molecular gastronomy'.

But the world turned, the statement did not make the front pages, and restaurants like Sublimotion continued to open across the world.

If chefs didn't like being slaves to the latest food trends, then the people who marketed them, their publicists, persuaded them that they should. And one of the biggest of those trends in 2019 was veganism.

For some, veganism brought together a perfect mix of global concerns, bestowing on oneself a badge of of-the-moment principles.

That vegan food is dairy-free means that it is good for the environment, as it results in fewer cows emitting the methane that is so damaging to the planet. Similarly, its meat-free status signals a stance against the industrialised factory farming that can be seen across the world, perpetuating a most unnatural process of intensive food production. And its cruelty-free label means that no calves are ripped screaming from their mothers, no beasts mercilessly taken to the slaughterhouse for death by metal bolt, no chickens decapitated on a conveyor belt, no eggs produced in a vast dark barn, no pigs forced to live cheek by jowl with thousands of others amid their own excrement, and no lives lived only for the unnecessary pleasure of humans.

Veganism wrapped humanitarianism up with care for the planet and human health (as an obesity epidemic raged), and, for some vegans, their choice of food was as political as the 1960s counterculture of the US (Chapter 15).

For certain activists, including those who badged themselves as BAME (black, Asian and minority ethnic), it was, according to one self-styled 'vegan ambassador', Jay Brave, 'an opportunity to make a stand against entrenched inequalities in British society':

> *[With] a lot of the black and African vegans I've met, [the decision to go vegan] comes from a place of personal autonomy and how can they take back control of their own diet in a system [in] which they are not in control of many of the things that we purchase.*

Between 2008 and 2018, according to the Vegan Society (an organisation founded in 1944), the number of vegans in Britain grew from 150,000 to 542,000. The number of vegan products sold by retailers doubled, and, according to a survey by market research firm Mintel, 42 per cent of UK consumers who ate meat-free products preferred them to be 'plant-based' (rather than containing eggs or dairy).

Across the UK, the US and beyond, cafés, bars and restaurants opened to satisfy the new lust for vegan food. In London, there were vegan pubs

Meat substitutes, cultivated in laboratories from biopsies on live animals, require 100 times less land and 5.5 times less water than conventional meat.

(the Spread Eagle, east of the City), a vegan doughnut shop, and a plethora of street-food stalls selling vegan food.

Vegan tasting menus appeared on offer at some of London's high-end restaurants – for example, at former Gordon Ramsay protégé Jason Atherton's Pollen Street Social (part of a global empire of restaurants he built) and at chef Theo Randall's restaurant at the InterContinental Hotel, Park Lane. In addition, mid-market restaurant chains, such as Wagamama and Itsu, piloted vegan menus, and, to counter the idea that vegan food was somehow unfashionably healthy, 'dirty vegan' food appeared – versions of fried kebabs or doughnuts. Food journalists could barely get through a day without being informed of new establishments, new menus or new dishes heralded as plant-based.

But, of course, there is much evidence of the contradiction within the philosophy of veganism: the lack of vitamins in such a diet; the fast-food and unnatural technologies used to engineer vegan products; the view of meat-eaters that vegan food can lack both flavour and texture. As the British writer Joanna Blythman wrote in 2019:

> *Be it vegan 'burgers' or 'chicken-less fillets', the recipe tends to be only variations on the same cheap ingredients: lots of water, some kind of protein powder (such as pea protein isolate, soya), a stiffening measure of chemically altered starch, powerful food glues, industrially refined vegetable oils, all this flavoured up with what's known as 'flavour modulators' – sugars, excess salt, synthetic flavourings.*

However, in the same way that purists of the organic movement of the 1990s and early 2000s encouraged diners and producers to think about the virtues of low-intensive farming, so, too, has veganism made people think about both the amount of meat they eat and the quality of it. And whether meat really needs to be culled from a live animal. Indeed, while Ovnew may have thought it was at the cutting edge of food trends, the real money in the future of food is not in molecular gastronomy or vegan dishes, but in meat substitutes.

Laboratory-grown meat, in which a biopsy taken from a live animal is used to grow muscle cells, has attracted the investment of billionaires such as the Microsoft founder Bill Gates. As he wrote on his personal blog:

> *Raising meat takes a great deal of land and water and has a substantial environmental impact. Put simply, there's no way to produce enough meat for 9 billion people. Yet we can't ask everyone to become vegetarians. That's why we need more options for producing meat without depleting our resources.*

Lab-grown meat requires 100 times less land and 5.5 times less water. But would a vegan eat it? Because of the biopsy needed, it is not wholly free of cruelty. But, for the fashionable, occasional vegan, it's likely to be a good option. Especially if it can be Instagrammed – that other driver of trendy restaurants across the world.

As the world reached peak Instagram, the social media platform began to influence both food and décor. London design studios working with would-be restaurateurs and chefs had to have Instagram high on their list of essentials when helping to plan a restaurant. 'It is something young entrepreneurs are always thinking about,' designer Hannah Collins said. So, in addition to the likes of tile mosaics, murals and neon lights, the food needed to be aesthetically pleasing or simply bizarre. If the stars of Instagram were the new 'influencers', then a chef had to entice them into their restaurant and ensure that they were rewarded with plates and décor that fitted the bill for their square-shaped Instagram window, and that the food suited the hashtags of the moment.

As the social media mantra stated: 'If it's not on Instagram, it didn't happen.'

When food is being cooked because it can be easily photographed in a square format, and when restaurateurs and chefs are creating food in environments where entertainment is everything, the very concept of eating out must be questioned. For, if the great pleasure of food is that people can commune over it, should we not switch off our phones, take pleasure in the moment, look into one another's eyes and enjoy the beauty of human interaction?

The future of dining out will doubtless mirror the present. There will be new food concepts, new cutlery, space-age environments, new-fangled digital booking systems based on your history of preferences and your current bank balance. But there will always be a place for the simple establishment. While some fantasise of merging science with ingredients, others will still have a dream about opening a little place with a small kitchen, a modest, seasonally changing menu, a functional wine list, cheerful staff, and the buzz of conversation and laughter. I'll take a table for two in that one, please.

Acknowledgements

Firstly, I'd like to thank Iain MacGregor, publishing director at Simon & Schuster, for asking me to write this book. I feel very lucky to have been commissioned to delve deep into the fascinating subject of eating out. For steadfast support and endless cheer at PFD, my agents, huge thanks to Caroline Michel, Jon Fowler and Vicky Cornforth. Thanks to my friends at the *Telegraph* – Vicki, Sasha, Amy, Claire I., Laura and Claire F. – for soliciting words from me on my favourite subject and for supporting our exciting programme of foodie events.

Much of this book was written at home at Weston in Northamptonshire, and I thank Dave and Jane for bringing order, calm, cheer (and walkie-talkies) and for making our home an even happier place. I'd like to thank the plumbers, Will, Andy and Alex, for making the house warm – well, I would if I knew where they were, or if the beautiful new radiators were actually connected. Retreating to the warmth of my mother-in-law Sarah's home in Somerset, I wrote vast acres of copy from her dining room, and I am eternally grateful to her for her cups of tea, biscuits, Briscoe lunches, telly suppers and Booja-Booja. Thanks also to our wonderful friends who supplied me with a chair, table and Wi-Fi in Lipari, Corsica and Ibiza: Carlo and Alexandra; Skippy and Lara; Lindy and Dan. Dan, mate, I'm still taking the concrete.

Thanks to Emily Ediger for sketching out a brilliant research pattern for the book, and to the erudite Melissa Bond, project manager at Simon & Schuster, who deftly copy-edited the manuscript. To my teenage children, Alice and Albert, I give massive hugs and admiration for the amazing commitment shown to your own endeavours. And, finally, thanks to my darling Emily for your endless, endless love, encouragement and support. And for popping out a new light in our lives: happy, joyful little Walter.

About the Author

William Sitwell is one of Britain's leading food writers. He is a restaurant critic for the *Daily Telegraph*, as well as a writer and commentator for the newspaper. He was formerly the multi-award-winning editor of acclaimed magazine *Waitrose Food* for sixteen years. William has authored three internationally successful books: *A History of Food in 100 Recipes*, *Eggs or Anarchy*, and *The Really Quite Good British Cookbook*. A frequent presenter and guest on TV and radio and a popular speaker at events, he is one of the longstanding critics on the hit BBC show *MasterChef*. He also entertains diners with William Sitwell's Supper Club, providing exceptional food in extraordinary locations across the UK. He lives in Northamptonshire with his wife Emily, and he has three children.

www.williamsitwell.com

Select Bibliography

Books and Citations

Adrià, F., *A Day at elBulli: An Insight into the Ideas, Methods and Creativity of Ferran Adrià* (Phaidon, 2008)

Adrià, F., Blumenthal, H., Keller, T., McGee, H., 'Statement on the new cookery', *The Observer* (10 December 2006)

Apicius, *Cookery and Dining in Ancient Rome* (Dover Publications, 1977)

Arellano, G., *Taco USA: How Mexican Food Conquered America* (Scribner, 2013)

Aubrey, J., *Brief Lives* (Clarendon Press, 1898)

Bala, P., Narayanan, J., *Secret Sauce; Inspiring Stories of Great Indian Restaurants* (Harper Business, 2018)

Ball, Professor M., Sutherland, D. T., *An Economic History of London 1800–1914* (Routledge, 2001)

Barber, L., 'Grouse, claret and a fag: Man of my Dreams', Interview with Simon Hopkinson, *The Observer* (23 September 2007)

Barton, R., '"An Influential Set of Chaps": The X-Club and Royal Society Politics 1864–85', *The British Journal for the History of Science*, Vol. 23, No. 1 (March 1990), pp. 53–81

Battuta, I., Husain, M. (trans.), *The Rehla of Ibn Battuta* (University of Baroda, 1953)

Beauvilliers, A. B., *The Art of French Cookery* (London, 1824)

Burnett, J., *England Eats Out: A Social History of Eating Out 1830–Present* (Pearson Longman, 2004)

Carême, M. A., *The Royal Parisian Pastrycook and Confectioner* (F. J. Mason, 1834)

Carlin, M., '"What say you to a piece of beef and mustard?": The Evolution of Public Dining in Medieval and Tudor London', *Huntington Library*

Quarterly, Vol. 71, No. 1, pp. 199–217 (University of Pennsylvania Press, March 2008)
Chelminski, R., *The Perfectionist: Life and Death in Haute Cuisine* (Michael Joseph, 2005)
Clarke, H., *Working Men's Clubs: Hints for their Formation, with Rules, etc.* (Working Men's Club and Institute Union, 1865)
Clayton, P., Rowbotham, J., 'How the Mid-Victorians Lived, Ate and Died', *International Journal of Environmental Research and Public Health* (March 2009)
Clover, C., *The End of the Line* (Ebury Press, 2005)
Coghlan, F., *A Guide to France, Explaining Every Form and Expense from London to Paris* (J. Onwhyn, 1830)
Collingham, L., *Curry: A Tale of Cooks and Conquerors* (Chatto & Windus, 2005)
Cowan, B., *The Social Life of Coffee: The Emergence of the British Coffee House* (Yale University Press, 2005)
Cowen, R., *Relish: The Extraordinary Life of Alexis Soyer, Victorian Celebrity Chef* (Phoenix, 2006)
Crowther, G., *Eating Culture: An Anthropological Guide to Food* (University of Toronto Press, 2013)
Cummings, P. R. et al., *The Role of Hospitality in the Lives of Individuals and Families* (The Haworth Press, 1998)
Cushing, C., *Letters, descriptive of Public Monuments, Scenery, and Manners in France and Madrid*, Vol. 1 (Newbury Point, 1832)
Cwiertka, K. J., *Modern Japanese Cuisine: Food, Power and National Identity* (Reaktion Books, 2006)
D'Israeli, I., *Curiosities of Literature* (Richard Bentley, 1838)
Dean, J. M. (ed.), *London Lickpenny* (Medieval English Political Writings, 1996)
Dunn, R. E., *The Adventures of Ibn Battuta: A Muslim Traveller of the Fourteenth Century* (University of California Press, 1989)
Egilsson, S. Y., *Romantic Travellers in the Highlands 1770–1830* (University of St Andrews, 1991)
Ellis, H., *What to Eat?: 10 Chewy Questions about Food* (Portobello Books, 2012)
Engels, F., *The Condition of the Working Class in England in 1844* (Herstellung & Verlag, 2018)

Evelyn, J., *Diary and Correspondence of John Evelyn, FRS* (George Bell & Sons, 1878)

Fag, F., *The Recess, or Autumnal Relaxation in the Highlands and Lowlands* (Longman et al., 1834)

Feinstein, C. H., 'Pessimism Perpetuated: Real Wages and The Standard of Living in Britain during the Industrial Revolution', *Journal of Economic History*, Vol. 58, No. 3 (September 1998)

Feltham, J., *The Picture of London, for 1802* (Longman et al., 1818)

Fitton, R. S., Wadsworth. A. P., *The Strutts and the Arkwrights, 1758–1830: A Study of the Early Factory System* (Manchester University Press, 1958)

Fitzstephen, W., *Description of the City of London* (B. White, 1772)

Forte, C., *Forte: The Autobiography of Charles Forte* (Pan Books, 1986)

Fraser's Magazine for Town and Country, Vol. 62, July–December 1860 (John W. Parker & Son, 1860)

Galigani, A., Galigani, W., *Galignani's New Paris Guide* (A. and W. Galigani, 1827)

Gillespie, C. H., 'Gastrosophy and Nouvelle Cuisine: Entrepreneurial Fashion and Fiction', *British Food Journal*, Vol. 96, No. 10 (1994), pp. 19–23

Gisslen, W., *Professional Cooking* (John Wiley & Sons, 2011)

Goody, J., *Cooking, Cuisine and Class: A Study in Comparative Sociology* (Cambridge University Press, 1982)

Goodyear, D., 'Jeremiah Tower: A Forgotten Father of the American Food Revolution', *The New Yorker* (1 May 2017)

Griffin, E., *A Short History of the British Industrial Revolution* (Macmillan, 2010)

Hailwood, M., *Alehouses and Good Fellowship in Early Modern England* (The Boydell Press, 2014)

Hanawalt, B. A., 'Medieval English Women in Rural and Urban Domestic Space', *Dumbarton Oaks Papers*, Vol. 52, pp. 19–26 (Dumbarton Oaks, Trustees for Harvard University, 1998)

Hare, J., 'Inns, innkeepers and the society of later medieval England 1350–1600', *Journal of Medieval History*, Vol. 39, No. 4 (2013), pp. 477–97

Harper's New Monthly Magazine, Vol. 3, July–November 1851 (Harper & Brothers, 1851)

Hopkinson S., Bareham L., *Roast Chicken and Other Stories* (Ebury Press, 1994)

Hopkinson S., Bareham L., *The Prawn Cocktail Years* (Michael Joseph, 1997)
Howgego, C., 'The Supply and Use of Money in the Roman World 200 B.C. to A.D. 300', *The Journal of Roman Studies*, Vol. 82, pp. 1–31 (Society for the Promotion of Roman Studies, 1992)
Hylton, S., *Leisure in Post-War Britain* (Amberley Publishing, 2013)
Isin, P. M., *Bountiful Empire: A History of Ottoman Cuisine* (Reaktion Books, 2018)
Issenburg, S., *The Sushi Economy: Globalization and the Making of a Modern Delicacy* (Gotham Books, 2007)
Jarnow, J., *Heads: A Biography of Psychedelic America* (Da Capo Press, 2018)
Jarvis, A. W., 'Old London Coffee Houses', *The English Illustrated Magazine* (May 1900)
Kamp, D., 'Cooking Up a Storm', *Vanity Fair* (October 2006)
Kay, E., *Dining with the Georgians: A Delicious History* (Amberley Publishing, 2014)
Kia, M., *Daily Life in the Ottoman Empire* (Greenwood, 2011)
Kingsford, C. L. (ed.), *The Chronicles of London – 1289* (Clarendon Press, 1905)
Lander, N., *On the Menu: The World's Favourite Piece of Paper* (Unbound, 2016)
Lane, C., *The Cultivation of Taste and the Organization of Fine Dining* (Oxford University Press, 2014)
Lee, Rev S., 'The Travels of Ibn Battuta: In the Near East Asia and Africa, 1325–1354', unabridged, from *Abridged Arabic Manuscript Copies*, first published by the Oriental Translation Committee, London, 1829 (Dover Publications Inc, 2004)
Lickorish, L. J., Middleton, V. T. C., *British Tourism* (Butterworth-Heinemann, 2005)
Lucas, E. V., *A Wanderer in London* (Methuen & Company, 1907)
Luhmann, T. M., *The Good Parsi: The Fate of a Colonial Elite in a Postcolonial Society* (Harvard University Press, 1996)
MacCulloch, J., *The Highlands and Western Isles* (London, various, 1824)
Mackay, T., 'Women at Work: Innkeeping in the Highlands and Islands of Scotland 1790–1840', *Journal of Scottish Historical Studies*, Vol. 37, No. 2 (October 2017)
Mackintosh-Smith, T., *The Travels of Ibn Battutah* (Picador, 2002)
McNamee, T., *The Man Who Changed the Way We Eat* (Free Press, 2012)

McNamee, T., *Alice Walters and Chez Panisse: The Romantic, Impractical, Often Eccentric, Ultimately Brilliant Making of a Food Revolution* (Penguin Press, 2007)

Melton, J. V. H., *The Rise of the Public Enlightenment in Europe* (Cambridge University Press, 2001)

Mennell, S., *All Manners of Food: Eating and Taste in England and France from the Middle Ages to the Present* (University of Illinois Press, 1996)

Milne-Smith, A., *London Clubland: A Cultural History of Gender and Class in Late Victorian Britain* (Palgrave Macmillan, 2011)

Mokyr, J., *The Enlightened Economy: Britain and the Industrial Revolution, 1700–1850* (Penguin Books, 2011)

Nichols, J. (ed.), *The Gentleman's Magazine and Historical Chronicle* (David Henry, 1785)

O'Gorman, K. D., 'Discovering commercial hospitality in ancient Rome', *Hospitality Review*, Vol. 9, No. 2 (2007), pp. 44–52

Oddy, D. J., *From Plain Fare to Fusion Food: British Diet from the 1890s to the 1990s* (The Boydell Press, 2003)

Palsetia, J. S., *The Parsis of India: Preservation of Identity in Bombay City* (Brill, 2001)

Pike, R. E., *Human Documents of the Industrial Revolution in Britain* (Routledge, 2006)

Pilcher, J. M., *Planet Taco: A Global History of Mexican Food* (Oxford University Press, 2012)

Pinchbeck, I., *Women Workers and the Industrial Revolution 1750–1850* (Frank Cass, 1977)

Ray, J., *A Collection of Curious Travels and Voyages* (Royal Society, 1693)

Robinson, E. F., *The Early History of Coffee Houses in England* (Cambridge University Press, 2013)

Rosen, A., *The Transformation of British Life, 1950–2000: A Social History* (Manchester University Press, 2003)

Roux, M., *Life is a Menu; Reminiscences of a Master Chef* (Robinson, 2003)

Singer, A., *Starting with Food: Culinary Approaches to Ottoman History* (Markus Wiener Publishers, 2011)

Solly, H., *Facts and Fallacies connected with Working Men's Clubs and Institutes* (A paper read before the Social Science Association, Sheffield, October 1865)

Solly, H., *Prospectus for the Working Men's Club and Institute Union* (Working Men's Club and Institute Union, 1862)
Somerville, A., *The Autobiography of a Working Man* (Robert Hardwicke, 1854)
Stacey, C., 'The Chef Formerly Known as Alastair Little', *The Independent* (15 June 2003)
Symes, R. A., *Family First: Tracing Relationships in the Past* (Pen and Sword, 2015)
Tannahill, R., *Food in History* (Paladin, 1973)
The New Monthly Magazine and Humorist (Henry Colburn, 1844)
Trépanier, N., *Foodways and Daily Life in Medieval Anatolia: A New Social History* (University of Texas, 2014)
Ukers, W. H., *All About Coffee* (Library of Alexandria, 1922)
Warde, A., Martens, L., *Eating Out: Social Differentiation, Consumption and Pleasure* (Cambridge University Press, 2000)
Waters, A., *Chez Panisse Café Cookbook* (Harper Collins, 1999)
Waters, A., *Coming to My Senses: The Making of a Counterculture Cook* (Hardie Grant, 2017)
Well-willer, 'The Women's Petition Against Coffee; Representing to Publick Consideration the Grand Inconveniencies Accruing to their Sex from the Excessive use of that Drying, Enfeebling liquor' (London, 1674)
White, M. P., Steen, J., *The Devil in the Kitchen* (Orion, 2006)
Wood, A., *A Life of Anthony à Wood* (Thomas Hearne, 1711)
Wood, A., *Athenae Oxonienses* (London, various, 1820)

Websites

www.academia.edu/444265/The_Rise_of_the_Coffeehouse_Reconsidered
www.muslimheritage.com
www.pompeiana.org
www.pompeiiperspectives.org/index.php/regio-ix-insula-1
www.sciencedirect.com/science/article/pii/S2352618118300180
www.turkishcoffeeworld.com/History-of-Coffee-s/60.htm
www.web-books.com/Classics/ON/B0/B701/11MB701.html

Picture Credits

2. Bridgeman Images; 11. Getty Images; 17. Bridgeman Images; 19. Wikimedia Commons; 20. Alamy; 23. Alamy; 25. Bridgeman Images; 29. Wikimedia Commons; 32. Bridgeman Images; 35. Alamy; 41. Bridgeman Images; 42. Getty Images; 45. Leiden University Libraries, ms or. 320; 47. Getty Images; 49. Getty Images; 52. Alamy; 56. Alamy; 61. Wikimedia Commons; 62. Bridgeman Images; 66. Alamy; 70. Getty Images; 73. Getty Images; 77. Alamy; 80. Bridgeman Images; 82. akg-images; 84. Alamy; 90. Mary Evans Picture Library; 94. akg-images; 97. Getty Images; 99. Bridgeman Images; 101. Bridgeman Images; 102. Brighton Museums; 106. Wikimedia Commons; 117. Bridgeman Images; 118. Bridgeman Images; 120. Alamy; 122. Alamy; 125. Getty Images; 126. akg-images; 129. Getty Images; 132. Alamy; 135. Mary Evans Picture Library; 137. AP/Shutterstock; 138. Shutterstock; 140. Getty Images; 150. Getty Images; 152. Mary Evans Picture Library; 156. Alamy; 158. Getty Images; 164. Getty Images; 167. © Adela Nistora, 2013; 168. Alamy; 172. Alamy; 178. Getty Images; 180. Getty Images; 184. Associated Newspapers/Shutterstock; 188. Alamy; 193. Alamy; 197. Getty Images; 201. Alamy; 203. Getty Images; 207. Alamy; 211. Getty Images; 213. Alamy; 218. Shutterstock; 221. Alamy; 222. Getty Images; 229. Getty Images; 233. Getty Images; 237. Getty Images; 242. Alamy; 244. Alamy; 247. Alamy; 250. © Nichole Rees

Index

à la carte, 55, 104
AA Guide, 224
Abbasid tradition, 23
ABC Caterers, 158
Abu 'Inan, Sultan, 34
ACBPR, 214–15, 216
Acton, Eliza, 100
Adrià, Ferran, 237–40, 242, 243
Adulteration of Food and Drink and Drugs Act (1872), 110
Afghanistan, 36, 129
Africa, 24, 36, 38
Ago, New York, 232
Ahmed I, Sultan, 27
Ahmed III, Sultan, 30
Alan Crompton-Batt Public Relations (ACBPR), *see* ACBPR
alcohol:
  covert consumption of, 31–3
  Danish custom of, 51
  -free culture, 31
  industrial scale, 113
  institutionalisation of, 57
ale, 48, 55, 62, 111, 150
alehouses/ale-pourers, 48, 54, 57, 63–4
Alexander I, Tsar, 103
Algeria, 23, 24
Ali, Mustafa, 28, 229
all-you-can-eat dining, 234
Altman, Elissa, 196
America (*see also* United States), colonies of, 55
American Automobile Association Guide, 224
Americanisation, 138, 166, 169
amphoras, 18, 19
ancient Greece, 13, 19, 101, 229
anti-establishment counterculture, 197–8
Apicius (Roman cook), 24
Archestratus, 229
Arellano, Gustavo, 144
Argentina, 137
aristocracy, 72–83, 92, 120, 123, 149
Arkwright, Richard, Jr, 95
Arkwright, Sir Richard, 95
army catering, 123, 137, 138, 148, 156–7
Aron, Jean-Paul, 82
Arun, Jean-Paul, 83
Asahi (brewer), 163–4
Asia, 42, 45, 56, 59, 110
Astor, Nancy, 177–8
Astylus (Pompeii bar owner), 16
Athenaeum Club, London, 119
Atherton, Jason, 189, 245
Athictus (Pompeii bar owner), 16
Atholl, Duke of, 126
Au Rocher de Cancale, Paris, 105
Aubrey, John, 60
Australia, 169, 235
Austria, 59
Aztec tradition, 143

Bailly, Sylvain, 101
bakeries, 81, 131
  Bombay, 128
  Roman, 15, 16, 20
Bala, Priya, 130
Balkans, 23, 24, 28
Ball, The (inn) 55
Ball, Prof. Michael, 89
Ballard Estate, Bombay, 126, 128, 130
balti, emergence of, 218
Balzac, Honoré de, 107
Bancelin (restaurateur), 79
Bangkok, Thailand, 226, 242
banqueting, seventeenth-century, 23
bar culture, 132
Barcelona, Spain, 234–40
Bareham, Lindsey, 208
barley bread, 55
Barry, Charles, 120
bars, Roman, 16
Bastani & Co., Bombay, 130–1
Bates, H. E., 154
Battettes, 215
Battistella, Antonio, 182
Battuta, Ibn, 6, 34–45, 48, 56
Bavaria, 19
BBC, 146–7, 190, 212
beans and seeds, importation of, 135–6
Beard, Dame Prof. Mary, 13, 14
Beard, James A., 230
béarnaise sauce, 187
Beauvilliers, Antoine, 79, 81–2
Beefsteak Club, London, 119
beer, 55, 80, 88, 90–1, 176, 185, 218
Bell, Dorothy, 139, 140
Bell, Glen, 138, 139–41, 142, 144

Bell, Kenneth, 179
Bell, Martha, 142
Bell, Rex, 139, 141
Bell Savage, Ludgate Hill, 96
Belle Meunière, La, London, 176
Benares, Mayfair, 227
Bennett, Caroline, 166, 167, 174
Bennigan's, 141
Bento, 168
Berlioz, Hector, 107
Bernardin, Tom, 136
Bertrand, Patrick, 221–2
Bianco, Francesco, 117
Bibendum, London, 206–19
Bibendum, M. (Michelin Man), 206
Bibliothèque Nationale, 101
Biddulph, William, 59
Bill of Rights (1689), 58, 65, 68
Bion, Ottaviano, 27
Bishop, Willy, 198
Bishopsgate, London, 80
bistro scene, 180, 195, 210, 212
Black Sea trade, 24, 26, 36
Black's Guide, 92
Blair Castle, Perthshire, 126
Blue Ocean Institute, 174
Blumenthal, Heston, 217, 228, 238–9, 242
Bocuse, Paul, 222, 225
Boiardi, Hector, 137
boiling, 49–50, 81, 121
Boissier, Louis, 105
Boleyn, Anne, 56
Bombay, India, 21, 124–33, 192
Bonaparte, Napoleon, 98, 105
Boodle's, London, 119, 120
Borrel (chef), 105–6
Bosi, Claude, 233
Boulanger (restaurateur), 79, 98, 234
Bourbon, Louis Joseph de, Prince of Condé, 76, 77, 78
Bourbon royal family, restoration of, 98
Bourdain, Anthony, 198, 202–3, 226
Bowman, Christopher, 61
branding, 137
Bras, Sebastien, 226
Brasserie Benoit, Old Bailey, 186
brasserie cooking, 209, 222
Brave, Jay, 245
Bray, Berkshire, 176, 185, 191, 217, 228
Brazil, 169
bread and butter, 130, 132
Brick Lane, East End, 217
Briggs, Richard, 80
Brillat-Savarin, Jean Anthelme, 8
Britalian joints, 180
Britannia & Co., Bombay, 124–33
British Empire, 124, 125, 159
British Raj, 127, 128, 130, 217
British Restaurants, 147, 148
broiling, 81
Brooks's, London, 119, 120
Broomfield, Andrea, 111
brothels, 14, 15, 16
Bruni, Frank, 231
Buckaroo Buffet, Las Vegas, 234
Buckingham Palace, 119, 151
budgeting, 25
Budrick, Jerry, 198
Buenos Aires, Argentina, 137
buffet froid, 151
burger joints/chains, 138–9, 166, 169, 196, 246
Burger King, 145
Burnett, John, 8, 148, 236
Business India, 131
Byzantine tradition, 23

Café Anglais, Bayswater 219
café culture, 104, 105, 128, 130–2, 140, 148, 155, 156, 181, 192, 203, 217
Café de Paris, Paris, 106
Café Royal, London 159
Cambodia, 136, 198
Camp, David, 198
Campion, Charles, 232
Canada, 169, 171
Canary Islands, 110
candying, 81
canned meat, 110
Canova, London, 182
canteens, 147–8
car culture, 139, 150, 159, 171
Caraccioli, Louis-Antoine, 81
Carême, Marie-Antoine, 6, 97, 98–109, 119, 121, 224
Carlin, Prof. Martha, 48, 49
Carlitz, Barbara, 198
Carlos-Clarke, Bob, 216
Cassius, Dio, 18
Catalonia, 236, 241
Caterer, The, 185
catering:
  high-speed expansion of, 146
  postwar, 149, 158
Cazalet family, 181, 182
Champagne, 55, 202
charcoal cooking, 103, 121
charcuterie, 179, 185
Charles I, 60, 64
Charles II, 23, 65, 67–8
Château de Chantilly, 76, 77
Chaucer, Geoffrey, 49
cheese factories, first opened, 110
Chef Boyardee, 137, 138
Chez Panisse, Berkeley, 7, 192–203, 212
Chicken George, 141
China, 36, 38, 40, 45, 59, 129, 169
Chinese restaurants, 145, 181, 218
chocolate houses, 117
Christian tradition, 42, 50, 53–6, 89

Churchill, Sir Winston, 147, 158
City of London, 46, 49, 50, 54, 61, 71, 166, 211
City of Westminster, 46–7, 50–1, 54, 157
civil liberties, development of, 58
civil unrest, 147
Claiborne, Craig, 229–31
Clancy, Margaret, 185
Clarendon, Earl of, 67
Clarke, Sally, 191, 205, 212, 219, 228
Claudio, Master, 55
Claudius, Emperor, 18
Clement VII, Pope, 56
Clerkenwell Boy, 233
Clover, Charles, 171–2, 174
clubs, *see* working men's clubs
coaching inns, 14, 15
coffee, 33, 149, 151
coffee houses, 58–71, 72, 116, 117, 218
Coffee Room, Mayfair, 118
Coghlan, Francis, 104, 107
Collingham, Lizzie, 217, 218, 219
Collingwood, Francis, 80
Collins, Hannah, 247
colonialism, 124–33, 134, 159, 217
Columbian exchange, defined, 135
Columbus, Christopher, 135
commercial hospitality, Roman-style, 14
commercial kitchens, 99
communal dining, 40
Community Feeding Centres, 147
community gardens, 136
Conagra, 138
Condé, Prince of, *see* Bourbon, Louis Joseph de
confectionery, Turkish, 25, 30
Congo, 136
Conopios, Nathaniel, 60
Conran, Sir Terence, 7, 181, 206–19
consumer aspiration, 173
consumerism, postwar rise of, 141
conversation, 173–5
conveyor-belt sushi, *see* *kaiten* sushi
cook shops, 30, 31, 48–9, 53, 54
cookbooks, 8, 136, 148, 199, 217, 241
cookery teachers, 138
Coq d'Or, London, Le, 176
Corbin, Chris, 228
Cordon Bleu, Le, Paris 205
Cornhill, London, 46, 60, 64
Cortés, Hernán, 134–5
Costello, Dudley, 81
Côte d'Azur, France, 176
Couilloud, Hubert, 224
counterculture, 197–8, 245
Country Pavilion, South Bank, 157
Cowan, Brian, 65
Cowen, Ruth, 120–1
Crimea, 123
Criterion, Piccadilly Circus, 157
Cromford, Derbyshire, 95
Crompton-Batt, Alan, 214, 215–16, 230
Crompton-Batt, Elizabeth, 215
Cromwell, Oliver, 64–5
Crown & Anchor Tavern, the Strand, 80
Crowther, Gillian, 165, 169
culinary restrictions, Nero imposes, 18
Cushing, Caroline Elizabeth Wilde, 108–9
cutlery, 46, 243
Cwiertka, Katarzyna, 165

Daily Mail, 212
Daily Telegraph, 110, 187, 216, 232
Dairy Bar, South Bank, 157
dates, 24, 26
Davey, John, 209
David, Elizabeth, 148, 149, 191, 200, 201, 211, 213
Dean Street, Soho, 151
decadence, 75
decaying produce, how to disguise, 137
Dekker, Thomas, 55
Denmark, 51
Diana, Princess of Wales, 212
'dirty vegan' food, 246
disposable packaging, 139, 141
Dissolution of the Monasteries, 56
Doggie Diner, 141
Doyen, Gabriel-Charles, 75–6
dried fruit, history of, 23
drugs/drug-taking, 93, 110, 198–9
Ducasse, Alain, 225
Dunkin' Donuts, 145
Dunlop, Fuchsia, 240, 241
Dunn, Prof. Ross E., 44–5
Dunn's, Paris, 107
Dwivedi, Sharada, 133

East India Company, 127, 217
Edible Schoolyard, 204
Edward I, 51
Edwards, Daniel, 60
eggs, 24, 26, 189
Egypt, 23, 24, 38, 42, 122
Ehrlich, Richard, 240
Eisenhower, Dwight D., 157
El Bulli, Roses, 236–40
El Cubano, Kensington, 179
El Rancho Vegas, Las Vegas Strip, 234
'elegant cuisine' front-page article, 230
Elizabeth I, 55
Elizabeth II, 124, 151
Ellis, Hattie, 173, 174
Ellis Island tours, 136
Ellis, Michael, 227
Empress, The, London, 176

Engels, Friedrich, 93–5
England:
  beer drinking, 90–1
  coffee houses, 60, 66, 68–71, 72
  French gastronome inspired by, 79
  medieval, 46–57
  mid-sixteenth-century, 23
  'most sumptuous and impressive meal' served in, 122
  postwar, 146–61
  seventeenth-century, 23
  six key pillars of, 57
  Victorian, 110–23
English Civil War, 64–5
entrepreneurship, 134, 247
environmentalism, 173–5
Estchepe (Eastcheap), England, 53
Ethiopia, 33
Eugénie-les-Bains, France, 209
eunuchs, 25, 27
Evening Standard, 155, 227, 232
execution, 30, 32, 33, 72, 73, 75, 89
Expo '70, Osaka, 165–6
export bans, 23

Fabre, Bernard, 223
factory food, 94–5, 137, 140, 141, 142, 150
Fai, Jay, 226
Falernian, 13
Falernus, Mount, 13
Farley, John, 80, 81
'farm to fork' mantra, 197
farmers' markets, 204
fashionable eateries, 8
fast food, 134–45
  first unleashed, 7
  most popular in US, 139
  vegan, 246
  Waters' campaigns against, 192, 196, 204
Fat Duck, Bray, 217, 228, 242
Feinstein, Charles, 92
Feltham, John, 92
Fermor, Patrick Leigh, 39, 40
Festival of Britain (1951), 146, 157
Fez, Morocco, 34, 44
Ffarr, James, 64
Filet-O-Fish, 174
Financial Times (*FT*), 172
fine dining, 51, 73, 98–109, 122, 243
Finegan, Robert, 199
Finland, 141
First World War, 153
fish:
  commercial wastage of, 173
  farms, 171
  raw, *see* sushi
Fishguard, Wales, 208
fishing industry, 171–5, 185
Fitzpatrick, James, 129
Fitzstephen, William, 8, 49–51
fixed-price menus, 104
Fleet Street, London, 62, 80, 156
flour mills, Roman, 20
Floyd, Keith, 191, 224
Fontainebleau, Paris, 105
food activism, 244–6
food guilds, 79
food magazines, 7, 153, 154, 161, 217
food science, 173
Fort, Matthew, 236
Forte and Company, 155
Forte, Charles, 146, 154–5, 157–61, 179
Forte Holdings, 159
Four Seasons, New York, 230
France, 50, 59, 98–109, 176, 178, 194
  bistro scene, 210
  British Embassy kitchens, 182
  English-style cookery in, 107, 148
  food guilds, 79
  middle-class, 72
  post-revolutionary, 98
  proliferation of restaurants in, 82
  sushi bars, 168
  Turkish cooks look to, 22
  wine appellations, 31
  working-class, 119
franchising, 141, 166–7
French Revolution, 72–83, 92, 98, 101, 104, 178, 194
Frenchification, 68
Frost, David, 147, 160, 209

G. D. Ritzy's, 141
Gagnaire, Pierre, 236
Gaitey, Stephanie, 220, 222
Gaitskell, Hugh, 158
Gallati, Mario, 148
Gambero Rosso Guide, 224
Gandhi, Mahatma, 124, 130
Garrett, Jesse James, 232
Garrick Club, London, 119
gas stoves, first use of, 121
gastro-anarchists, 235–6
Gates, Bill, 246
Gateway of India, 125, 129
Gault, Henri, 222
Gault Millau Guide, 222–3, 237
Gavroche, Le, London, 7, 176–91, 199, 209, 211, 215, 236
Gaylord, Fitzrovia, 219
Genlis, Madame de, 83
Genroku Sushi, 164
gentlemen's clubs, 116, 119
George IV, 103
George, The, Stamford, 96
George V, 125
Germany, 128
Gervais, Eugène-Eléonore, 76
Gill, A. A., 9, 232
Giraldin, Silvano, 190
Giraldo, Jon, 235
Gisslen, Wayne, 99

globalisation, 134, 169, 170, 173
Globe Tavern, Fleet Street, 80
Glorious Revolution, 58, 68
gluttony, 20
Godley, Manchester, 112
Goin, Suzanne, 199
'gold', 21
Good Food Guide, The, 7, 153, 154, 161, 178, 219
Goodyear, Dana, 199
Gore House, Kensington, 123
Gothic Revival, 116
Gourmet, 200, 229
gout, 61
grace, tradition of, 27
Gradwell, Cath, 212
Grampian Mountains, Perthshire, 126
Grand Bazaar, Constantinople, 28
Grand Café, The, Oxford 64
Grande Taverne de Londres, La, Paris, 81
grandeur, 50, 76, 120, 178, 209
Great Britain, *see* United Kingdom
Great Exhibition (1851), 123, 157
Great Fire of London (1666), 51, 64, 67
Great Reform Act (1832), 72
Greece, 13, 19, 23, 42, 60, 168
Greek mythology, 13, 127
Greenpeace, 174
Greg, Robert Hyde, 112, 113, 114
Greg, Samuel, 112
Griffin, Emma, 88
Grignon's, Paris, 106, 107
Guadalupe Hidalgo, Mexico, 144
Guardian, The, 159, 210, 236
Guerard, Michel, 209
guesthouses, 152
Guinness, Alec, 210
Gulf of Tonkin, 193
Gyngell, Skye, 226

Habermas, Jürgen, 65
Haines, J. T. A., 114
Hajj, 38
hamburger shacks/stands, 28, 134, 138, 140 (*see also* burger joints; Burger King; McDonald's)
Hamlyn, Paul, 206–8
Hard Rock Hotel, Ibiza, 241
Harper's Magazine, 105, 106
Harris, Henry, 210, 212
Harris, Matthew, 210, 212
Harrods, London, 170
Harry Cipriani, New York, 231
Harvard Club, New York, 170
Harvey, Dr William, 60
Harvey, Eliab, 60
Harveys, Wandsworth, 189, 213
Henderson, Fergus, 217
Henry II, 50
Henry IV, 53
Henry VIII, 55–6
Herculaneum, 17, 20
Hermosillo, Sonora, 144
Hibiscus, London, 233
Higashiōsaka, Japan, 162
Hilaire, London, 206, 208, 214
Hindoostane Coffee House, London, 217
Hindu tradition, 127
Hispanic tradition, 141
Hitler, Adolf, 156
Hogarth, William, 72
Holconius's crossroads, 10
Hole in the Wall, Bath, 179
Holland, *see* Netherlands
Hong Kong, 203, 226
Hopkinson, Simon, 191, 205, 206–19, 228
Hotel de Condé, Paris, 76
Hôtel de la Côte d'Or, Semur-en-Auxois, 220
House of Commons, 66, 67
Howard Johnson's, 141
Howard, Phil, 189, 210
Hungary, 24, 178, 187
Hutchinson, Col. Hon. Henry Hely, 89

Ibiza, 241
ice carvings, 99
ice-cream parlours, 155
Ilkhanid tradition, 22
immigration, 9, 135–6, 138
Imperial Hotel, Torquay, 151
import costs, 137
imported food:
  in Roman times, 21
  into US, 135–8
Independent, The, 168, 219
India, 36, 38, 41, 44, 110, 217, 218, 219
  bar culture, 132
  bureaucracy, 128, 129–30
  culinary heritage, systematic loss of, 132–3
  independence, 124, 131
  modernisation, 132
  property boom, 132
  restaurants of, 124–33
  slums, 128
Indian Mutiny (1857), 127
Indian restaurants, 181, 227
Indo-Iranian cuisine, 131
Industrial Revolution, 84–97, 109, 110, 112, 121
Inn of Primus, 10, 16, 21, 48, 192, 234
inns, 48, 54, 55, 62, 81, 229
  female proprietors of, 96–7
  Industrial Revolution, 88
  Pompeii, 10, 16, 21
  Scottish, 85
Innulus (Pompeii bar owner), 16
Instagram, 233, 247
InterContinental Hotel, Park Lane, 245

interwar period, 148
Iran, 23, 24, 42, 125–6
Iranian cafés, 131
Iraq, 23, 24
Islamic tradition, 31, 37–8, 124, 126
Isle of Man, 156
Italian café culture, 137
Italian trattoria, 18
Italy, 45, 59, 136, 155
Itsu, 245
Ivy, The, West End, 228

J. Sheekey, Covent Garden, 228
Jacob the Jew, 60, 64, 65
Jacobin Club, 83
Jacobs, Sherelle, 149
James II, 68
Japan, 129, 162–75, 225
Japanisation, 169
Jarnow, Jesse, 198
'Jeremiah Tower's Montpelier Butter', 208
John, Duke of Bedford, 53, 54
Johnson, Cirques, 64, 65
Johnson, Lyndon B., 193
Johnson, Samuel, 8, 81
Jones, George Matthew, 31
Juzayy, Ibn, 34, 36, 41, 44

kaiten sushi, 165, 166, 170
Kanishka, Mayfair, 219
kebabs, 30, 246
Keller, Hubert, 242
Keller, Thomas, 243
Kennedy Brooks, 214
Kennedy's, Kings Road, 215
Kentucky Fried Chicken (KFC), 166, 196
King, Jeremy, 228
King, Tom, 72
Kiss, Dr Ladislas, 224
kitchen brigades, Ottoman structure of, 25–6
Kliman, Todd, 198
Kochhar, Atul, 219, 227–8
Koffmann, Pierre, 186, 187, 189
Kohinoor, Bacha, 131
Kohinoor, Boman, 124–33, 192
Kohinoor (Bombay restaurant), 128
Kohinoor, Merwan, 130–1
Kohinoor, Rashid, 125, 126, 128, 130, 192
Kroc, Ray, 138–9
Kyani & Co., Bombay, 131, 133

laboratory-grown meat, 246–7
Ladenis, Nico, 215
Lambert, Constant, 154
Lambert, Don, 136
Lander, Nicholas, 8
Laskin, David, 199
Laud, William, the Archbishop of Canterbury, 60
Lebanon, 42
leftovers, history of, 28
Leigh, Rowley, 188, 191, 205, 211, 212, 213–14, 219, 228
Lemardelay, Paris, 107
Leoni, Peppino, 148, 151
L'Estrange, Roger, 67
Levant, 27, 72
Levin, Bernard, 147, 160, 161, 179, 190
Levy, Joe, 157
Levy, Paul, 210
L483, 19
liberty halls, 14
libraries, 116
Lickorish, Leonard, 149
Lieberman, Jaime, 235
Little, Alastair, 191, 205, 211, 212, 214, 219, 228
Livy, 14
Lloyd's Coffee House, 70, 71
Lloyd's of London, 71
logistics, 134
Lois Weedon, England, 89
Loiseau, Bernard, 220–4, 233, 237
Loiseau, Dominique, 220, 222, 223, 224
London, England, 21, 49–51, 96, 97, 113, 147, 189, 205, 206–19 (*see also* City of London; City of Westminster)
  beer drinking, 91
  clubland, 121, 122
  coffee houses, 60, 66, 68–71
  dining scene, 7
  eating houses, 53
  fashionable eateries, 87, 150
  Feltham's vivid description of, 92
  first restaurants emerge in, 51
  French restaurants, 176–91
  immigration affects, 217–19
  medieval, 46
  milk bars, 155–7
  Paris lags behind, 80
  postwar, 149–50
  sushi bars, 166–9
  taverns, 80
  Victorian, 119
  Wittet's 'recreation' of, 126
London Gazette, 68
London Tavern, Bishopsgate, 80
Louis XVI, 75
Louis XVIII, 92
Lucaris, Cyril, 60
Lucas, Edward, 119
Lucullus (politician), 82
Ludgate Hill, London, 96
Ludlam, Bob, 113
Lydgate, John, 46
Lyons Corner Houses, 156, 183
Lyttelton, Lord, 115

MacCagie, Kenneth, 87, 88
MacCulloch, John, 84–8, 97, 229
McDonald, Maurice, 7, 138, 139–40
McDonald, Richard, 7, 138, 139–40
McDonald's, 140, 196
  Filet-O-Fish, 174
  first opened, 138
  in Japan, 166
  in Mumbai, 132

McGee, Harold, 243
McIntosh, Hon. Hugh D., 155
Mackay, Theresa, 96–7
Mackintosh-Smith, Tim, 37
Maclarty, Mrs (inn keeper), 85, 86
McNamee, Thomas, 198, 229–30
Macpherson, James, 96
Madame Guillotine, 72, 73, 75
Magno, Alessandro, 55
mail coaches, introduction of, 96
Maldives, 40, 44
Maldonado, Juvencio, 7, 142, 143, 144
Manchester Guardian, 110
Marie Antoinette, 75, 81
Marie Louise of Austria, 103
Marine Conservation Society (MSC), 174
Marinetti, Filippo Tommaso, 241
markcting know-how, 6
markets, 49, 148
Martin (chef), 107
Mary, Queen, 125
Maschler, Fay, 215, 232
Masciaga, Diego, 190
Mazouz, Mourad, 236
Meades, Jonathan, 232
Meadow Milk Bar, West End, 155
mechanisation, 143, 162–75
medieval England, 46–57
Mediterranean cuisine, 13, 27, 148, 202, 241
Mehmed II, Sultan, 24, 30
Mehmed III, Sultan, 33
Memluk tradition, 22
Méot (restauratcur), 79, 82, 83
Mercier, Louis-Sébastien, 78
Mercury Street tavern, 18
Methodist Recorder, 157
Methodist tradition, 89
Metropolitan Water Board, 110
Mexican cuisine, 140, 142, 143, 144
Mexican tradition, 134–45, 138
Mexico, 142–3, 144, 204, 235
Michelin, André, 225
Michelin, Edouard, 225
Michelin Guide, 187, 189, 190, 219–28, 233, 237
Middle Ages, 46–57, 58, 75, 99
middle class:
  French, 72
  nineteenth-century, 115
  Roman, 21
  US, 141
Middle East, 141
Middleton, Victor, 146, 153
migration, 135–6
Mikes, George, 147
milk bars, 155–7
Milk Marketing Board (MMB) (UK), 157
Millau, Christian, 222
Miller, Mark, 199
Milne-Smith, Amy, 117, 118, 122
Ministry of Food (UK), 147, 156
Mintel, 245
Mirk, John, 54
Misson, Francis, 71
Mister Donut, 166
Mitla Café, 140
Mitsubishi, 171
Mogadishu, Somalia, 38, 43
Mokyr, Joel, 89
Moldavia, 24
molecular gastronomy, 243, 244
monasteries, 42, 48, 56–7
monastic taverns, 57
Mongolian tradition, 22, 127
Monkey Gland cocktail, 149
mono-cultural society, 153
Mooragh Camp, Ramsey, 156
Morning Chronicle, 120
Morocco, 34, 37, 38, 44
Moshi Moshi, London, 166, 174
motorways, first built, 150
Mrs White's Chocolate House, Mayfair, 117–18
Muhammad, Prophet, 31, 36, 41
multi-sensory dining, 234, 235–40, 239, 242–3
Murad II, Sultan, 24
Murad IV, Sultan, 33, 60
Muslim cuisine, 125
Mussolini, Benito, 156

Naegellen, M., 223
Nancy, Lady, Viscountess Astor, 177–8
Naples Market, 16
Narayanan, Jayanth, 130
Naret, Jean-Luc, 227
National Convention (1794), 73, 74, 82, 83
Native American tradition, 135
negotiating talent, 6
Nero, Emperor, 18
Netherlands, 39
neurogastronomy, defined, 234
New Empire, Bombay, 132
New Excelsior, Bombay, 131
New World, 135
New York Magazine, 230
New York, NY, 10, 15, 71, 134, 142, 226, 242
  immigration, 135
  restaurants critiqued, 230–2
  theatre district, 143
New York Times (NYT), 170, 198, 199, 200, 229, 231
New Yorker, 199
News Review, 155–6
Nicolas, Grand Duke, 103
Nicolson, Sir Harold, 153
Nightingale, Florence, 123
Nobu, London, 174–5
Norman Conquest, 53
nouvelle cuisine, 236–7
NPR, 198

Obama, Barack, 204
obesity, 38, 43
Observer, The, 188, 231
Old World, 135
Oldys, William, 60–1
olive oil, Greek trade in, 24
Oliver, Jamie, 242
Olney, Richard, 213
Optati, L. Rapinasi, 15
opulence, 74, 83
ordinary food, defined, 54–5
organic produce, 204
Orient-Express, 241
Ottoman Empire, 22–33
  'collapse' of, 22
  1502 law, 31
  mutes and buffoons, 27
  royal household cooking staff, 24, 25–7
Ottovari, Farhad, 133
Ovnew, Barcelona, 235–6, 241
Ozinda's (coffee house), 66

Pacific Rim, 169
Palais Royal, Paris, 105, 106, 108
Palsetia, Jesse S., 127
pamphleteering, 68, 71
Papilio (Pompeii bar owner), 16
Pardulus (Pompeii bar owner), 16
Paris, France:
  London ahead of, 80
  notable restaurants in, 98–109
  proliferation of restaurants in, 82
Parisien, Le, 222
parliamentary papers (1833), 94
Parsi tradition, 124–33
Partridge, Frances, 148
Pasha, Ibrahim, 122
pastries, ancient, 33
Paz, Octavio, 144
Peak Café, Hong Kong, 203
Peart, Fred, 185
Peet, Alfred, 195
Peet's Coffee, 195
Peggy (serving girl), 85
Pepys, Samuel, 64, 68, 71
Perry-Smith, George, 179, 191
Persia, 24, 38, 41, 126
Phelps, Henry, 93
picnics, 30
pig's trotters, 189
Pilcher, Jeffrey, 142, 144
pilgrimage, 34–45, 48, 56, 136
Pizza Hut, 145, 166, 196
Place du Châtelet, Paris, 107
plagiarism, 36
Platter, Thomas, 55
Pliny, 10
poets/poetry, 10, 14, 16, 33, 44, 46, 46–7, 59, 103, 144, 229
Poilâne, Lionel, 194
Point, Fernand, 200
political ideology, 22, 33, 58
Pollen Street Social, 245
Polo, Marco, 36–7, 45
Pompeii, 7, 10–21, 192, 234
Poole, Bruce, 210
Popham, Peter, 168, 170
Port Trust, 128, 130
Portugal, 128
Postgate, Raymond, 153–4, 178, 179
postwar:
  Britain, 146–61
  consumerism, 141
  dining scene, 7
  Japan, 166
  US, 134
potting, 81
Poulbot, Le, City of London, 186, 211
Pownall, Elfreda, 199
pre-packed food, 168
preserving, 81, 111
price controls:
  medieval England, 54
  Ottoman Empire, 31
  postwar, 149
Pricus, Podiscus, 16
principles of cooking, 243–5
Privy Council, 68
prix-fixe menus, 201
prostitution, 14, 30–1
Protestant reformation, 56
Provençal dishes, 82
prunes, Egyptian trade in, 24
Prunier, London, 176, 182
Prunier's, St James's, 150
Prupas, Jessica, 235
public baths, 15
public houses (pubs), 88, 113
public kitchens, 27
puff pastry, 209
pugilism, 73
Pup 'N' Taco, 141

Quaker tradition, 119
Queen's Lane Coffee House, 64
Quo Vadis, 148, 151

Racine, Knightsbridge, 212
Radio Times, 146
Rainbow Coffee House, 63, 64
Rainbow Corner, West End, 156, 157
Ramsay, Gordon, 188, 189, 213, 217, 225, 227, 231, 241, 245
Randall, Theo, 245
rationing, 147, 148, 149, 156
Rauwolff, Leonhart, 27, 31–3, 59
Rayner, Jay, 188
Raz, Guy, 198
Red Barn, 141
Red Guide, 220
Reddish Working Men's Club, 112
Redzepi, René, 240
Reform Act (1832), 110
Reform Club, London, 119, 120, 122
refrigeration, 110, 173
refugees, 135–6
Reichl, Ruth, 203
Reign of Terror, 74, 81, 83
religious communities, 42, 48, 56, 56–7

religious travel, *see* pilgrimage
Remy, Pascal, 225
restaurant(s):
critiqued, 220–33
French, 78, 98–109
Industrial Revolution foundation of, 84
postwar, 149
sustainable menus, 175
Restaurant Elizabeth, Oxford, 179
Restaurant Gordon Ramsay, Chelsea, 227
restaurant guides, 7, 92, 98–109, 153, 154, 161, 178, 187, 189, 190, 219, 219–28, 237
restaurant PR, 206, 214–17
Restoration, 65, 67
restoratives, 79
Richard's (coffee house), 66
Rignon's, Paris, 120
Ritz, The, London, 149
Ritzkrieg, 149
Robert (executive chef/restaurateur), 76–9, 82
Robespierre, Maximilien, 7, 72, 74, 75–6, 83
Rodgers, Judy, 199
Roman Empire, 7, 10–21, 23–4, 33, 39, 48, 49, 82, 192, 234
Barbarian invasions, 13
middle class, 21
Roman mythology, 13, 50
Romania, 24
Romulus Augustulus, 13
Ronay, Egon, 178–9, 208, 214
Roncero, Paco, 241–2
Rosebery, Lord, 114, 115
Rosée, Pasqua, 60, 61, 64
Roses, Catalonia, 236
Rothschild, Cécile de, 177–8, 182
rotisserie, 99
Roux, Alain, 191
Roux, Albert, 7, 176–91, 192, 209, 215, 236
Roux, Cheryl, 191
Roux, Françoise, 176
Roux, Germaine, 190
Roux, Michel, 7, 176–91, 192, 209, 236
Roux, Michel, Jr, 191, 236
Roux, Monique, 176, 185
Roux Restaurants Ltd, 181
Roux, Robyn, 191
Royal Exchange, London, 68
Royal Pavilion, Brighton, 103
Rue de Richelieu, Paris, 78, 81, 107
Rufo, Marco Epidio, 15
Russell Hotel, Dublin, 151
Russia, 136, 141 (*see also* USSR)

Sackville-West, Vita, 153
Safavid tradition, 23
St Augustine's, Canterbury, 54
St Edmund Hall, Oxford, 64
St John the Baptist, 53
St Loys School, Northampton, 89
St Margaret's, Westminster, 54
St Mary & St Peter Church, Northampton, 89
St Michael's, Cornhill, 60, 61, 64
St Xavier's College, Bombay, 131
salad cream, 160
Saladino, Dan, 212
Salle des Machines, 73
salmon farms, 171
salt trade, 24, 28, 127
salting, 43, 44, 87
sandwiches, 125, 130, 132
Sandys, Sir George, 59
satirists/satirisation, 146–7
Saturday Review, 115, 116
sauce dispensers, 140
Saudi Arabia, 36
sausages, 18, 30
Savoy, The, London, 149
Scarborough Working Men's Club, 114
school lunch, 204
scorched-earth policy, 149
Scotland, 84–7, 96, 112, 126, 155, 160, 229
Scott, Sir Walter, 85, 97
Second World War, 7, 131, 137, 147, 148, 149, 162, 178, 217, 218, 229
Selim II, Sultan, 24
Seljuk tradition, 22
Serendipity 3, New York, 242
service stations, 159
sewage, Roman, 20–1
sex workers, 14, 30–1
Shams al-Din Abu'Abdallah Muhammad ibn'Abdallah ibn Muhammad ibn Ibrahim ibn Muhammad ibn Yusuf al-Lawati al-Tanji ibn Battuta, *see* Battuta, Ibn
sharing plates, concept of, 40
Shiraishi, Yoshiaki, 7, 162, 163–7, 171
Sikh tradition, 129
silver salvers, 122
Singapore, 203, 214, 224, 226
Sirocco, Bangkok, 242
Sitwell, Sir Sacheverell, 154
Sketch, London, 236
slavery, 14, 38
Smith, Rev. Samuel, 89
Smyrna, Greece, 60
Snowfox, 168
snuff, 55
Soboul, Albert, 75
social levelling, 19–20, 21
social media, 233, 247
Soler, Juli, 237
Somalia, 38, 43
Soup Kitchen, Chelsea, 181
soup kitchens, 110
sous-vide, 243–4
South America, 135, 136–7, 141, 169
Soviet Union, *see* USSR
Soyer, Alexis, 119, 120–3, 157, 224

Spain, 108, 234–40
Spectator, The, 121
Spence, Prof. Charles, 238, 243
Spencer, Colin, 111
spice trade, 24, 28, 31, 111, 127
sponsorship, 157
Sprang, Rebecca, 79
Sprott Road, Bombay, 124
Sri Lanka, 38, 44
Stacey, Caroline, 180, 219
Stalin, Joseph, 149
Stanley, Lord, 115
Starbucks, 33, 195
Stars, San Francisco, 202, 203, 208
Stone Age, 84
street vendors, 49, 62, 116, 134, 226
Sublimotion, Ibiza, 241
Subway, 145
Suetonius, 18
suffrage, 68
sugar, 24, 26, 147
Suleiman the Magnificent, 24, 59
Sullivan, Steven, 199
Sully, Henry, 113–16
Sumatra, 40
Sunday Times, 7, 232
Sunni Islam, 38
supermarkets, 148, 168, 175, 194–5
sushi/sushi bars, 7, 162–75 (*see also kaiten* sushi)
sustainability, 173–5
Switzerland, 191
symbolism, power of, 126
syphilis, 135
Syria, 31, 36, 42, 59

tablecloth, 46, 86
tableware, 25
Tabriz, Iran, 24
taco(s):
  bastardisation, 169
  first sold, 142
  machine, 7, 134–45
  shops, 138
Taco Bell, 140–1, 145, 196
Taco-Tia, 142
Taiko Foods, 168
Tailhade, Laurent, 103
Taj Mahal Palace Hotel, Bombay, 128
Taloyr, John, 114
Tamarind, Mayfair, 219
tandoor, 30, 219
Tangier, Morocco, 37, 44
Tanis, David, 199
tap rooms, 116
Taste of India, 217
'Taste of the Five Continents', 235
Tata, Jamsetji, 128
tavern food, Roman, 18, 19–20
taverns, 46, 48, 54, 55, 59, 61, 63, 80, 81
  food first served in, 57
  London, 8
  monastic, 57
  Roman, 14, 17–20
Tavola, Westbourne Grove, 219
taxation, 67
tea trade, 73
tearooms, 156, 183
technological innovation, 93
teetotal cause, 113–14
Telegraph, The, India, 131
Temple Coffee House, London, 80
Thailand, 136
That Was the Week That Was, 146–7, 160
Thatcher, Margaret, 170, 210
Tiberius, Emperor, 17
Tilbrook's, Paris, 107
Tillyard, Arthur, 64
Time, 205, 230
Times, The, 115, 217, 232
Times of India, 124
Tom King's Coffee House, 72
Topkapi Palace, 24
tourism, 149
Tourism Society, 146
Tower, Jeremiah, 199–204, 208
Town & Country, 198
transportation, 134, 147
Transylvania, 24
Travellers Club, London, 119
Treaty of Guadalupe Hidalgo (1848), 144
TripAdvisor, 233
Trois Frères Provençaux, 79
Trump, Donald, 67, 139, 151, 204
Turkey, 22, 24, 36, 39, 42, 48, 59, 60, 62
Turkish coffee houses, 33, 59
TV cookery, 213
TV dinners, 141
TV shows, 224, 242

Uffenbach, Zacharias Conrad von, 65
UNESCO, 144
United Kingdom (UK), 84–97, 129, 174 (*see also* England; Scotland; Wales)
  bistro scene, 180, 212
  car culture, 149–50, 159
  food reputation abroad, 160–1
  government-run canteens in, 147–8
  milk bars, 155–6
  postwar, 146–61
  rationing, 147, 148
  restaurant revolution, 176
  vegan awareness in, 245
United States (US), 128, 129, 140, 169, 229 (*see also* America)
  burger joints, 138–9, 139
  car culture, 139
  community gardens, 136
  counterculture, 197–8, 245
  drive-thrus
  fast food, 134–45, 192
  immigration affects, 134–45
  Mexico invaded by, 144
  milk bars, 156
  packaged foods, 138
  postwar, 134
  sushi restaurants, 169–70

Upper Regent Street, London, 155
Upper West Side, New York, 142
US Army, 137, 138, 156–7
USSR, 149 (*see also* Russia)
Uzbekistan, 37

Van Houten, Peter, 194
Vanity Fair, 198
Vegan Society, 245
veganism, 8, 244–6
Verney, Sir Ralph, 68
Vesuvius, Mount, 10–12, 13, 16, 20
Victoria, Queen, 110, 119
Victorian era, 109, 110–23, 125–33, 157
Villas, James, 198

Wagamama, 245
Wagner, Martin von, 19
Waines, David, 38
Wales, 88, 90–1, 147, 208
Walker, Rev. E. M., 114
Wareing, Marcus, 188, 225, 227
Waters, Alice, 7, 192–203, 212
Waterside Inn, Bray, 176, 186–91, 199, 209, 228, 236
Waxman, Jonathan, 199
White Hart Tavern, Holborn, 80
White Lion, Bath, 96
White, Marco Pierre, 188–9, 213, 214, 215–16, 226, 227, 228
White's, Mayfair, 117–18
William and Mary, 65, 68
William II, 51
William the Conqueror, 51
Williams, Bryn, 189
wine(s):
  ancient, 13, 15, 18, 19
  appellation, 31
  Bordeaux, 78
  Champagne, 55, 107, 202
  Chardonnay, 107
  English tavern, 80
  French, 82–3, 176
  palm, 40
  postwar, 151
  Soyer's kitchen, 122
  vin ordinaire, 104
Winner, Michael, 7
Wittet, George, 125, 126
Wolseley, The, London, 228
Wood, Anthony, 60, 64
Woodroffe, Simon, 167–9
Woodstock, 197–8
Woollams, John, 80
Wordsworth, Dorothy, 96
Wordsworth, William, 96
working class, 90–1, 92–6
Working Men's Club and Institute Union, 113
working men's clubs, 112–16
World Wildlife Fund (WWF), 174
Wren, Sir Christopher, 65
Würzburg, Bavaria, 19

Xochitl, New York, 143

Yemen, 23, 24, 33, 43, 59
YO! Sushi, 166, 167–9, 173, 174

Zafar, 43
Zagat restaurant survey (2016), 170
Zaila, 43
Zoastrian tradition, 126–7
Zuni Café, San Francisco, 199